SAVAGE WEST

▫   ▫   ▫

SAVAGE WEST

□ □ □

The Life and Fiction of
THOMAS SAVAGE

O. Alan Weltzien

UNIVERSITY OF NEVADA PRESS Reno & Las Vegas

LIBRARY OF CONGRESS CATALOGING-IN-PUBLICATION DATA
Names: Weltzien, O. Alan (Oliver Alan), author.
Title: Savage West : the life and fiction of Thomas Savage / by O. Alan Weltzien.
Description: Reno ; Las Vegas : University of Nevada Press, [2020] |
   Includes bibliographical references and index. | Summary: "Savage West is a literary
   biography chronicling the life and works of neglected Montana novelist, Thomas Savage
   (1915–2003). The author seeks to restore Savage to a higher position in the ranks of West-
   ern American, let alone Montanan, literature"— Provided by publisher.
Identifiers: LCCN 2020017794 (print) | LCCN 2020017795 (ebook) | ISBN 9781948908863
   (hardcover) | ISBN 9781948908870 (ebook)
Subjects: LCSH: Savage, Thomas. | Gay authors—Montana—Biography. |
   Authors, American—Montana—Biography. | Authors, American—20th century—
   Biography.
Classification: LCC PS3569.A83 Z934 2020 (print) | LCC PS3569.A83 (ebook)
   | DDC 813/.54—dc23
LC record available at https://lccn.loc.gov/2020017794
LC ebook record available at https://lccn.loc.gov/2020017795

ISBN 9781647790677 (paperback)

The paper used in this book is a recycled stock made from 30 percent post-consumer waste
materials, certified by FSC, and meets the requirements of American National Standard for
Information Sciences—Permanence of Paper for Printed Library Materials, ANSI/NISO
Z39.48-1992 (R2002). Binding materials were selected for strength and durability.

Manufactured in the United States of America

To Sandy (R. Alexander) James, founder of Dillon Junior Fiddlers and fiddle teacher extraordinaire, family historian, Savage's nephew, and my friend for many years who has always shared generously about his uncle

and

In memory of Sue Hart (1936–2014), longest-serving professor at Montana State University Billings, who knew everything about Montana writers, who knew many as friends, and who told me to read Tom Savage long ago

Contents

Illustrations

SAVAGE WEST

□ □ □

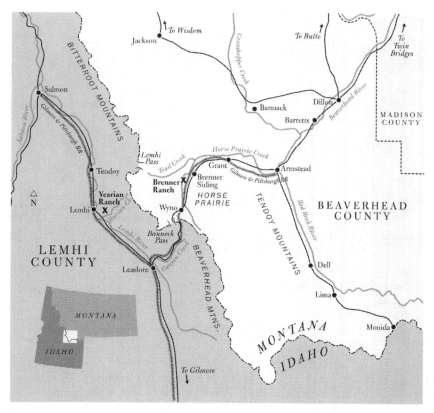

Thomas Savage country, in southwest Montana, winds across the Continental Divide into Idaho's Lemhi River valley. Map of Thomas Savage County, southwest Montana. Courtesy of *Montana the Magazine of Western History*, designer Diane Gleba Hall. It first appeared in O. Alan Weltzien, "Thomas Savage, Forgotten Novelist," *Montana The Magazine of Western History* (Winter 2008): 22-41.

Introduction

The West is a kind of touchstone for myself

THOMAS SAVAGE to interviewer John Scheckter,
(April 15, 1983, during his final Montana visit)

Something aching and lonely and terrible
of the west is caught forever on his pages.

ANNIE PROULX, afterword to *The Power of the Dog* (rpt. 2001)

Of mountains and valleys
of cold and cruelty
of stony silence
writes Thomas Savage
queerly

SANDY JAMES (Savage's nephew, September 30, 2008)

T HOMAS SAVAGE resisted fitting in though he was, by all accounts, a brilliant conversationalist, a chameleonic voice who could easily adapt and play a range of roles. Growing up a century ago in rural, high-elevation country in the northern Rockies that remains remote even in the early twenty-first century, he presented himself as an urban sophisticate, and he was that. He loved flashy scarves, smoked (until quitting, at age seventy-three) with a cigarette holder à la Franklin Roosevelt, and favored showy sports cars. He knew Montana ranches and small towns from its southwest corner as a native (though he was born in Salt Lake City), and until his early twenties he worked on the Brenner cattle ranch all seasons. He broke a wild horse named Grizzly, taught riding at dude ranches, and found himself, on his twenty-first birthday (April 25, 1936), herding sheep in Montana's Bitterroot Valley. Later he relished exotic seafood and classical music, above all Mozart—one cousin claimed Savage knew more classical music than most music professors—and he built a huge record collection. An interior decorator, according to Russell Savage, his surviving son, he preferred "Russian samovars, brass student lamps, Toulouse-Lautrec prints, and epergnes," all carefully placed above a big Persian carpet.

He drank a lot, like many writers, yet kept strict nocturnal writing habits, and he always knew his novel's openings and closings when he began a new one. He professed to read little, claiming to know nothing about most other writers, Montanan or otherwise. They returned the favor. Above all, as a gay man who married, fathered three children (two sons then a daughter) whom he adored all his life, and loved extended family deeply, he embodied a powerful contradiction, or set of tensions, wherein his sexual orientation chafed against accepted heterosexual conventions. His wife, fellow novelist Elizabeth (Betty) Fitzgerald Savage, put up with a lot yet they remained extraordinarily close, both personally and professionally, until her dying day.

In her *Publishers Weekly* interview with Savage (July 15, 1988), Francesca Coltrera called Savage "a balladeer, almost, of the American scene." If so, Savage's ballads, like many of the best known, sing sad stories, but it's more than that. Particularly in the eight novels set in southwestern Montana and Idaho's Lemhi River Valley, Savage wields an acidic brush, one that goes against the grain of triumphal stories of white pioneers and their prospering or floundering descendants. Savage prefers anti-heroic, acerbic flavors. His stylistic wit and play, especially his essayistic interludes, expose grim realities and lonely spaces: spaces swollen by gender stereotypes that precluded, for the most part, sexual minorities such as himself.

After Savage died (July 25, 2003), *The New York Times* obituary, published a month later, referred to his "spare novels of the American West, without six-shooters and gunsmoke, [which] found wide acceptance in the 1940s and a whole new readership in his later years." (Wolfgang Saxon, August 25, 2003) The Savage revival, insofar as his faded reputation is changing in the current generation, can be dated from 2001, when Emily Salkin Takoudes, a then young editorial assistant at Little,

Brown and Company, persisted and, with Savage's friendship and blessing, republished his two best novels (*The Power of the Dog* and *I Heard My Sister Speak My Name*, the latter re-titled *The Sheep Queen*) in Back Bay trade paperback editions (June and November 2001, respectively).

The *Los Angeles Times* obituary also cited Savage's "spare, sensitive Western novels." I take "spare" to mean the kind of unsettling, discomforting plot that subverts the usual claims of self-congratulating western narratives from the Manifest Destiny doctrine through the present, endemic in popular cultural production and local histories. Savage's West presents a tougher story of unbending gender boxes and stifling provincialities, of personal or social failure. In his West, meanness and ostracism and hatred surface more frequently than love. For these and other reasons, Savage's career comprises a story of neglect, which the *Los Angeles Times* obit conceded: "although Savage enjoyed universal critical acclaim for all of his novels, he never became well known and never had a best-seller." (Myrna Oliver, August 30, 2003) His novels, among other things a calculated subversion of genre fiction (i.e., westerns), sold poorly.

Savage's greatest commercial success came with his second and third novels, which he considered his weakest ("too sentimental"). Almost all of his thirteen novels, published 1944–88, earned him high praise in *The New York Times Book Review, The New York Review of Books*, and other newspapers. After the publication of *I Heard My Sister Speak My Name* (1977; hereafter *The Sheep Queen*) a *New Yorker* reviewer concluded, "There are few American novelists now active who have produced a more distinguished body of work." One of his champions, *The Washington Post*'s influential critic, Jonathan Yardley, called him, in the late 1970s, "a writer of real consequence . . . a masterful novelist" and included him with the likes of John Cheever, John Irving, Larry McMurtry, Toni Morrison, Peter Taylor, John Updike, Larry Woiwode, and Eudora Welty. Yet Savage sold far fewer than these other writers and his name is unknown by comparison. Yardley's praise matches his incredulity: "it is a shame, bordering on an outrage, that so few readers have discovered him." Savage received a Guggenheim Fellowship in 1980, between his tenth and eleventh novels, but public recognition still eluded him.

Writing in *The American Scholar* at the height of Savage's career, literary critic Roger Sale, another Savage champion, labeled him "perhaps the most striking instance among my [survey of] authors of the uses and disasters that are liable to accompany the unknown." In Sale's scheme, novelists collectively occupy a pyramid, the lowest, fifth level constituting the "unknowns." He documents Savage's sadly unknown status: "The novels of Thomas Savage have been borrowed from [my local library] about once every other year." Nor was Savage better known in professional circles since Sale declares, in a footnote, that no one in the Western Literature Association, the primary scholarly organization devoted to literatures of the American West, had even heard of him. (*The American Scholar,* Winter 1973–74, pp. 86–104) That's astonishing. More than a decade would pass before one scholarly article appeared (John Scheckter's "Thomas Savage and the West: Roots of Compulsion") in *Western American Literature* (Spring 1985), and none have appeared in that journal since. Furthermore, the Montana literary establishment that emerged after the 1960s has ignored Savage.

This study aims to reverse his sad tale of obscurity.

Perhaps it's too easy to label him a writer's writer, but he's found some powerful allies since then. He was closely admired by Annie Proulx, who wrote an essay about what she calls classic American landscape fiction, at the center of whom is Savage. This essay became the afterword to the reissue of *The Power of the Dog.* And just a few years ago, novelist Tom McGuane, another Savage fan for decades, declared, "It is incomprehensible that. . . Savage is so neglected. . . In my view, Savage may be the best of all the western novelists, after Cather."

High quality, low sales. The paradox goes to the heart of the matter. There are several reasons for Savage's relative obscurity in his lifetime, which this introduction enumerates. Chief among these, his strident writing against the grain of not only the popular western but of literary fiction in the northern Rockies, and his steadily harsh tone, best explain his coterie reputation. In Savage's West, ranches—a sine qua non in the national imagination—destroy rather than ennoble families. Savage foregrounds loneliness on ranches and in small towns as no other writer I know. His fiction makes us squirm and revise common understandings about life in the rural West. Townspeople in Savage's world often appear stupid rather than endearing.

Takoudes, the editor who resuscitated Savage in 2001, has told me she doubts *The Power of the Dog* sold more than 1,000 copies when first published. He remained largely unknown in his native state and region, and he knew his sales figures remained low. You won't find his name in the primary critical books about Montana literature—none of them. Montana's well-known state literature anthology, *The Last Best Place* (1989), neither names nor includes him in its 1,200-page survey: a shocking fact given the length of Savage's career and high critical reputation. But that absence signifies, tragically, the near-silence surrounding his name in his home region.

Thomas Savage Country, as I've called it for years, straddles a section of the Continental Divide, running from Dillon, Montana, southwest through Horse Prairie, Montana, across Bannock Pass and down to Leadore, Idaho, then northwest along the Lemhi River drainage to Salmon, Idaho. It covers the southwestern section of giant Beaverhead County, Montana (at more than 5,500 square miles, Montana's largest) and Lemhi County, Idaho, one of Idaho's largest and most remote from population centers. To this day it remains an acutely rural section of the country and certainly no other writer has claimed it. Savage Country includes Butte, Montana, and Salt Lake City, and in a few fictions, Boston or suburban New England, but mostly it's this high dry lonesome country he knew as a native son. He knew it inside out and possessed, apparently, a photographic memory. At least, he never seemed to forget faces, foibles, voices, buildings. Like James Joyce and Willa Cather, among so many writers, he left home in order to write it.

That near-silence within which he grew up dogged his career, and he couldn't entirely explain it. In his *Contemporary Authors* interview with Jean W. Ross (January 11, 1989), he states, "One strange thing is that I have never been considered a Western writer in Montana, where I come from. There are lots of people who are considered Montana writers who are not even Montanans. I don't know why I haven't been; I think I was among the first of them." Apart from the irony of his label, "Western writer," and the always-suspect nativist assumptions of

"Montana writer": in the inexplicable processes of canon formation, Savage's neglect in Montana represents the most astonishing element in his story of neglect.

After all, *The Pass* (1944), Savage's first novel, was published with good notices three years before A. B. Guthrie Jr.'s *The Big Sky*. In his home state, why isn't he assigned the same rank as Guthrie, whose first two novels (*The Big Sky*, 1947; *The Way West*, 1949) commenced an historical sextet that occupies an honored and indisputable position? The arc of Guthrie's sextet, spanning roughly a century and a half, provides a triumphant, foundational settlement story. Guthrie's title adorned Montana license plates for two generations (actually, a slight modification: *Big Sky Country*).

Yet after *The Pass* was published, one significant Montana writer, Joseph Kinsey Howard, who compiled Big Sky Country's first literary anthology, *Montana Margins* (1946), took note. As though confirming Savage's early promise, he included part or all of four chapters in his anthology (in the ninth, penultimate section, "Travel and Transport"). Yet after his thirteenth novel (published 1988), Savage couldn't sell another and by his death, his slender reputation had further drooped, though the republication of *Power* and *Sheep Queen* helps reverse that trend. At present four of his novels are in print. First editions can be bought cheaply.

The story of neglect, of low name recognition despite extravagant critical praise, forms an essential contradiction this study addresses and explains. Why was Savage little more than a footnote in serious fiction about the Intermountain West in the twentieth century's second half? Why wasn't he at least a midlist novelist? Why isn't he included in the ranks of the Wallace Stegners and Ivan Doigs? Why doesn't he receive classroom and critical attention (apart from a few instances, e.g., my own) and enjoy a devoted readership and leading position among the ranks of novelists?

This biography seeks to answer these questions and in doing so, place Savage in the front rank of twentieth-century Western American fiction, where he deserves to be.

Savage pushed against the settler-colonial narrative, which might explain his unpopularity. In the only publication devoted to the husband-and-wife novelists published during his lifetime, *Thomas and Elizabeth Savage* (*Western Writers Series*, 1995), Sue Hart cites Savage's preoccupation with the "dark side" of the American West as explanation for his lousy sales and slight reputation. A few years later, in the afterword to the reprint of *The Power of the Dog*, Annie Proulx lauds Savage's tough lens, which she believes puts off most readers. Proulx excellently surveys Savage's West—the myriad tragedies of settlement—and the total fusion of life and work:

> [The] family complexity of names and identities, of east coast culture and western mountains, of manual labor and writing, of a lost past and private secrets, characterizes Savage's life, his novels, and the people in them. The tangle of abandonment, loss, broken families, and difficult emotional situations is in Savage's work and, to a considerable extent, is related to his own life...Savage developed an exquisitely keen eye for nuances of body language, intonation, silence. (*Power,* p. 283)

But there's more to it than this. In his career-long chronicle of loneliness and strained communication, Savage repeatedly decries the plight of oddballs, particularly if oddballs include gay men such as himself. Over and over, his fiction implicitly protests stifling gender and sexuality stereotypes with their rigid proscriptions and taboos governing what can and cannot be expressed or desired. He argues that ranch and small-town life box men and women into preformed cells—straitjacket habits that stifle their affective and creative selves. These cells kill diversity.

Savage condemns much more than he praises and in his calling out, he suggests a more inclusive, more tolerant rural West than he grew up in or later wrote about. He knew that he could not produce western genre fiction. Moreover, he knew that his West disputed that social milieu celebrated by pop culture. He opens *The Sheep Queen,* his most overtly autobiographical novel, with a nonfictional confession that declares his independent road and resolve. The first-person authorial surrogate, Thomas Burton, a middle-aged novelist married to a novelist, affirms,

I am too difficult for some readers and my sentences are sometimes more than statements. Many readers are comfortable only
with the simple sentences, and prefer books that reward a belief
in the happy ending and the pot at the end of the rainbow, even as
the rainbow retreats and those who follow are footsore. There is
no ending, happy or otherwise, only a pause.

This defiant credo, with its closing note of disillusionment as though
even unhappy endings have no place in western plots, confirms the
value of his aesthetic, in which the marketplace has little bearing. He
makes no apology. This tough credo also explains his unpopularity.

   Savage knew his own quality; knew, for example, he was writing a
West that upended the formula western of Owen Wister and Zane Gray.
His occasional self-assessments appear accurate. Eleven years later in
that *Publishers Weekly* interview (1988), Savage sounds the same note,
simultaneously lamenting his unpopularity and defining his coterie
appeal. He opens the interview with his appraisal: "I'm a pretty good
writer. But I'm not rich and famous, I'll tell you that." His compara-
tive neglect bothered him: "I wish I could write cheaply or popularly,
because I need the money . . . [but] I don't know how to go about it." Even
if he knew how, he would have refused that well-worn path. He admitted he knew next to nothing about book promotion, and elsewhere he
describes a typical book launch as consisting of one Manhattan cocktail
party. Savage knew where he stood and for whom he wrote, and again,
makes no apology: "I'm writing for rather highly educated people, and
I think my writing is only going to appeal to people who have extreme
sensitivity. This can come by birth or it can come by education. And if
you don't have it . . . you'll never understand *me*." (ital. original)

   The arrogant, condescending tone in these passages suggests this
writer's marginality; his abrasive satire, plots of acute disillusionment,
and cri de coeur about the plight of gay men in the rural West explain
it further. That *Publishers Weekly* interview, published within weeks of
what turned out to be his final novel (*The Corner of Rife and Pacific*, 1988),
forms a swan song, in fact. Characteristically, *Corner* garnered praise
from several quarters. For example, the Literary Guild selected it for its
Critic Corner; and in 1989 he received the Pacific Northwest Booksellers
Association Award for it. But as a writer, Savage was finished.

Half a year later, in the *Contemporary Authors* interview with Ross, Savage said he was working on "a novel about a young man with acquired immune deficiency syndrome (AIDS)." Nothing came of this, but in old age Savage wrote a novella, "Buddies," chronicling a same-sex love story set before and during World War I, that his agent couldn't place nor his final editor, Harvey Ginsberg of William Morrow, accept. At this exact time there was an explosion in gay men's literature, but it predominately focused upon city life. Little was published about queer rural life, and the World War I setting might have also been a deal breaker. In the *Contemporary Authors* interview with Ross, glancing over his long career—thirteen novels in forty-four years—Savage ruefully admitted, "I don't know why it is, I have never had a wide audience and I suppose I never will." An old widower who moved to San Francisco for a few years and lived with a little boxer, Savage was increasingly neglected though he lived for another decade.

During his final visit to Dillon (April 1983), surveying his career to date, he denied any autobiographical basis to his novels, stating "nobody is actual, of course." That pose belies the fact that his fiction is acutely autobiographical, a series of family dramas in which various members are imaginatively repurposed to play various roles, and in which Savage himself appears in differing stages of his life. That tendency reinforces the idea that the life and the work cannot be separated since both, together, expose frictions between his sexuality and traditional heterosexual gender roles.

□   □   □

This study seeks to reverse his marginal position in letters during his lifetime and expand the modest Savage renaissance of the early twenty-first century. It reviews all his fiction though concentrating on the eight western novels. Most of the other five novels, set in New England, bear western seeds within them, and their protagonists display facets of "western" identity. It seeks to open his Savage West, and the fraught position of gay men within it, to new audiences and thereby restore him to the literary rank he so richly earned in American, let alone Montanan, letters.

In the American West as it's been theorized and conceptually

opened, further and further, in the current period—a West recogniz-
ing and celebrating sexual and racial minorities, and anti-foundational
narratives of failure and dispersal that complicate our common understanding and appraisal of our recent and not-so-recent past—Savage
finds his place. His idiosyncratic, courageous, sustained reinterpreta-
tion of the twentieth century's first half from the vantage of its second
recommends him as a significant precursor to the more inclusive, if not
tolerant, rural American West of the present.

To the extent that this biography is an act of recovery, Savage's West
belongs in a central position in our understanding of the Intermountain West as a literary region. The American West in the twenty-first
century is nothing if not diverse and inclusive, usually disruptive and
migratory, and Savage's astringency belongs in our ever-more plural-
istic canon. At the very least, readers of northern Rockies fiction gain
a far more nuanced, more ambivalent knowledge of twentieth-century
rural life and the ways in which that life follows characters into cities.
Savage complicates rural stereotypes in salutary ways for an increasingly urban population.

Savage's harsh and sometimes gay West is long overdue recognition, and critical esteem and embrace, in Western American literature.
He merits a high place in the canon, and his fiction deserves to be far
more widely read and taught and reviewed. Not that long ago, *Western American Literature* devoted a special issue (vol. 5, no. 2, Summer
2016) to "Queer Wests." Guest editor Geoffrey W. Bateman traces the
"painful legacy of violence that marks the history and representation
of queerness" in the American West. The four essays that follow his,
he argues, "strive to find something meaningful, if not redemptive, in
this violence, to provide insight into the queer legacies of resistance
and transformation and to imagine different ways of desiring, iden-
tifying, or embodying sexualities or genders that move beyond our
familiar structures." (p. 138) Savage clearly holds a place in early and
mid-twentieth-century representations of queerness in the rural West
(and urban Northeast, for that matter).

His daughter claimed he "hated Montana" and in the opening of *The
Sheep Queen* (1977) the authorial surrogate, narrator Tom Burton, states,
"I believe I lived in Maine because Maine is about as far as I could get

from the ranch in Montana where I grew up, and where my mother was unhappy, my beautiful, angel mother." (p. 7) He couldn't wait to leave it behind, but that's not the whole story, as is the case with many writers. In more than one place, Savage claimed that writers write best about what they dislike or even loathe. But that's not the whole story either. No doubt Savage regarded his home country similarly to British conductor Sir Thomas Beecham's disdain for Seattle, where he briefly landed in 1941, pronouncing it "a cultural dustbin." Or recall Gertrude Stein's famous pronouncement about her past in Oakland, California: "There is no there there." Yet Savage remained imaginatively loyal to his first geography for the majority of his career.

In the author's note concluding *A Bargain With God* (1953), his third novel, which likely outsold all the others, Savage stated that he feels nostalgia more strongly than any other emotion. Savage never did research for his fiction; rather, he opened the floodgates of memory and brought his photographic recall to canny use. Particularly in his eight western novels, he created what I've called a near-historical novel: fictions removed one-three generations from the writer's present that depict the period of the writer's childhood or young adulthood. Savage subscribed to Willa Cather's credo "that we are most sensitive to the world around us between the ages of eight and 16. And so I keep going back to the period when I was that age." (*Publishers Weekly* interview) While New England novels like *Daddy's Girl* (1970) and *A Strange God* (1974) are set in the present, the western novels focus, usually, upon the first half of the twentieth century, often the interwar period (1918-39). He kept returning to his first decades—a period during which Montana suffered major economic misfortunes and diaspora—to write queerly, as nephew Sandy James put it.

He wrote queerly not only as a gay man committed to heterosexual marriage. In old age, he denied he was bisexual, a different sexuality from homosexuality, to his daughter: Savage stayed true to his queer self. But he wrote about the Intermountain West from odd, sour angles, or at least angles that undercut the usual triumphalist narratives however light or dark. I know of no fictive world exactly like Savage's—though as a critical regionalist he belongs to a high tradition of American writers casting a hard glance at their home ground. He wrote a species of top-shelf anti-western that affords a much-needed corrective view among received notions of literary fiction about the American West. His audience—those with "extreme sensitivity," as he put it in 1988—has vastly expanded.

A 1974 author photo of Savage—my favorite, and which appears on the back dust jacket of *Midnight Line* (1976), his ninth novel—shows him age fifty-nine, at the top of his game. He sits at his ease on a wooden desk chair, his arms casually draped along its wide arms, his left leg crossed over his right above the knee of his dark slacks. Savage wears a white shirt, the top two buttons opened and the sleeves rolled up to just below his elbows. In his right hand, propped between index and middle fingers, a recently lit cigarette, firm in its short white holder, burns. His left hand cradles a Jefferson cup (pewter cups with circular rim designed by Thomas Jefferson, usually seven or eight ounces), no doubt filled with what he called gin or milk punch (half of each). His sweat socks match his shirt though his dirty sneakers do not.

Relaxed, he faces the camera directly without smiling but with no grimace, his tanned face and neck exposing some middle-aged wrinkles. He looks right at you but he doesn't stare. His eyes might suggest he's bemused, ready to engage you. Relatives and friends repeatedly attested to his good looks as though he were, say, a Rock Hudson lookalike. A nephew's wife called him "drop-dead handsome": one who attracts our gaze as soon as he appears. Savage knew he was a looker who exuded generous helpings of charisma and charm, just as he knew his relative neglect. He knew he commanded any room he entered. As his second son and middle child, Russell Savage recalled that his father had an air of imperial Caesar in him, always ready for his audience.

He set his own course and stuck to it. Savage's love of exotic European luxury or sports cars, particularly in the 1950s and 1960s, was well known. He illustrated a pattern wherein gay men use cosmopolitanism to mark their identity in a way that the hostile heterosexual majority might not discern. During his Boston years he enthusiastically belonged to the Veteran Motor Car Club of America, and it meant a lot to him to have owned a Rolls-Royce for a brief period after 1952. Not too many years ago, Russell told me of his father's contempt for Cadillacs and the businessmen who drove them. Savage judged himself superior to the big rancher, a luxury American sedan stereotype, one he grew up with in Dillon.

For a year or two in the mid-1950s, Savage, then living in Waltham, Massachusetts, flaunted a sporty "British racing blue Porsche speedster coupe," and on one occasion he recruited Russell to ride with him north, along US Highway 1 (no Interstate 95 yet existing) into southern Maine—ultimately, to Georgetown, where Savage moved the family in 1955. In Russell's story about the trip, Savage imagines a P-51 dogfight with a white Cadillac Coupe de Ville up ahead—those extraordinarily long 1950s Caddies sporting sleek, flanged fins. Savage voices the challenge: "'Let's see if we can get past him!'" Russell writes, he drove "like the very wind" but the Caddie accelerates farther and pulls away. The writer mutters, "'Son of a bitch may be able to keep ahead of us on the stretches,' the corners of his wide mouth turned down in a grimace, 'but we'll catch him in the curves and when we get to the right place, we'll pass him.'" But Savage doesn't pass the Caddie as "the road ahead, no matter how hard he drove himself, would always be for him cruelly, inexorably, straight."

Russell's conclusion perfectly captures Savage's use of sports cars as symbol of his sexual difference, as well as the symbolic sense of the road to popular approbation being denied him.

He lived and wrote as a divided self—a gay man mostly happily married to a woman—who embodied and manifested a series of sharp contradictions. As I've been noting, Savage wrote against the mainstream, both western and American, in a number of ways. For that fact alone, he merits critical attention and name recognition. Given his unusual edge as a rural gay westerner, his life and fiction reveal perspectives that invite our assessment. In the far more complex American West we've come to know, his sharp voice and counter-narrative have a place. His time has come.

CHAPTER ONE

Childhood and Adolescence, 1915–1936

My God! Here was my life!

THOMAS SAVAGE, April 1983

URING THOMAS SAVAGE's final visit to his home country, he drove up Horse Prairie, forty miles southwest of Dillon, Montana, and 1,500 feet higher, to Bannock Pass (7,684 feet) on the Continental Divide and Idaho-Montana border. He held a can of beer and looked near and far at this intimately familiar panorama—and dividing line—from his childhood. There's nary a building in sight, in 1983 or now, for that matter.

The scene's grandeur and tiny traces of human presence astonished him as though he cannot believe he sprang from such country.

Bannock Pass separates Horse Prairie, a high dry valley of scattered ranches, from the Lemhi River Valley just west beyond the Beaverhead Mountains, another high dry valley with scattered ranches. Given Savage's later New England life, urbane manner, and career as a writer, well might he have doubted his improbable origins in this remote corner of the northern Rockies. Yet Savage was a son of the sagebrush with town a far distance. The Yearian Ranch of Lemhi, Idaho, home of his mother's family, and the Brenner Ranch of Horse Prairie, home of his stepfather's, remained the psychic centers of his long life. He wrote about them repeatedly.

The Gilmore and Pittsburgh Railroad, a spur line built 1909-10 between Armstead, Montana, and Salmon (and Gilmore), Idaho, and informally known as the "Get Off and Push," regularly stopped at the Brenner siding, which included a post office and tiny store (until the

1930s). It linked the cattle ranch into which Savage's mother married and the sheep ranch run, mostly, by his maternal grandmother. Savage claimed, even late in life, to still dream regularly about this railroad, which ceased operation in 1939. He fondly recalls the ride over Bannock Pass, winding down Canyon Creek through a canyon to Leadore ("Junction"), Idaho, where the track split and where, with his mother and little sister, he'd ride the northwest spur some miles farther to the Yearian Ranch. He recalled boxed lunches, maybe fried chicken and oranges. The G&P in effect launched Savage as a novelist since he centered *The Pass* on the construction of the G&P and its triumphant arrival in "Salmon City," Idaho.

That little railroad, which backed through a tunnel just below Bannock Pass, connected sparsely settled country only a couple of generations after initial white settlement. Elizabeth (Beth) Yearian Savage (1890–1957) gave birth to Thomas, her second child, in Salt Lake City (April 25, 1915), and soon brought him home to Lemhi, Idaho. By that time her marriage to Tom's father, Benjamin Harrison Savage (1889–1971, title character of *The Liar*, 1969), was floundering. By all accounts the headstrong Beth, the oldest child, returned to the Yearian fold with baby and without Ben Savage—a man as handsome, in a period way (i.e., an "Arrow Collar man"), as he was superficial and unsuccessful: "all show and no go," it was said. In a letter written in old age, Tom Savage claimed Beth gave up her first baby, a daughter (born February 25, 1912), for adoption in response to her mother's (Emma R. Yearian's) deep grief upon the death of Beth's younger brother, Tom-Dick (Emma's favorite child), of appendicitis at age eleven (September 18, 1911). Savage would not discover this sister, Patricia ("Pat") McClure Hemenway, until middle age. His headstrong mother and grandmother became the models for all Savage's strong-willed female characters.

Savage's tenth novel, *I Heard My Sister Speak My Name* (1977)—a.k.a. *The Sheep Queen* (2001)—has long been judged his most autobiographical novel, and as I'll claim, though it's a fiction, Savage stays remarkably close to unchanged family history throughout it. Autobiography is masked as autobiographical fiction. Thus, *The Sheep Queen* provides unique, detailed insight into his life story, however fictionalized. Regarding his parents' divorce, for example, we read in *The Sheep Queen*,

"When [Beth] left him, my father was a salesman for a cigar company, a job that took him into poolhalls and bars; there they would have found him charming with his looks, his stories and comic monologues. His scenes from Shakespeare were impressive." (p. 216) Savage inherited the same wit and charm.

His most trenchant rendition of his parents' failed marriage occurs in *The Liar* (1969), Savage's sixth novel.

Beth Yearian divorced Ben Savage in 1917 on the grounds of infidelity (cf. *The Liar*, p. 218; *The Sheep Queen*, p. 216) and returned home to Lemhi, Idaho, from Seattle, where the Savages had temporarily lived. The same year, Savage married his second wife, Hazel Baldwin whom, after nine years, he divorced, soon after marrying his third, Marjorie Wood. He stayed married the longest to his fourth wife, Dorothy "Dottie" Ritchie who, after his death, would live with Tom and Betty Savage for a while. Beth took little Tom up Yearian Creek with her as she herded a band of her mother's sheep (there being a manpower shortage because of World War I enlistments; cf. *Sheep Queen*, pp. 216-17). Savage much later summarized his mother's endless ranch work in her three years between marriages: "Three summers my mother herded sheep. Three winters she tended to the big house and scrubbed the floors on her hands and knees. Three springs she cooked for the lambing crew and little later for the sheepherders. She was the last one in bed at night." (*The Sheep Queen*, p. 217) Her steady hard work manifested itself in her son's discipline in his writing career.

Savage retained a sharp memory of the 1918 influenza epidemic, which struck months after his third birthday. Reminiscing, he wrote his cousin, Janet N. S. Moore, "Then the Flu hit, and we wore gauze masks that my mother washed each day and hung to dry over the fireplace. And then she got the flu, and I recall my terror when the ambulance came to take her to the hospital. She survived..." (May 15, 1998)

Soon after the flu epidemic, Beth changed Tom's world at the Yearian Ranch. Just before he turned five, Beth married Charles (Charlie) Brenner, third and youngest son of Horse Prairie's Brenner Ranch, on March 23, 1920, in Butte, Montana. They honeymooned in British Columbia's Fraser River Valley. Savage would later characterize Beth's remarriage as her double duty—to her mother, the Sheep Queen, and to her son without a father. In *The Sheep Queen*, he states, "I believe my mother looked on the marriage as her duty to me. I think she hoped Charlie would adopt me, and I would be secure forever." (p. 219) This marriage brought the Brenner (cattle) Ranch into Tom's life, and it would remain his prototype of all that's destructive in the ranching world.

The landscapes of Tom's childhood and adolescence remain almost as unpopulated now as in his day. Montana remains one of the largest and least populated states, and Beaverhead County sprawls across its high, mountainous southwest corner. Larger than Connecticut, the county takes more than half a day to transit from northwest to southeast (incl. today's Interstate 15). Cattle considerably outnumber people per square mile a century after Savage's childhood, since Beaverhead County counts well under 10,000 people and features three traffic lights (all in Dillon). Today it's fewer than two people per square mile and a century ago, fewer yet. Most Americans would judge the Horse Prairie ranching community as the proverbial back of beyond. It's a forty-five minute drive from Dillon, the distant county seat, even factoring in Interstate 15 for the first eighteen miles.

The preponderance of sagebrush, with willow browse lining Horse Prairie Creek and its tributaries, its dun slopes giving way to broad bands of lodgepole pine and rocky ridges above them, might disenchant those accustomed, say, to verdant landscapes. This little north-south valley, like Bannock Pass capping its south end, viscerally represents Big Sky Country where landscape looms and people don't. We're tiny inside it, as are the infrequent sheds, barns, or houses. In these visual panoramas—and the Yearian Ranch, above a narrow swatch of the Lemhi River with the Lemhi Range rising immediately west (and the Beaverheads just east and above it), affords similar panoramas—people barely figure.

These big, open landscapes feel unimaginable to Americans from either coast, or the Midwest or South for that matter. The scale and the paucity of built environment scare most away. Savage's son, Russell, provided a hyperbolic outsider reaction when he wrote, "my father. . .was raised on a cattle ranch in a part of Montana which closely resemble[s] something which can be seen, with the help of a strong telescope, on the mountains of the moon." As a teenage New Englander, Russell claimed "it looked to me a lot like the dark side of the moon—red dirt, rock, and sagebrush and not much else." Russell Savage's incomprehension, if not outrage, typifies those accustomed to smaller scale, more settled and populated topographies—or those who have difficulty, to borrow a title, getting over the color green. Outsiders from any distance typically fail to enlarge their aesthetic lenses: those who spend any time in Horse Prairie usually love it and remark about its big open scale.

During his final visit to Dillon and Horse Prairie, standing atop Bannock Pass (7,684 feet) with a can of beer and surveying his past in this panorama almost entirely bereft of human sign, he exclaimed "My God! Here was my life!": a comment later repeated to Dillon interviewers. By then it felt both intimately familiar and impossibly remote. Out of that tension Savage defined his American West. That last visit to Dillon (April 1983) proved a crucial episode in Savage's psyche, further loosing the floodgates of memory. This biography repeatedly references that visit, which sheds bright light on the writer's harsh ambivalences about his first geography and its fraught presence in his fiction.

But the sense of seemingly impossible remoteness, Savage's birthright, never left him. He addresses it in the *Contemporary Authors* interview (January 11, 1989) published the year after his final novel: "I think the difference in Westerners has to do with the fact that they feel it's impossible to look at the Rocky Mountains—or to look at the horizon, which is equally vast—and consider that there is such a thing as Europe or neighbors or anything else." Savage compensated for rural remoteness with European sports cars and decor. A dozen years earlier in *The Sheep Queen* he'd stated the same thing: "it was difficult for some to look out on the awesome Rocky Mountains and consider the prosaic fact of Europe." (*The Sheep Queen*, p. 93) Most Americans—urbanites or suburbanites—can't imagine such remoteness. The valley's population likely peaked in the homesteader boom (1900-20), after which surviving ranchers bought out abandoned places, and the population shrank as holdings were consolidated. Savage hailed from a place with few, widely scattered neighbors.

Having lived in southwest Montana for over a quarter century, I understand Savage's perspective, one difficult for outsiders to accept. That peculiar combination of size and apparent emptiness constitutes a fundamental image and lure in the Intermountain West apart from its cities and suburbs. This image, of course, iconically defines notions of Western American frontier that held sway for generations—and still do in vestigial versions of pop culture. Savage repeatedly painted this canvas, as it came naturally to him, and in the foreground he anatomized particular strains of loneliness and frustration ensuing from it.

Yet students of American history, let alone Montana history, have actually heard passing reference to what I call Thomas Savage Country because it constitutes a small strand of Lewis and Clark's Corps of Discovery route west. What we call Horse Prairie represents part of Sacajawea's Lemhi Shoshone tribe's home country, and the home place of what would become the Brenner Ranch forms the spot where the Corps turned west, following Trail Creek up to Lemhi Pass (7,373 feet) where they first stood on the Continental Divide (August 12, 1805). On their route east William Clark's contingent of the split crew returned to lower Horse Prairie, recovering a cache that included tobacco. For most of the nineteenth century, geographers believed Meriwether Lewis's verdict that Lemhi Pass, west of Horse Prairie and ultimately a stagecoach route, constituted the headwaters of the Missouri River system. It's not. But apart from this famous white passage in the early nineteenth century, and the Nez Perce passage in August 1877, following the Battle of the Big Hole, this high remote valley remained unknown except to prospectors and ranchers. It remains little known beyond Beaverhead County.

When Beth Savage brought her toddler home to Lemhi, Idaho, she brought him to a family ranch begun by her grandparents forty years earlier. Thomas Yearian (1864-1963), Savage's maternal grandfather, was a cattleman, lifelong Democrat, and second fiddle to his wife, Emma Russell Yearian (1866-1951), known in the family as "Big Mama." Tom Yearian's family reached Bannack, Montana Territory, from Illinois in 1866, moved south to Horse Prairie two years later, and later moved across the Divide, having purchased the Joseph Pattee Ranch at Lemhi, Idaho Territory. The grandson-writer named after him claimed that Tom Yearian's father, George, discovered gold in Jefferson Davis Creek in 1870 and ultimately bought three ranches in the Lemhi River Valley. He likely sold some claims initially to William A. Clark, who became the first of Butte's three Copper Barons and a famously corrupt politician.

George Yearian sold other claims to John Brenner, Savage's paternal step-grandfather, who managed to lose $100,000 on a dredge-boat operation there. In a letter Savage stated, "after the dredge-boat failed in its search, the heavy machines, the generators and so forth, ended up in sheds beside the big log barn where also was stored silver and china from the house that burned in 191[3]." It amused Savage that both sides of his family crossed paths in a remote gold diggings in Horse Prairie, on a creek named after the Confederate president, and that the Yearians emerged much more flush as a result. Savage wrote the archetypal story of a prospector finding gold more than once.

Tom Yearian met Emma at a country dance (he played fiddle, and Emma, a determined young schoolteacher, played piano), and they married April 15, 1889. In good, nineteenth-century rural American fashion, they produced six children in the next eleven years, the author's mother, Elizabeth (Beth), being the firstborn. In 1901, having decided to get into the sheep ranching business, Emma secured a loan in a Dillon bank and, with her husband's help, trailed their first 1,200 sheep over the Continental Divide to Lemhi. Tom deeply admired his grandmother who broke ground as a businesswoman and sheep rancher. Emma, a lifelong Republican and the first woman to represent Lemhi County in the Idaho Legislature (1931–32), was tagged "the Sheep Queen of Idaho" by a *Salt Lake Tribune* reporter, and it stuck. As affirmed in *The Sheep Queen*, "she knew long ago what her life would be, how she would manage it." (p. 101) And she stuck to her plan.

Of the author's grandparents, the Sheep Queen was easily the dominant one. Short and broad, she always towered over Savage's imagination, particularly in the ways she pushed against gender conventions. The *Idaho Statesman* ran a lengthy retrospective about her (January 29, 1978) twenty-seven years after her death. She proved a canny rancher and family boss, eventually running 6,000 sheep on both the Yearian Ranch and leased land. The winter of 1918 brought so much cold and snow that the Gilmore and Pittsburgh Railroad hauled hay (with a 400 percent cost spike from 1917) that helped save the Yearians and other ranchers, an episode Savage borrowed for the climax of his first novel.

Emma was never refused a bank loan because of her track record and self-confidence, and she brought the ranch through the Depression. She secured her bank loans in Dillon through her reputation, and never mortgaged anything. In her day journal of February 21, 1916, she noted, "Fifty years old today and feel no older than at 25." She bred Rambouillet rams with Cotswold ewes to maximize wool production. In a pair of posthumous profiles (January 22, 1978; January 29, 1978), *Idaho Statesman* staff writer Betty Penson quotes an old-timer who said, "She was so smart she just brained her way through anything." At a dinner in Switzerland in 1929, Emma was introduced as a representative of the (52,000-member) National Business and Professional Women's Club. By the early 1930s, the Yearians owned 2,500 acres. A Utah reporter who interviewed her in the 1930s, according to Penson's retrospective, stated, "She looks like a mixture of the late Queen Emma of Holland and Mme. Schumann-Heink" [a stout German opera diva]. She was short and broad, one relative referring to her as "5' by 5'."

Tom Yearian, in extreme old age, sold the ranch in 1961, a decade after his wife's death on Christmas Day, 1951. By then he'd also lost his favorite child: Beth, his firstborn.

According to Savage, Big Mama's personal credo was captured in W. E. Henley's poem, "Invictus" (1888), particularly the lines, "I thank whatever gods may be / For my unconquerable soul." In old age, corpulent and with bad knees, she declared, "my spirit will never be broken." In *The Sheep Queen*, Savage's narrator-avatar adds, "She sometimes quoted the entire poem in a quiet, sepulchral voice—she had been trained in elocution. At the words, 'My head is bloody but unbowed,' she inclined her own head slightly and then snapped it up on her spine." (p. 150) Savage also quotes stanzas from "Invictus" in *Daddy's Girl* (1970), his seventh novel. Emma thus proved a model of deep civic involvement, lending her weight to many local organizations and charities. Emma was as easy with sheep shearers as political or religious leaders. Writing of her in his late essay, "Why a Pilgrim Traveled to Boston, and His Implausible Arrival There," Savage stated, "When later on my grandmother went to Europe, she got along with Ambassador Dawes in Germany and with the Pope in Rome." (*A Book for Boston*, 1980, p. 14) He inherited her drive for success and her flair.

The Yearians receive their most extended fictional treatment in *The Sheep Queen*—a re-titling he blessed in old age, as it honors his remarkable, high-octane maternal grandmother. That novel's autobiographical narrator, with shrugging admiration, describes the Sheep Queen as unstoppable: "Emma was like a brushfire. When you checked her in one place, she flared up over there." (p. 108) And in "Why a Pilgrim Traveled to Boston," Savage paints the annual sheep shearing scene at the Yearian Ranch, when ten shearers arrive an early June evening and "Big Mama" greets them by name and inquires after their kin, eventually admitting to her grandson that she has been to Boston, addressing a convention at the Copley Plaza Hotel. Grandmother and grandson proved at their ease anywhere.

The Yearian grandparents embraced fundamentally different parenting philosophies, Tom proving the gentle one. As stated in *The Sheep Queen*, "He wanted his children to be happy. She wanted them to be a success." (p. 77) The daughters particularly favored their father's view. In one day journal entry two months after the birth of Tom, her oldest grandson, she voiced rare frustration: "My children are all —— phules [damn fools]" (June 22, 1915). It took her years to recover from the death of her favorite child, Tom-Dick, at age eleven (September 18, 1911) — likely the roughest blow in her life. *The Sheep Queen* records the horror of his death: "After she buried him she stood in the middle of her dining room and screamed. And except for a little humming sound, that's the last sound her mouth made for two months. She could not speak but only hum, and that she did night after night. She sat on the edge of Tom-Dick's bed, humming a lullaby she had sung when he was a baby." (pp. 234–35)

Savage's mother, Beth, was feisty and independent growing up. She studied piano along with her siblings—a younger brother, three younger sisters, and a baby brother, Tom-Dick—and Big Mama kept a willow switch behind the upright to reinforce their practicing. She and her sisters were sent to boarding schools (St. Margaret's, Boise, Idaho), and college, where she led an active social life. The beauty of the family, she was described as a "Girl of the Golden West" who'd been "presented at Court in Ottawa" at age eighteen. (*The Sheep Queen*, p. 78) At age twenty-one (1911), Beth taught school at the mining settlement of Gilmore, Idaho. She had met this handsome young salesman, Ben Savage, and when she found herself four months' pregnant, she and Ben hastily married, on September 25, 1911, in Salmon, Idaho. Her father and favorite sister, Edwina ("Weenie") were in attendance; her mother was not. Tom-Dick Yearian had died one week earlier. As Savage suggests in his novels and letters, Beth's guilt in defying her domineering mother by marrying Savage, coupled with her guilt about Tom-Dick's death, doomed the marriage. Indeed, Savage stated that "It was on that fact that I wrote my novel I HEARD MY SISTER SPEAK MY NAME." (April 23, 1998, letter to cousin Janet Moore)

Growing up under such a powerful mother was tough for this pretty first-born daughter, and coming home after a busted marriage proved tougher.

Savage revisits his parents' love affair and failed marriage in both *The Liar* and, to a lesser extent, *The Sheep Queen*. She gave birth to a girl February 25, 1912, in Seattle, whom she immediately gave up for adoption. *The Sheep Queen* suggests that Beth's guilt compelled the adoption. (p. 241) Some combination of Beth's complex relationship with her mother and her sense that Ben Savage was a dud might explain her decision. The baby was immediately adopted by an affluent couple, Walter and Amy McClure, and named Amy Patricia McClure: she would go by her middle name, to distinguish herself from her mother. McClure was a prominent Seattle attorney, and "Pat" grew up in a lovely neighborhood near Seattle's Leschi Park.

Five years later (1917) when Beth returned home with Tom as a toddler, she would take her turn tending sheep or working in the fields, her baby strapped on her back like a papoose. Her independence later inspired her son's. At that time Beth befriended some of the Lemhi Shoshone band, learned some of their language, and wrote a dictionary. Back then their reservation boundary bordered the ranch, and some families used to summer camp there, as well as on the Brenner Ranch in Horse Prairie. The Yearians employed Lemhi Shoshone on the ranch. In *The Sheep Queen* we're told,

Each Christmas she sent the Indians boxes of food; they often visited the ranch where she gave them sides of beef and sacks of flour. The squaws came in and had coffee and cigarettes with her in the living room and they talked Shoshone. *Zant-nea-shewungen* means I love you. She bought their gloves and moccasins at twice the price the stores paid for them, and distributed them among her friends. (p. 136)

Tom Yearian was a close personal friend of Chief Tendoy (1834–1907), who reputedly died just a few miles up Agency Creek above the village that bears his name.

The home she returned to, a comfortable Dutch colonial house built in 1911, remains intact, as does the Yearian barn with a large "Y" painted above the front sliding door. As a child Savage loved this home and never forgot its nooks and crannies: in letters written late in life, he recounted particular hiding places and furniture details and pranks to his cousins. Among the Yearians he was the oldest known cousin of the third generation, and "always had a few French phrases to impress his younger cousins," according to one of them.

As adults, the Yearians developed a reputation for lively parties and alcohol was never in short supply though Big Mama never touched it. Beth in particular developed a fondness for drink that likely shortened her life and that she passed on to her precocious son. She used to hide bottles in dining room cupboards at the Brenner Ranch, and her brother-in-law, William—a bachelor and model for Savage's most notorious character—didn't take kindly to her. Beth loved horseback riding and camping, and one summer in the 1930s, she ran the Salmon River ("River of No Return") with a famous local guide. According to one grandchild, she liked to shoot magpies off a nearby fence from an open dining room window, using a .22 Remington pump action. One version of this behavior shows up in *Daddy's Girl*, when the narrator, Chris, describes his mother: "She was a good shot, and often picked off magpies with her .22 rifle out the kitchen window where, just beyond, there was usually a piece of spoiled beef for bait." (p. 32)

Like her mother, Beth displayed additional gender-bending interests, including a taste for unfiltered Camel cigarettes; moreover, she "could ride and shoot as well as any man and she rarely smiled." In most surviving photos, Beth Brenner looks harried, not happy. Pressures of gender conformity likely took a toll. Both tomboy and Marlboro (or Camel) Girl, Beth proved as tough as her mother, the Sheep Queen, though Beth outlived Emma only six years (Beth was eighteen years younger when she died).

Savage remained acutely close to his mother whom he often called "my beautiful angel mother." He named the tragic wife in his first novel, Beth Bentley, after her, and Beth fictionally reappears in later novels. When she died of pneumonia (cf. *The Sheep Queen*, p. 229) at age sixty-seven (April 6, 1957), Russell Savage recounts his father sitting on a stairwell landing, weeping—the only time he ever saw his father cry. In *The Sheep Queen*, Savage accurately depicts his mother's final years, after she and Charlie quit the ranch, moved to Missoula, Montana, and occupied a sixth-floor apartment in the historic Wilma Building (1952): years blighted by her alcoholism and lung cancer, including two failed surgeries. (chap. 12)

Savage's grandmother and mother influenced him more profoundly than did the men in either family. Savage ultimately developed a modest, pitying relationship with his birth father, an itinerant salesman, sometime actor, and labor union staff employee. Benjamin Harrison Savage comes off badly during a visit to the Brenners and Yearians recounted in *The Sheep Queen,* when his car, a "Roamer," gets stuck and, without chains, he requires help (pp. 157–67). When Beth married Charlie Brenner, young Tom became Tom Brenner—his name until 1942, when he was twenty-seven and decided to revert to his birth father's surname before his first child was born. By then he was well along with his first novel, and linked his professional identity with his birth surname.

At age five, Horse Prairie, Montana, became his primary residence.

Although some relatives question the closeness of the stepfather-stepson relationship, most believe Charlie acted in warm, generous ways toward his stepson, treating him as his own and teaching him the ropes on a cattle ranch. He provided a solid presence his birth father never provided.

The Brenner Ranch, purchased in 1883 by John C. and Isabel White Brenner, proved a different kind of operation than the Yearians'—more different than cattle from sheep. The patriarch wanted to be a Gilded

Age tycoon though not necessarily a Beaverhead County cattle baron—
and, as it turns out, there weren't a lot of Montana cattle dynasties
anyway, largely because of prevailing economic factors. Both John and
Isabel came from wealth, Isabel more than he. She commanded a fortune of more than $300,000, as did both of her sisters, bequeathed them
by their Pennsylvania timber baron father. Son of a big wholesale hardware businessman in Philadelphia, John Brenner, "in trade," had been
sent to the West Coast to open a branch there, but when he reached
Helena, a wealthy friend convinced him to buy this cattle ranch in Montana Territory's southwest corner for $60,000. He was the third owner
of what was then a dairy ranch, to which the Brenners moved in 1885.

John Brenner was much more interested in horseflesh than cattle.
Though he was never seen riding a horse, he wanted to raise Hamble-
tonians and other trotters, and spent the next three decades burning
through his wife's fortune in pursuit of equine excellence. The patriarch receives his most extensive portrait in *For Mary, With Love* (1983),
Savage's twelfth novel. It's the unflattering portrait of an arrogant, selfish bully who "married up" and never got over a root sense of inferiority. He posed as a derisive example of a ranch patriarch. He was said
to resemble Kaiser Wilhelm II, particularly in his sharp-bladed nose—
a feature that recurs in *Lona Hanson* (patriarch Burt Bart), *The Power
of the Dog* (the "Old Gent"), and *For Mary*. In a late letter to a cousin,
Savage harbored few fond memories of this paternal grandfather: "the
Old Man...was arrogant and selfish, which I came to know later. As a
child of five I kicked him in the shins because of a remark he'd made to
my mother." Young Tom's fierce loyalty to his mother never abated, as
is seen in Peter and Rose Gordon in *The Power of the Dog*.

Isabel proved as kind and well-mannered as she was patrician,
keeping her upper-class sensibility intact in this high lonesome valley.
Visitors remarked her eastern elegance in her remote place, and young
Tom took note. The marriage proved trying and her husband, obdurate
to the extent that, according to Savage in a late letter, "Many times Mrs.
Brenner was about to 'go to Indiana' which in those days meant to get a
divorce. Indiana in those days was lenient like Reno today. She didn't, of
course, because nice people didn't, then." Likely Savage associated her

class and taste with the East Coast, where he'd live most of his life. Her love of books inspired his devotion to encyclopedias and dictionaries.

The first beef cattle grazed on the ranch in 1906; thereafter, the dairy operation became the Brenner Livestock Company. They raised three sons, Henry ("Hal"), William ("Bill"), and Charles ("Charlie"). In 1926 they turned over the ranch to their sons and retired to the Finlen Hotel in Butte, Montana. John died the following year and his widow, eleven years later (the same year as her middle son, William). By this time, John Brenner had run the ranch into considerable debt, leaving his third son, Charlie, and his wife, Beth Yearian Brenner, the hard work of returning it to profitability. Bill and Charlie Brenner proved as steady as their father, John, was profligate.

Hal, oldest of the three Brenners, married Mary Skoning, the headstrong and beautiful daughter of an Illinois dairy farmer and schoolteacher in Medicine Lodge Valley, a tributary of Horse Prairie, in 1910, and their son John (Jack) S. Brenner, was eventually raised by Charlie and Beth Brenner after his parents divorced (1925) and his mother departed for California. Cousin Jack differed considerably from Tom, but both "proved up" on the Brenner Ranch. Hal suffered from multiple sclerosis, ultimately retiring to Walla Walla, Washington, where he died (1943). This strand of the Brenners forms the basis of *For Mary*, where the step-nephew's close identification with the glamorous, independent Mary becomes clear.

Bill Brenner, John and Isabel's middle son who became a peculiar bachelor and eccentric recluse, proved a mechanical genius and fine banjo player. He disliked women and kept to himself. He was sent to New England for prep school (St. Paul's, Concord New Hampshire), then to Stanford University (Palo Alto, California), which he apparently disliked. A craftsman with wood and easy mechanic, one time he built a power mower from a Model T (or A) chassis. He favored his niece, Isabel Brenner (Charlie and Beth's daughter), and carved wooden dolls for her. Apparently his personal hygiene was minimal, according to some relatives. Bill, who died (September 16, 1938) from blackleg, a cattle disease he inadvertently contracted from a sliver (while building stackyards), left a huge impression on his step-nephew, Tom, who later created his most infamous character, *The Power of the Dog*'s Phil Burbank, based on him. Bill Brenner's death inspired the horrific climax of *Power*.

In 1939 the Ranch was split in half, Jack Brenner, Hal's son, running one half and Charlie Brenner, the other.

Bill Brenner avoided women. It was likely that Tom, a young gay man, might have detected subtle cues about Uncle Bill's departure from heteronormativity. Even if Bill Brenner were gay, he never came out and silence—his family's and the rural ranch society's silence—surrounded him. He preferred it that way. In *The Power of the Dog* Savage limns Phil's loneliness and sexual attraction to his mentor, Bronco Henry Williams: "He felt strangely remote, even lonely, and sort of wished he wasn't a Burbank, something like that, something." Savage imagines his uncle remaining stifled and unfulfilled. On Saturday nights or holidays when ranch hands head to town for drink and women, Bill-as-Phil remains behind, trapped by proscribed, same-sex desire: "Wasn't it on such a day he'd first laid eyes on Bronco Henry?...hot time in the old town tonight." (*Power*, pp. 62–63)

Silence ruled on the Brenner Ranch and elsewhere about such matters, and that silence shaped both Savage's adulthood and his fiction.

In old age Savage retained precise memories of the ranch since he worked there in his adolescence and off and on up through his twentieth year. He remembered lots of dairy equipment, a butter tub that doubled as a pond raft, and various pastures: "First Field, Second Field, Big Field, Horse Field, Cabin Field and Dairy Field."

Bill's younger brother, Charlie, followed him to Stanford University but like him, only lasted a year or two. Charlie lived the cowboy role, his forehead displaying a permanent dent from a childhood accident: as a toddler he'd stepped between a mare and her colt, and the kick fractured his skull, yet he survived. By all accounts he was a quiet, steady man who took Tom on the autumn cattle drives from the ranch northeast down to Armstead, Montana, the nearest shipping point. In *The Sheep Queen*, Savage surveyed Armstead ("Beech," which would later disappear under the waters of Clark Canyon Reservoir in 1964), in typically harsh, sharp focus:

> Nothing grew. The town was nothing. A combination grocery and
> dry-goods store: canned goods, overalls, housedresses, gingham

stuff. Two saloons did a good business...when the ranchers drove in their cattle in the fall; the stockyards huddled down by the stinking creek that ran through them so the cattle could drink. The hills around the place were steep and bare; wild horses wandered up the sides, half-starved. The wind was never still and whined like some living thing. (p. 115)

Savage's bleak view of Armstead serves as a rough draft for his sustained satirical portraits of Dillon.

Charlie Brenner became a steady anchor for young Tom. Savage later acknowledged his closeness with his stepfather, who appeared dauntingly irreproachable—of "frightening rectitude":

He held all the cards as one does who is not known to have sinned or erred like the rest of us...a man who has never been known to weep. I had both admired and feared him and—quite without his permission—I had as a child begun to call myself by his last name instead of my father's name. I tried to acquire his swift, precise handwriting. To this day I see something of him in my signature. (*The Sheep Queen*, p. 146)

Despite his "frightening rectitude," Charlie showed young Tom how to be a rancher and to "man up." This proved crucial in helping Tom disguise his gay self. Charlie—his name unchanged in *The Sheep Queen*— was a master carver at table, "the sure mark of a gentleman": "He now sat at the head of the mahogany table—so vast that it had its own horizons; he carved the twenty-pound chunks of beef served up one day as roasts on a silver platter and the next as stews or hashes." (*The Sheep Queen*, p. 222) Once Tom reached adolescence, Charlie bought him shots with the others at the Armstead bar. Unsurprisingly, Tom called him "Dad"; looking back he judged him "a fine man." Charlie filled the bill as a reliable father.

The Brenner home, a big log house (forty-nine by eighty feet, incl. a back "L") that Tom, at age five, moved into with his mother, was built in six months (1914–15) after a fire burned its smaller predecessor. Savage describes the fire and building the new house in *For Mary* (pp. 112–13), and in *The Sheep Queen* and *For Mary* he calls it a sixteen-room log cabin. It included two big bedrooms (incl. the master bedroom), bathroom and powder room, an office, kitchen, and two dining rooms (the back one for the "help") on the main floor, and five big bedrooms and another bathroom upstairs. Savage chronicles its haphazard design:

> Mr. Bower [i.e., John C. Brenner], who was not comfortable in small rooms, ordered the carpenters to add a few feet here and a few there, and since he disliked being confined to a handful of rooms, he caused others to be added. Thus the new house, like the old one, remained under the high, sagebrushed hill that obscured all but the highest sun, and on the edge of the ranch instead of at the center. (p. 113)

Bill Brenner did custom log and filigree work on the front porch, which faced the driveway with a concrete walkway and yard fence.

A year after his mother's remarriage, a sister was born, Isabel Brenner (1921), named for her paternal grandmother, Isabel W. Brenner. Weird Uncle Bill favored her, carving wooden toys for her. Isabel seems to have inherited her maternal grandmother's commanding persona. She was described by one relative as "a lonely little fat girl with no friends." Perhaps Uncle Bill, consummate loner, recognized her as a kindred spirit. She later showed great musical talent, exceeding her mother's at the piano. Isabel married Robert ("Bob") James, a musician she'd met in Missoula during World War II, and they had four children, ultimately owning and running Charlie Brenner's half of the ranch. Recalling his talented sister in old age, Savage said Isabel played the piano "magnificently"—she might have had a concert career—but that her multiple sclerosis, of which she began to show symptoms in her mid-forties (like her Uncle Hal Brenner in the early 1910s), ended her prospects. Isabel was bedridden most of her final years and died in 1978. One relative claimed that Isabel James, who favored her father, never felt close to her exotic writer brother, though they shared a deep love of music. He differed too much from the usual ranch culture.

Once while he was in elementary school, Tom demonstrated his emerging flair for interior decoration, a sign of his declared independence from that ranch culture with its prescribed gender roles. He made clear he wanted his bedroom painted in stripes; no one took him seriously, so he found the paint he wanted and did it himself.

Somewhere between childhood and adolescence, Tom discovered he was gay: the salient truth of his life, one that impinged on his fiction in sundry ways. He carefully cloaked his homosexuality, as I've never found a single reference, however oblique, to it in any surviving letters or other documents. Instead, he played the part of ladies man, cowboy, and cowboy entertainer, and he played them well. Not until his courtship with his fiancé, Betty Fitzgerald, did he declare his true self, and not until the eventual move to the Maine coast (1955) did he gradually come out, according to his surviving son, Russell.

Tom's physical world, then, was far removed from town, and his mother's family proved close, warm, and tumultuous. He grew up surrounded by strong-willed, independent-minded women, hard-working men, bluebloods and eccentrics, partiers and drinkers. Outdoors brought endless space, endless chores, endless adventures; indoors opened the worlds of music, books, and other cosmopolitan delights. Writing much later to a nephew, Savage recounted the quantity of magazines and books in the Brenner Ranch house, testimony to Isabel W. Brenner's literary interests: "the house was alive with just about every magazine published at the time... In the bookcase to the left as you entered were several addictive volumes called *Living Races of the World* [*The Living Races of Mankind*] and *Living Animals of the World* [*Hutchinson's Animals of all Countries*], profusely illustrated... The 11th Edition of the Britannica [complete set] was in that shelf. There I began my education." (December 16, 1997) All his life, Savage remained loyal to the Britannica 11th Edition (1910), which also profoundly influenced major Modernist writers such as Ezra Pound, T. S. Eliot, and James Joyce.

When he began school he didn't have far to travel because the Brenner School District #30 (1908–23) —a typically tiny, rural Montana district that was born and died in the homesteader era—was close by. After third grade, he had to ride much farther. For his sixth-grade year he lived in Salmon with his great aunt, Nora Yearian Whitwell, and attended the local elementary school. He remained close with her the rest of her long life, as she embodied the generosity and warmth of the Yearians.

Though he knew the Brenners and Horse Prairie intimately, and spent more time in Dillon than Salmon, his heart remained with the

Yearian tribe in the Lemhi River Valley. Given all that Savage's daughter, Betsy Savage Main, heard about Horse Prairie, she believes the Brenner Ranch worked "like kryptonite: it destroyed a lot of people." By contrast, the Yearians worked hard but played hard, not always under the watchful eye of Big Mama. Savage thus grew up with alternative models of ranchers: in his fiction the negative model predominates. In *Power*, for example, we watch several characters destroyed by the Burbank Ranch.

As an older brother and oldest cousin, Tom loved playing pranks and demonstrating his mischievous streak. His cousin, Ralph Nichol, recounts that Tom "delighted in reading *Dracula* to [another cousin] and me and scaring the hell out of us." On another occasion, he draped himself in a tiger skin and head (complete with teeth) acquired by the Brenners, hid in a closet until his younger sister opened it, and "scared her to death!" Tom loved to control entertainments.

During his eighth- and tenth-grade years he had tutors at the ranch, as did Isabel. Otherwise, he followed a time-honored Montana tradition of "boarding in" (i.e., living in town) for school. Like many prep school students in the East or England, he was thus shipped out to Dillon during the week, and he developed this split identity between week and weekend, town (Dillon) and home. The swing back and forth stamped his most impressionable years à la Willa Cather. The schoolboy boarded with the Boones (who appear as the Booths in *The Sheep Queen*), but he also stayed with one Dr. Tragitt in the "Pierce House" just east of the Episcopal Rectory (East Glendale Street, Dillon). From this house he walked three blocks north to enter Beaverhead County High School (BCHS), where he graduated as valedictorian in the class of 1932.

As a boy then teenager, Savage often roamed at night, as does Peter Gordon in *Power*, and he never forgot what he saw, heard, smelled. In a letter sent a few months before *The Sheep Queen* was first published under the original name, he wrote, "When I was in high school in Dillon, Montana we used to play pool in the Pheasant. In Shithouse you counted any ball you got in the pocket, no rotation, no pattern. I wish I were back there now." Exceptionally observant, he was both lonely and socially active when he chose to be.

Presumably Tom's writerly habits of observation and sexual

identity kept him vigilant and removed at times, even or especially amid others. Yet his natural gregariousness and savoir faire also made him a lead conversationalist.

He would later claim, for example, that during the 1920s, Dillon boasted fifteen whorehouses, though that number seems inflated. In his fiction he would foreground some of these, varying the names and numbers. Despite the various opportunities Dillon provided, during the week he felt incredibly lonely for the ranch and yearned for the weekend return. He studied long hours, listening to what he later recalled, fondly and frequently, as the "Three Ones"—the sound, that is, of the county courthouse clock chiming 12:30, 1:00, and 1:30 a.m., of "that magic hour when time stopped," as he wrote in a letter generations later. His nocturnal habits later prevailed in his writing.

At BCHS Tom "Brenner" developed a few friends (Ed Kellner being the closest) and delved into some high school activities. He was part of the school newspaper staff, for example: in the October 7, 1930, issue, he was listed as one of thirteen reporters; in the January 27, 1931, issue, he was listed as one of eight assistant editors. And he wrote a satiric column for *The Beaver* called "Balloni." He presented baloney as a miracle food and "Balloni"—malarkey—as an indispensable advice column: without both, no guy could advance with the ladies as he wishes. One column shows the high schooler satirizing a typical product testimony with self-mockery. Tom Brenner is a changed man because of baloney: "'I appreciate what Balloni has done for me, and that is why I write this column, so everyone can try it and be a changed person like I am'. . . We are certainly glad that Mr. Brenner discovered Balloni and hope he remains as full of grace and Balloni as he is now." (May 11, 1931). The witty self-mockery helped mask his closely guarded gay identity. He loved to sing his version of the high school football cheer: "Go get a rat trap / Bigger than a cat trap / Cannibal cannibal, siss boom bah / [Beaverhead] High School, rah rah rah." (cf. *Sheep Queen*, p. 174)

By high school, Savage knew he wanted to be a writer—his mother noted "Tom's typewriting" in letters and much later, he claimed "My mother worried because I was a dreamer and left the ranch and security and wanted to write books." (*Sheep Queen*, p. 133) According to Ralph Nichol, a close cousin, "Tom loved people more than he loved animals.

That is why I think he loved to write more than he loved the cowboy life." (letter, June 22, 2018) He needed social contact and preferred town or city diversions to back pastures. In a 1980 profile and interview by Edgar Allen Beem, Savage stated he "feels that what prompted him to write in the first place was his family": "I was a stepchild and I wanted out. I had to do something that was absolutely my own." ("The Savages of Georgetown," *Maine Sunday Telegram,* June 22, 1980) This writer, particularly close to extended family on his mother's side, explained his career by pointing up his obsession with family—real rather than imagined—which he continually evokes and celebrates in his novels. The stepson compensates by limning real family members, and ranching and small-town life. He wanted an identity "absolutely my own" beyond his sexual identity.

But his route to becoming a writer wasn't always clear. Savage told others he wanted to be a diplomat and wrap himself professionally in current European and Soviet affairs. Ironically, to the best of my knowledge he never traveled abroad.

Looking back on BCHS, he repeatedly extolled his high school education, claiming it the best he ever received. He praised particular teachers, remembered their details in letters and in *The Sheep Queen* where, after discussing three individuals, he pauses, "I look back with wonder at the excellence of those teachers in that small town under a high hill on whose slope you could sometimes see wild horses grazing. I want here to express my appreciation for what they did for me." (p. 175)

In a letter to Blanche Gregory, his longtime literary agent, written the same year *The Sheep Queen* was first published (1977), Savage wrote, "I've heard from a lot of old schoolmates who wrote me through Little, Brown. Odd to think so many of them have followed my books all these years. I have a picture of the entire faculty in 1931, all of them lined up in front of the bricks of the school. It is wonderful what good teachers they all were, and I learned more there than I ever did later on." (May 9, 1977) So not all Montanans ignored Savage's career. During his final visit to his hometown, Savage gleefully recounted his favorite high school memory, of witnessing a "terrible row" between the "flippant French teacher and its serious English instructor. The ladies screamed and called each other names, all in French . . . Fortunately, I had studied the language." ("Savage Comes Home Again," *Dillon Tribune-Examiner*, April 20, 1983) He never forgot anyone.

Savage claimed he never read much. In letters or interviews he often stated he gained inspiration, in the 1930s and 1940s, from John Steinbeck, Robert Benchley, Dorothy Parker, T. S. Eliot, and Tennessee Williams.

As a child Savage loved music, his budding obsession with classical music alternating with his absorption in 1920s–30s pop tunes, the lyrics of which he recounted from memory over half a century later (e.g., "My Blue Heaven," 1927). In his "near-historical" fiction set during his childhood or young adulthood, he often cites pop hits from the late 1920s or early 1930s: a recurring example of his infallible memory and his uncanny historical texturing. In *Daddy's Girl* the narrator, Savage's autobiographical surrogate, confesses, "the musical baggage I brought with me to college was but maudlin bunkhouse ballads I pretended to scorn but half believed in, popular tunes picked up from the Atwater Kent radio like *Valencia* that accounts for my still-cockeyed idea of Spain; and the even earlier military marches—Sousa's band and Pryor's band . . ." (pp. 101-2). But grounded as he was in pop music of his youth, Savage was already learning classical music from the piano and from his budding record collection.

On the Brenner Ranch he grew up with some measure of affluence in the big house and as he lengthened, he cowboyed up as well as anyone, according to Ralph Nichol, who worked on the Brenner Ranch several summers. Nichol claimed, "[Savage] never saw the glamour in cowboying and his heart was never in it. I don't think he hated the ranch life but I don't think he ever felt he belonged there." (letter, July 28, 2009) Savage/Brenner replayed his marginal status on the Brenner Ranch, his being not quite family both as a stepchild and as a gay man, in several novels, above all, through Peter Gordon in *Power*, who feels a misfit in several ways.

He did his share of all the chores including wrangling horses, driving cattle to Armstead, Montana, and winter feeding. He helped with hauling salt blocks, dehorning, calving, tuberculosis testing, milking and "separating" milk, cutting two-year olds, breaking horses, haying, and at the Yearians, lambing. Ranch life, his first world, ultimately

receded far in his rearview mirror, but he never forgot any of it. In the
Publishers Weekly interview (1988), he reminisced, "You get up on winter
mornings when it's as cold as 60 degrees below zero and ride six miles
across the fields to where you've got your team fenced in, in a haystack
yard, hitch up the team and feed 200 head of cattle. It's so cold you have
to light a little fire with a bunch of hay and then warm the pitchfork
handle so you can bear to touch it." For most Americans, the climate
Savage grew up with feels as inconceivable as his geographical remoteness. He transferred his hard work as a ranch son directly to his daily
(nocturnal) discipline as a novelist.

After his freshman year at what was then called the State University of Montana—now the University of Montana (Missoula)—in 1932–
33, Savage left, having mixed minds about his fit there. He wanted to be
a history major focusing upon modern Europe—unsurprising, perhaps,
in the 1930s—but soon abandoned this plan. He returned to the university as a student for parts of 1934–35 and again in 1936–37 as an "Unclas-
sified" student, studying writing and taking a reduced load.

His academic transcript reveals Savage to be an inconsistent student who increasingly turned his attention to writing. During his
freshman year he earned As in Freshman Composition and Advanced
Spanish, but Bs and Cs in Elements of Journalism and World Literature
(and low grades in Greek Literature, English, and Military Drill); his
second year he did poorer (e.g., a D in Advanced Reporting and Editing),
and he withdrew partway through winter quarter. During his third
go-round, though he earned only a C in Shakespeare, he received a B
in Advanced Composition and As in his other writing courses, reflecting his increasing focus and discipline. Of his Missoula faculty, Brassil
Fitzgerald, a writing instructor and ultimately, his father-in-law, influenced Savage the most, as he recognized his talent and modeled for him
the identity of a writer.

In a series of letters penned in 1935–36 to a close friend from Salmon,
Idaho, Elizabeth (Bess) Carlson, Savage repeatedly voices a restlessness not uncommon for a twenty-year old. He mentions occasionally
a desire to move south to Mexico; at one stage, tired of ranching, he
claims to have lined up a job learning the lumber business at a big Portland, Oregon, yard, but nothing came of it; in another letter he states

he's enlisted in the Marines, but because he's not yet twenty-one that enlistment is contingent upon his a parent's signature. Beth Brenner didn't sign off.

Savage's psychological contradictions during this period stack up sharply, torn between the two ranches he knows and the cities he imagines. He claimed to love Horse Prairie and the Brenner Livestock Company: "This is absolutely the best place in the world. I'll never leave again no matter what. I know now. This is where I belong." (March 22, 1935) He even goes so far to assert he wants no more contact with "the outside world" (other than riding to tiny Grant, Montana, to post or fetch the mail). Savage confidently announces his happiness as a recluse who rarely bathes—as though imitating weird Uncle Bill: "Life is the *grandest* thing if you can live it where you want and not be bothered with people, and damned 'civilization.'" (ital. original, May 22, 1935) He claimed to hate Missoula: "Missoula seems so far away from me. It is hard to think that I was ever *cooped up* in such a hell-hole. I will always think of Missoula & hell-hole in the same moment." (ital. original, April 29, 1935) At the same time his letters attest to the number of good friends he'd developed in his first college town. Both of these attitudes represent poses—partial truths at best. Savage had developed habits of both solitude and extreme sociability, and one habit never precluded its opposite in him. Like Walt Whitman, he contained multitudes including sharp-edged contradictions.

In the summer of 1935, twenty years old, he'd taken a job at The Highlands Riding Academy just outside Portland, Oregon, teaching riding and training horses, but that autumn saw him back home, the job not outlasting the season. He wearied of the Brenners, voicing a dislike of Bill Brenner in particular (November 19, 1935) that would later spike as he transforms this uncle in *Lona Hanson, Power,* and *The Sheep Queen.*

Yet, having returned to the Brenner Ranch (autumn 1935), Savage was soon on the move again. Just after the Christmas holidays in 1935, he abruptly quit home and rode over the Divide—with two horses including Grizzly, whom he'd broken because no one else would—to the Yearian Ranch to work, much to his relief: "You don't know how supremely happy I feel now that I am over here—God it was awful at home." (January 24, 1936) So much for "the best place in the world." He later elaborates the difference between the two ranches he grew up on, content with milking and lambing: "Am becoming well *adjusted* to this life where *people* laugh & have a good time & don't worry about anything much." (ital. original, February 2, 1936) The Yearian Ranch symbolized conviviality; the Brenner Ranch, grim loneliness. His grandmother, the Sheep Queen, ran a tight ship but there always seemed to be time for parties. At the least, good times existed at his mother's family's place that did not on the Brenner Ranch. He later wrote, "at the ranch I was never sure how I stood": "How I would like to see my horses & the people—but I won't be around for a long time," he declared. (May 20, 1936) He missed Charlie and, especially, his mother, but, at age twenty-one, felt more uncertain than ever about his legal position at the Brenner Ranch. In adulthood Savage never entirely forgot that he was not born a Brenner; compared to his slightly older cousin, Jack, whom he sometimes regarded as a brother, he felt an outsider.

Savage's love of horses was genuine and stamped his years in Horse Prairie. He frequently mentions "his" horses and his longing for them in letters, and details saddles and tack, work and dress clothes and boots. His intimate knowledge would inform his fiction set in his home country. He frequently describes his early bedtime because of dawn feeding and herding chores. Yet after the summer of 1937 when he quit Montana, he left that love behind him along with the rest of his rural life in high lonely valleys.

By April 1936 he'd left the Yearian Ranch and taken a job "working on a sheep-ranch 5 miles out of Missoula." On this operation well away from family, he's able to take control: "It seems good to be the *important guy* around the lambing sheds—all the operations are mine." (ital. original, April 11, 1936) For the first time he's an independent boss, as he will be as a novelist. In early May he was out herding with other shepherds for two weeks and professes his love of the rough outdoors life—farther away from amenities than his Brenner Ranch life he'd claimed to love most. Obviously he's learned a lot about sheep ranching which, para-doxically, will guide his writing career.

Savage told Ralph Nichol, "if I hadn't herded sheep, I would have never learned to cook," which Ralph always thought funny.

But by the late summer he left it far behind, having taken a job at the Half Diamond S Ranch, a dude ranch in Skookumchuck, British Columbia (near Cranbrook). Brenner got along famously with the managers and loved training racehorses, teaching riding to the dudes, and partying with them as well. Again writing to Bess Carlson, he ordered a polo saddle from Calgary to complement his racing bridle. (September 12, 1936) He loved the English-style clothes and gear: "I have 2 new bridles—a full polo bridle with double reins and a racing bridle with rubber hand grip up next to the bit. Both are of English leather. Also I have a new show leather, and a new exercising saddle." (September 12, 1936) He wanted his appearance to match his riding.

The dude-ranch season ending, Savage left the Half Diamond S before September's end, having "put the finishing touches on five horses." (September 17, 1936). He fully intended to return the following late winter, but a woman ultimately changed his plans. While north of the border, "Brenner" confessed his fervent desire to rodeo as a bronc rider, "which is what I have had in the back of my mind *anyway,* for the last 5 years." (August 30, 1936) "Brenner" wanted to develop further his cowboy credentials, but instead he soon turned his back permanently on ranches and rodeos. Instead, his planned career as bronc rider inspired his first professional piece of writing.

Tom Savage proved, like his mother and her family, fond of the drink. He mentions various brands of whiskey and, in early autumn, 1936, gleefully describes a two-week drunk while working on a harvest crew near Idaho Falls, Idaho. Usually in his confidences to Bess Carlson he treats his drinking bouts in a hush-hush way, swearing her to secrecy. Alcohol will play a major role in his life and his wife's, and as with many writers who are alcoholics, they published steadily despite the extended cocktail hours.

He never breathed a word about his sexuality, as far as I can determine, to his mother, Bess Carlson, or anyone else. Though he had flings with girls and later led a heterosexual life, he was gay. Savage also evinced some self-awareness of his easy role playing—and role switching. Advising his close friend, Bess, about putting on the charm and wit and increasing her popularity on the Missoula campus, he confesses, "Seriously I don't know how I did it; didn't know I could be such a damned hypocrite." But given his facility with his high school "Balloni"

newspaper column and persona, neither his charisma nor his irony
come as a surprise. Brenner wore diverse hats as an entertainer and
few disputed his deft impersonations, including cowboy balladeer or
popular songster. He memorized several songlists. Ralph Nichol labeled
him "the entertaining cowboy" who "loved to sing and play his guitar
and . . . entertain people with his stories." (letter, June 22, 2018)

Possessed of a fine voice, young Savage traveled with a guitar and
played cowboy songs, a local Gene Autry. On the university campus he
participated in "The Montana Masquers" and played Valentine in a production of *Twelfth Night*. He'd pledged Sigma Alpha Epsilon fraternity—
the Beta chapter was founded in 1927—his first year and, like many
students, eagerly anticipated the drinking and dancing at the annual
Foresters' Ball. He also played the part of hell-raiser, lassoing, with his
friend Al Decker, a saddle in the basement of Decker's boardinghouse
(owned by Decker's sister, Ida Maxey), or taking a fiddle bow to a saw
and drunkenly serenading the boardinghouse. Savage was restless, an
unfocused student apart from writing. Budding romance prompted him
to board a Greyhound bus in Butte, Montana, in the early fall of 1937,
and he effectively abandoned his native state. He was twenty-two.

□   □   □

How were Montana and Beaverhead County faring during the writer's
coming of age? As all state or regional historians note, the Great Depression arrived in Montana years before the 1929 stock market crash. Dry
years meant hard times, and the twenties didn't roar. The abnormal
cycle of wet years, primary lure during the state's major homestead-
ing boom (the twentieth century's first two decades), ended after 1919,
and many small farms or ranches dried up and blew away. From 1920
to 1940 Montana lost more than 50 percent of its ranches. During the
same period, Beaverhead County lost population, while Dillon, the
county seat, grew. During his final Dillon visit, Savage recalled that
the big ranch families had nothing during the Depression. The Roe
Ranch (twenty-five miles south of Dillon), for example, kept one heated
room, with a stovepipe venting out a window; on the Brenner Ranch
they hung a big blanket between the living and dining rooms, and used

a "heat troller." The Dillon banks would not foreclose properties, else they'd fold.

By 1950 the county had lost almost 10 percent of its 1920 population; the county seat, by contrast, increased by more than 17 percent. Those who didn't move far away often came to town to try another life apart from running cattle and growing hay. As noted earlier, the Yearian Ranch survived the Depression as did the Brenner Ranch, the latter in part because of the hard work of Charlie Brenner.

Tom Savage grew up in Horse Prairie, Dillon, and Lemhi, Idaho, just as local life got harder and harder. During his final visit home he recounted what it was like for the ranchers, land-rich but cash-strapped. Savage expresses the belt-tightening in *Lona Hanson*. As he flourished in high school and college, the world nearby shrank. When he boarded that bus in Butte, he took all his sensory experience of childhood and adolescence with him. Ultimately he inhabited that commonplace writer's paradox: he moved far away in order to come home. And he came home obsessively.

CHAPTER TWO

Thomas Savage's Emergence: The Early Novels, 1936–1953

B Y THE SUMMER OF 1937, age twenty-two, Tom Savage (then still known as Tom Brenner) busily corresponded with a pen pal, Eliza-beth ("Betty") Fitzgerald (1918–89), the daughter of his favorite profes-sor in Missoula, Montana. She had moved back to New England with her parents and enrolled at Colby College in Waterville, Maine. Betty's father, Brassil, had encouraged both her and Tom, who soon became romantically involved with her, in their writing careers. Savage was interested enough that he decided to follow Betty to New England and, specifically, Colby College, where she'd matriculated. From a Boston Irish family, Betty grew up in Utah and then Missoula, which she loved, and she judged herself a westerner.

When Savage boarded that Greyhound bus in Butte, Montana, at summer's end in 1937, he made a fateful decision to turn his back on his native state. Thereafter he returned with his own family, pri-marily to visit relatives. For over forty years he would be an adopted New Englander though he maintained a split regional identity, in part because he persistently returned to the northern Rockies in his fiction. He left behind rodeo and ranching and turned himself into the sophis-ticate latent inside him. He played the social host as easily as he did horse wrangler or backcountry shepherd. Savage switched identities as easily as he did clothes, and these contrary lives, both native to him, competed for attention.

He also brought along his intense ambitions as a writer as well as his sexual orientation, which he'd shared with no one. Rather, his

Missoula seasons yielded more than one girlfriend (one named Lila) and common heterosexual interests in the opposite sex. He crowed in one letter "A number of the girls seem to think I'm OK." (March 22, 1935) He also boasted of his familiarity with at least one Dillon, Montana, whorehouse in another: "[Alma] is dandy. And was she glad to see me! She appreciates me more than my other girls. I certainly do know the best people." (April 4, 1935) That final sardonic comment, vintage Savage, typifies the generous attitude toward prostitutes that recurs in his novels set in Dillon. And Savage honored Alma by making her proprietress, name unchanged, of the "Dixie Rooms" in *Lona Hanson*.

Of course, this bragging likely served as the best camouflage for his homosexuality, his own closest secret revealed, as far as I can find, to no one in his youth. Savage, like most sexual minorities, kept counsel in his psychic closet, the safest retreat for so many generations. To my knowledge, he made no references to being gay until his deepening relationship with Betty, whom he married after their junior year in 1939. Many years later, Betty told their daughter she'd known about Tom being gay since "the Missoula days."

According to Sarah Pruitt, a frequent history.com contributor, in the 1930s "LGBTQ culture and community began to fall out of favor," and because of "newly enforced laws and regulations" as well as a series of sensationalized sex crimes wherein the sex criminals were equated with gay men, "homosexuality seem[ed] more dangerous to the average American." (www.history.com) While gay and lesbian communities thrived in New York's Greenwich Village and in Chicago, Missoula was a long ways away. Tom locked his gayness precisely as gay Phil Burbank, in *Power*, guards his bathing hole: "The spot was precious, and must never be profaned by another human presence . . . Even now as a grown man, he never failed to leave it without a sense of innocence and purity; the brief communion there with himself made his step lighter and his whistle as gay as a boy's." (p. 171) In the fiction, Phil is spied upon, found out; not until his forties did Savage come out.

Nonetheless, his gayness undoubtedly tinctured his ranch youth, creating an insider-outsider double perspective he would put to fictive use. His hearty protests about Horse Prairie being the best place anywhere, which he soon enough discarded, belie his sense of isolation and detachment, as do his boasts about girls. Perhaps he even felt affinity on some level with weird Uncle Bill Brenner, clearly the odd duck at the ranch: an affinity presented in the changing relationship between Phil Burbank and Peter Gordon in *Power.* Savage could and did "pass" with ease—an indispensable safety net.

Savage scrupulously kept his homosexuality under wraps; he was quite public about his writing ambitions, however. Correspondence in 1936–37 reveals his increasing preoccupation with writing. Enrolled at the State University of Montana in Fall quarter, 1936, Savage tells his close friend, Bess Carlson, he's bought a "noseless Remington" type-writer: "I have spent hours and hours everyday writing, and some of the things are good. My style if you can call it that is getting better and better all the time." He claims, "I am sticking to the old things [i.e., humorous pieces] that I can do," which includes "some 70 poems," and he boasts, "I think I might be able to sell them." (November 12, 1936) Savage fancied himself a protégé of the Algonquin Wits and thought he might become another James Thurber or S. J. Perelman. He wouldn't.

At Thanksgiving 1936, Savage confides that for the past month he's been "working working working on the Book . . . called Geography of the World, and Other Jokes, which is very good, being a parody of all Geographies of the world, and very funny." He claims two professors endorsed it, and he plotted its success: "I will give Doubleday-Doran or some other company the copyright of this book, and they will publish it, and I will get 15% royalties, and the book will take, and I will make more than a thousand dollars, I hope." (November 26, 1936) In this and sub-sequent letters Savage described this book as a done deal. The aspiring writer expressed great self-confidence in a variety of breezy, satirical wit he'd first displayed in his high school "Balloni" column.

He'd more recently worked a light humor vein in a piece, "Find the Orchestra," published the following summer (1937) in *Frontier and Midland: A Magazine of the West,* a respectable literary journal edited by H. G. Merriam, a foundational name in Montana letters. In this toss-off "Brenner" salutes what he calls the "Traveling Ghost Orchestra," the artfully hidden orchestra accompanying actors or actresses moved to song in movies. Perhaps he subliminally recognized an analogy between his hidden orchestra and his hidden queer self. He speculates about its cold location in a romance between a member of the Royal Canadian Mounted Police and a woman in the Canadian Rockies and flaunts his amateur wit: "But hazarding guesses as to how the orchestra gets where it does is merely confusing, and is not leading to anything but the end of this article." (vol. 17, no. 4, p. 276)

Even in his juvenilia, Savage worked nights. He'd already developed the nocturnal writing habit he would maintain, "up until four or five in the morning, working" (February 4, 1937) on this manuscript.

"Geography of the World, and Other Jokes," which occupied him in 1936–37, ultimately came to naught, though apparently he thought it was in the can. He brags to Bess Carlson, "My book is already [sic] for publication. I heard from Harpers and Brothers but have written to Simon & Schuster in hopes that they will be interested. They push a book much better than H. There doesn't seem to be any doubt about people liking it. . .Most people have hysterics when they read it. It ought to sell—according to professors—about two hundred thousand copies, then that means fifteen percent to me, or about thirty thousand dollars, enough to live on for a year, anyway." Savage reveals detailed knowledge and brash self-confidence about publishing, yet he's a complete greenhorn. Missoula helped prop his glowing castle in the air: "Great interest in writing has of course been aroused because of my success and professors and people are trying to start up the old national literary fraternity again—Sigma Upsilon. I am head of the bunch." Missoula faculty, especially Fitzgerald, had puffed up his ego and convinced him he had a future in glib satire. He desperately wanted the publication for self-validation, unsurprisingly. He dreamed of buying an L-29 Cord, a luxury car.

The young writer reveals a breezy and unwarranted optimism since no one published his juvenile manuscript. Bound copies of the work from McIntosh and Otis, Inc., a New York literary agency established in 1928, survive (misspellings intact), apparently to the subsequent embarrassment of Savage. In its short preface, he wrote, "This manuscript came back again today. It's been coming back so often that I'm getting sick and tired of looking at it. Evidently the editors are getting pretty sick of it, too, the way they keep sending it back." The young writer pictures one particular editor "blithely dismissing thirty-five thousand words with a terse 'sorry,' blasting my life's hopes," and imagines reversing roles and shooting him in a duel ("gun-shots at five paces"). The self-mockery is not entirely tongue-in-cheek. This manuscript, another road not taken for the later novelist, shows Savage deep under the influence of Robert Benchley. In a letter written much later, he admits "My mother gave me a copy of one of [Benchley's] books every birthday." The nonsensical humor of "Geography" ranges from out loud funny to labored to dull and pointless. The further one reads, the more the "other jokes" wear thin.

In his future he modulated his fondness for the one-liner or the silly anecdote into a far more nuanced, sometimes mordant, satiric key, one that manifests itself through his penchant for essayistic comment, a central element in his style. Biting humor remains one hallmark of Savage's West.

In fact, whatever his number of submissions, Savage only published a short essay, "The Bronc-Stomper," in *Coronet* (August 1937), a general interest digest magazine founded the year before (1936). Savage fondly recounted, in later years, that he was paid seventy-five dollars for this piece, the only money he received from writing for seven years, until his first novel was published. Of his payment, he gave twenty-five dollars to a cousin, Janet Nichol, so she could buy a red prom dress, and invested the rest in gold stocks in Missoula, which lost all value within one week.

"The Bronc-Stomper," with its strongly accented, assonant title, describes the process of haltering and then saddling an unridden horse. The hyperbolic title, evoking a badass competitor in a standard rodeo event, also intimates serious cruelty in the business of breaking a horse. An ode to his rodeo path not taken, the piece distills his proud young career breaking and training and riding horses (e.g., Grizzly at the Brenner Ranch, whom no one else tackled). Savage privileges and historicizes his class of horse breakers as though they're part of the romantic, vanishing West of popular culture, only surviving in rodeos. Bronco Henry Williams in *Power* represents Savage's best member of this class. "I guess horse-breakers like me will be the next to go," Savage announces: "most rodeo riders are not horse-breakers. Horse-breakers are born, not made." The vaunted boast is matched by some sensuous description, all illustrating the essay's epigraph: "A good time is to have a bronc alone in the middle of a corral."

This first publication reifies popular western imagery rather than subverts it. Only in his (published) beginning does Savage glorify the life represented by his work at the British Columbia dude ranch the previous summer and fall. Never again would he sing a familiar refrain about the Old West; instead, he mocked it for the most part. Yet he writes respectfully about Bronco Henry in *Power* and *For Mary*, his respect linked with Phil's sexual desire in the former.

"The Bronc Stomper" had just been published when Savage made his fateful decision to quit the West. He forgot nothing about that first cross-country trip to New England. He'd never stepped anywhere east of the Rockies, so the sight of Lake Erie shocked him. In the *Contemporary Authors* interview over half a century later, he characteristically remembered all the details: "I left Butte and got into Boston ninety-six hours later. It costs fifty-six dollars for the bus trip. I was getting very tired toward the end—I couldn't sleep on the bus at all. . . I arrived in Boston and I met at the Greyhound station the girl who was the reason that I went East. We had been pen pals all the previous summer, and finally we met, and that night I hung my fraternity pin on her." A mutual friend had introduced them as likely pen pals since they burned with the same passion for writing. Tom and Betty Fitzgerald had exchanged drafts and critiques that summer, and the relationship grew serious quickly.

He told the story slightly differently to professor Sue Hart (in the Western Writers Series booklet, *Thomas and Elizabeth Savage*). Betty and her mother, Mildred, met Tom at the bus station, their opening exchange a romantic cliché from a script: he asked, "Are you the one I'm looking for?" and she answered, "I think I am." Savage and Fitzgerald grew close through their letters; it was not primarily a physical attraction. He fell in love with Betty's hunger and ability as a writer, which matched his own, and he stayed loyal to his original epistolary, "inscribed" closeness with her.

The three repaired to Copley Plaza's Merry-Go-Round bar where, after a misunderstanding with their waiter, mother and daughter huffed away, sans shoes, and Savage caught up to them with their high heels. He loved this story, as he recounted it in his late essay, "Why a Pilgrim Traveled to Boston" (in *A Book for Boston*, 1980). A few weeks later, he gave Betty his SAE pin for their engagement.

In Missoula Savage had been inspired by Betty's father's attention. Savage would dedicate his third novel to his father-in-law. Brassil Fitzgerald was also a bad drunk and, likely, abusive. In 1972 Betty Savage told her daughter that she'd briefly married a pilot at age sixteen (1934) to escape further sexual molestation from her father. This may shed further light on her motives for marrying Tom five years later.

Colby College—founded in 1813 and the twelfth oldest liberal arts college in the country—cost $125 for a year's tuition in the late 1930s. Tom joined Betty in Waterville, Maine, as a student and they married two years later—apparently the first Colby undergraduates to marry, in the process securing permission from the dean of men and dean of women, respectively. Before this occurred, the couple exchanged extraordinary confidences about Tom's sexual orientation, as Betty later confided to her daughter. In a *Colby Alumnus* reminiscence published many years later (Spring 1975 issue), Savage recalled those semesters at the end of the 1930s, when most students were poor and lacked cars: "On the way back from the railroad yards one Saturday afternoon in 1939 I suggested that if we got married we wouldn't have to walk so much." The young writers "were married at the end of our junior year, and we walked very little after that." More Savage irony. They could be together all the time and, as the first married couple, gained great distinction.

They married on September 15, 1939, in Boston. Savage states in *The Sheep Queen* that, upon his marriage, his mother "gave me a pair of white silk pajamas, five hundred dollars, and a mandolin." (p. 137) Sue Hart quotes Savage saying that as newlyweds, they could live a "real life" which included weekend grocery shopping and "dream[ing] of having an income of $5000 a year and being rich." Underneath these fantasies, they started out in a cockroach-infested apartment, living the life of poor artists à la G. Puccini's *La Bohème*. They would "get by" even as their children came along, though a $50,000 check received in 1948 eased their worries.

Betty Fitzgerald was inducted into Phi Beta Kappa her junior year—

a measure of her academic success. Her fiancé referred to it as "Phi Beena Krappa": evidence of Tom's pride in Betty, satiric contempt, and more than a dash of envy. Betty would be the intellectual and well-read writer of the two. Additionally, Betty twice won Colby's Mary Low Carver Poetry Prize. Queer Tom would define himself as cosmopolitan elitist and impersonator who commanded conversation and insistently sought high praise in his fiction.

Tom arrived at Colby with sombrero and guitar, ready to play any western or Mexican role, and matriculated as a sophomore. According to a *Colby Alumnus* review of *The Pass* (May 1944), Savage "blew into Colby from Montana...and straightaway took over a column in the *Echo* [the student newspaper] and a spot on the college radio program which left trails of chuckles behind." Savage hadn't abandoned his role as humorist begun in high school, even as his fiction shifted into sardonic satire: a consistently bright color in Savage's palette, presented through a range of characters and asides.

At Colby, he demonstrated both academic and athletic ability, though their transcripts reveal that Elizabeth usually earned higher marks than Tom. He won the Foster Memorial Greek Prize his senior year (1940), a twenty-dollar prize awarded to a student in the men's division "for marked excellence in interpreting Greek authors." In *Power* Phil Burbank, who's also studied Greek, corrects Dr. Johnny Gordon's mistaken Greek. (p. 40) And Savage proved his mettle as an amateur boxer in Colby's intramural boxing program, on one occasion knocking out his opponent. Clearly the Montanan retained some of his tough guy/bronc-stomper persona. He uses his prowess in Greek and in the boxing ring later in his fiction to upend stereotypes firmly embraced in genre westerns, particularly stereotypes about "hick" westerners.

Much later he gleefully recounted that, based on aptitude tests he took his junior year, he should have become a dentist because he was meticulous, patient, and liked working with his hands. In a retrospective published in *The Colby Alumnus* in 1962, twenty-two years after his graduation, Savage admitted "I could write a little" but stressed his differences from the majority, which come as no surprise: "I think I can look back on myself, dispassionately, as if I were a stranger...I was a strange sort of person. It was obvious to me that I'd never succeed in business. Neither money nor competition meant a thing. I was gauche and fearful of what people thought of me." ("Colby History & Dean Marriner")

The betrothed couple spent two months out west in the summer of 1939—likely Betty's introduction to Horse Prairie, Lemhi, and Salmon, all the Brenners and Yearians, all a world away from Missoula. They returned in the summer of 1941 before moving temporarily back the following year.

Tom and Betty, married less than a year, graduated on June 17, 1940. They treasured their Colby College years and maintained connections with their alma mater. Betty would later teach a few years at Colby; and Colby certainly publicized each new novel by this celebrated pair of alums. In April 1945, when he returned to host a discussion for students, Savage was described as "probably one of [the most] gifted writers who has graduated from Colby in some time" (*The Colby Echo*, March 21, 1945); on March 11–12, 1949, Savage served on the Journalism panel in Colby's "Second Annual Career Conference"; at the spring 1954 commencement he was awarded an honorary master's degree, along with thirteen others; and in March 1964, both Savages returned to campus and, with other alumni panelists, participated in a conference discussion of "Maine's! [*sic*] Cultural Heritage" (*The Colby Echo*, March 20, 1964). Colby College esteemed the Savages and their work.

Their early years as a couple were not easy. Hart's *Thomas and Elizabeth Savage* (1995) provides the best biographical summary of the newlyweds and their young family in the 1940s. The crucial fact of Savage's gay self does not appear in Hart's streamlined, twin biography. After they graduated from Colby they moved to Chicago where Savage worked as an insurance company claims adjustor for a $1,500 annual salary—well above the average income in 1940. He got his first taste of urban poverty, tending to settlements and favoring poor claimants. The World War II years saw the couple starting a family and moving according to jobs Savage landed. With the depletion of men following Pearl Harbor and massive enlistments, the couple moved back to Horse Prairie, Montana, in the early spring of 1942 to help on the ranch. That year saw Beaverhead County, Montana, ship more beef than any other American county. Their first child, Robert Brassil Savage, was born in

Butte, Montana (May 29, 1942). They were busy on the ranch and as brand- new parents. Additionally, while back home Savage finished the final draft of his first novel. In a letter to a Colby professor, he said "Houghton-Mifflin is interested in my first novel and I'm doing some revamping on it now," though Doubleday would publish it. He wanted to enlist in the Navy or Marine Corps as an officer and confessed, "This country is now strangely silent, for everyone of my age is gone, it seems." (September 17, 1942)

Savage remembered that the Brenner Ranch kept no sheep or pigs, and lacked a produce garden. In 1942 they were gifted a couple of pigs, but after Tom fed them fresh milk, they died in seven minutes. He told this story in the spirit of self-mockery, as a cattle ranch's son ignorant about pigs.

A year later, feeling crowded by relatives at the ranch, they moved back to Massachusetts to be close to Betty's folks, where Tom worked as a welder in the Hingham shipyard on a shift that allowed him to keep writing. Their second son, Russell Yearian Savage, was born in Cohasset, Massachusetts (November 23, 1943). Classified 1A, Savage quit that job and prepared to be drafted, but a rules change kept him out: as a married man with two babies, he was exempt. Queer men, if discovered, were denied service; Savage, a closeted homosexual with two sons, was exempted because of his family. He then took a job with the New York, New Haven & Hartford Railroad as a brakeman, "the most dangerous job" he'd had, that lasted through the war's end. Following the war he worked briefly at Cushing Hospital in Framingham, Massachusetts, then changed gears and worked as an instructor of English at Boston's Suffolk University (1948–49). The seemingly random job changes suggest Savage took what opportunities presented themselves: he knew his real career didn't depend on any day job. After the war, enrollment at Suffolk boomed because of the GI Bill and the university expanded its already broad night-school curriculum. Savage very much liked the mature and enthusiastic students he taught there.

For a period of years after age thirty-three, the young novelist worked as both a teacher and a fundraiser at Brandeis University, which had opened its doors in Waltham, Massachusetts, in 1948: more amenable occupations than his seasons as adjustor, hayer, or brakeman.

After Savage confessed to Betty that he was homosexual, she accepted it, claiming, as have many in comparable situations, that that was not a problem and that they could raise a family anyway. Ultimately, Betty told this story to their daughter, Elizabeth ("Betsy") St. Marks Savage (born December 20, 1949), who in turn told her brothers. There is no surviving evidence that, in his first decade of marriage, Savage acted upon homosexual desire. Instead he played the heteronormative roles of husband and father, and beyond his series of day jobs, worked to establish his career through his first two novels. In *Lona Hanson,* with the character of Clyde Barrows, Savage satirizes the Owen Wister writer stereotype (upper-class easterner comes west for health and self-discovery as writer) and more broadly, the stereotype of writers as effete, thereby mocking, to an extent, himself. Yet Barrows is heterosexual.

A fundamental contradiction, a cracking tension, existed in the family from the outset. Tom made it abundantly clear that he loved relatives and his family members deeply, yet in his aging his sexual orientation became increasingly manifest, at a great psychic cost to Betty. He was a deeply committed family man and yet, unsurprisingly, a core part of him was not fulfilled by wife and children; this family masked his true nature. Russell Savage described his parents' "arrangement": Savage's sexuality cast a deep shadow across their family life and variably colored the lives of their sons and daughter, who grew up with a father "split at the root," in Adrienne Rich's memorable phrase.

The Pass (1944)

During his final visit to Dillon, Montana, Savage recounted the slow genesis of what became his first novel, *The Pass.* That spur railroad, the Gilmore and Pittsburgh, which crossed the Continental Divide and connected his mother's and stepfather's families, occupied his imagination through his life. The railroad, completed in 1910, five years before Savage's birth, and lasting only one generation (abandoned 1939), became central to the plot of a story he drafted and sent to Edward Weeks, then editor of *Atlantic Monthly Press.* Savage recounted that after Weeks held the story a good while, he returned the manuscript suggesting Savage turn it into a novel and add characters, for the story on which it was based lacked any people in it, as if setting—landscapes and climates—were insufficient interest. Eastern publishers traditionally had a hard time accepting the prominence of these key elements of western literary fiction. The prominence of setting in *The Pass* clearly locates it in American naturalistic fiction. Savage expanded his material slowly over the next six years while working that series of blue- and white-collar jobs.

Savage had a contract with Doubleday for his first novel, which he finished revising in 1942–43. One night in June 1943, when Savage returned home at midnight after his welding shift (at the Hingham shipyard), Betty held out a telegram from Doubleday that read "REVISION [of *The Pass*] EXCELLENT. Offering $750.00 advance." Savage couldn't sleep that night and decades later, claimed that there never was anything as exciting as his first novel's acceptance. To celebrate, they booked a suite at the Copley Plaza Hotel, and Betty bought two hats and a coat at Bonwit Teller. Looking back, he deemed it "a pretty good book" that "just vanished." He wryly commented, "I wasn't old enough to make mistakes" but *The Pass*'s disappearance off American fiction's screen foreshadowed the fate of most his novels, though not the next two.

Published three years before A. B. Guthrie Jr.'s more famous *The Big Sky*, *The Pass* serves as Savage's foundational Western American narrative, and his version of the white settler-colonial story underscores the heavy costs of establishing a cattle ranch and ranching community. He conflated two geographical passes—Lemhi and Bannock Passes—in his title, and his reference to "the prairie" within the story, his first use of "Horse Prairie," is based on the Yearian Ranch in Idaho's Lemhi River Valley. This novel's naturalistic flavor is set right from the opening paragraph. The "prairie," bad medicine for vanished natives, takes a heavy toll upon those who would settle and build a community. It kills Billy Blair for his questionable masculinity: he owns two milk cows and a cream separator, and dairying appears to be no man's business. Milking is supposedly women's work. Savage stated in a 1981 interview that he, for years and years, did the milking at the Brenner Ranch because "the cowboys wouldn't do it, you see." More significantly, neither Jess Bentley's baby nor his wife, Beth (named after Savage's mother), survive, so

Savage's settlement story strips the protagonist of his family—though the cattle survive.

Savage built *The Pass*'s climax—the dry cold autumn and endless winter blizzards, set (as is the final third of the novel, chapters XXVI-XXXIX) in 1924—upon the "starvation" winter of 1918-19, when the Gilmore and Pittsburgh, the Little Hay Train that Could, hauled enough hay for the ranchers, including the Yearians, to survive. The climax underscores the remoteness of the novel's setting as well as the sense in which landscape and climate loom as protagonists—perhaps unsurprisingly, given the novel's origins as a short story without people.

As he would do throughout his career, Savage altered historical details to serve his own purposes in his near-historical novels set during his childhood or young adulthood. In this case he rewrites the decade of his birth, since the novel spans thirteen years, 1911-24. The Gilmore and Pittsburgh Railroad, quietly funded by the Northern Pacific Railway (rival of the dominant Great Northern line), was built over thirteen months, beginning from Armstead, Montana (razed and underwater since the 1964 Clark Canyon Dam) in April 1909 and reaching the mining settlement of Gilmore, Idaho, and, on its other (i.e., northwest) branch, Salmon (City), Idaho, in May 1910. Savage shifts the completion ahead six years, and the railroad's arrival (1916) spans his novel's center. He paints a typical scene of a small town's extended celebration, one only undercut by Jess Bentley's dissenting opinion (e.g., chap. VIII).

Montana writer Joseph Kinsey Howard, who single-handedly compiled and published Montana's first literary anthology, *Montana Margins* (1946), recognized the strong promise of Savage's early career and called out the young novelist. In Howard's penultimate section, "Travel and Transport," he included the final section of *The Pass*'s chapter XVI, chapters XVII-XVIII, and the first section of chapter XIX—one of the longest excerpts in the anthology, Salmon residents' celebration of the train's arrival and the town's much faster connection with the outside world.

Against everyone else's eager embrace, protagonist Jess Bentley's skepticism about the railroad and, later, the telephone provides the only critical voice about inevitable ambivalences accompanying technological change and thus, modernity. Far beyond the patriotic bunting, speeches, toasts, and hurrahs, relationships will change beyond anyone's imagining and only Jess dreads the unforeseen consequences. Later, the telephone similarly changes the community: "the hum of the telephone wires brought a new sound of loneliness to the prairie." Jess's complaint—"It seemed that all the new things, all the new ways, spoiled something" (chap. XXXIII)—suggests in a different way that, in this version of the Jeffersonian citizen farmer, ranching is a far more mixed bag than any popular, heroic accounts about it claim: a theme he sustains throughout his career. To found a ranch and lionized rural life, Jess loses his family as well as an earlier sense of connection if not intimacy, one replaced by the train's speed and the party line.

Savage thus paints a darker, more somber portrait of settler colonialism than that provided by most local histories or popular western cultural production. Of course, Jess Bentley "sticks" while Guthrie's *Big Sky* protagonist, Boone Caudill, quits paradise (i.e., Montana's Upper Teton River country) and wanders, condemned, like Richard Wagner's Flying Dutchman. Jess still has his cows but no family, and the phone makes him apprehensive. Instead of ever bigger family and ranch, he ends resolutely desiring a West before train tracks and phone lines, and lonelier than ever.

The Pass's chief cowboy, a fastidious, gay ranch manager named Slim Edwards ("'sort of an old woman,'" p. 49), is treated satirically. In an early bar scene when Jess woos Slim to be his ranch manager (chap. IV), we encounter a fussy old codger who complains equally about women, sloppy young ranch hands, and his kidneys. With his name and temperament he's nothing if not a comic version of a "hand" waiting for hire, a stock western character. More broadly, both Cy and Amy Pierce are treated with broad-brush humor through gender stereotypes, with Amy as the chatty, good-hearted gossip and Cy, the stolid solid man, kind but mostly mute. For example, they and other characters listen to the speech by the railroad executive, on the occasion of the railroad's arrival in Salmon City: "[Cy] was deep in thought. The whole celebration seemed to rest on his shoulders. Amy said, 'Cy, you missed the first part of the speech. He said the mountains are going to flower. Isn't that nice?' 'Yes,' he said absently. 'There you go thinking again!'" (p. 154) Such satiric sketches, among other effects, usually render characters more endearing than condemned by the reader.

Savage's West differs markedly from the pop western initiated by Owen Wister's *The Virginian* (1902). In chapter VIII Jess and Beth receive a copy of *The Virginian* as a "whimsical" wedding present, and if Jess read it he'd find few affinities between Wister's romantic lead couple and him and Beth. At the Masonic Hall's winter dance, the middle-aged spinster-schoolteacher, another cliché, introduces Jess as "a rancher, but a cowboy also!" to the young new schoolteacher fresh from Minneapolis who "has been reading *The Virginian* and wants to know all about cowboys." (chap. XX) In *The Virginian,* the railroad connects the title character's coal interests with industrial markets and assures personal wealth, vast resource exploitation, and mobility, and at the climax Wister uneasily poises a clichéd romantic idyll with his lead couple and that business empire barely offstage. By 1944 when *The Pass* was published, the Hollywood western was in the ascendant so Savage's West comprised a minority view, a counter-narrative that didn't win popular favor.

Savage thus criticizes the naïve, insistent romanticization broadbrushed by Wister and countless others before and since and eagerly championed by schoolteachers and everyone else at any distance from the felt realities of ranch life—the vast majority of us, even in the 1940s. Barely two generations after Wister, Savage, who knew it intimately from the inside, would have none of it.

In an interview during his 1983 Dillon visit, Savage stated, about his first novel, "I was after loyalty, love, hope: all the good things, you know." Surveying his career, he added, "the two greatest things are loyalty and generosity," and that the only good writing is about family—a credo he adhered to, whatever the psychic cost, given his gayness. In *The Pass* the community pulls together to avoid cattle die-off and rallies around Jess in his loss and sorrow. Jess's devotion to Beth, as well, reflects Savage's loyalty to his wife and young kids, which trumped his loyalty to his queer self for many years. Besides, Savage's heteronormative definition of family precluded, for him, versions of family led by gay or lesbian couples.

New York Times reviewer Hoffman Birney stressed the novel's rejection of the pop western and its realism: "there's no killing, no rustling, no schemes to steal the ranch" and little romantic intrigue, yet "Savage has not written a negative story." Birney stressed Savage's "very real people" whose "lives and their sorrows and their sometimes pathetic pleasures are real, not fictional," and he concluded the novel "will not be forgotten quickly." (April 23, 1944) The *Los Angeles Times* reviewer argued that its "grim realism" is offset by "the courage of the people you have met and the beauty you have seen through their eyes." In the novelist's insistent deromanticization readers gain a matured, fraught version of that favorite, nineteenth- and twentieth-century American westering narrative. It would seem a ranch dynasty always "spoils something."

Lona Hanson (1948)

Lona Hanson, Savage's second novel (1948), continues *The Pass*'s foundational story, fictitiously shifting ahead a few years (1928–33). Bigger ranches by that time had bought out smaller ones, and dry years and worsening economic conditions forced everyone to tighten their belts. The Depression, bear in mind, began in Montana in the 1920s. Before *Lona*, Savage had started a book about Bannack, site of Montana's first gold rush (1862) and territorial capital (1864), and part of the writer's geographical backyard, but nothing came of it.

In his late sixties Savage called *Lona* a "deterministic" book which he hadn't looked at in a long time. He also judged it sentimental, one of his weaker novels, though it and his third novel, *A Bargain With God* (1953), outsold all his other fiction. About this pair of novels, he declared, "I was just learning, for God's sake." He rightly judged the former as too melodramatic and the latter as a cloying piety.

He'd switched publishers, and Simon & Schuster published both of his most commercially successful novels. *Lona Hanson* was optioned by Columbia Pictures for $50,000, and Rita Hayworth was cast as Lona but her pregnancy and temporary residency in Switzerland (with Prince Aly Khan, her third husband) jettisoned this project. She left after two weeks. When that $50,000 check arrived at their "tacky" Waltham,

Massachusetts, home, Betty was sewing strips from her grandmother's carpet for curtains.

In a well-publicized anecdote, Savage, still an instructor at Suffolk University, was turned down for a $500 (Boston) bank loan in April 1948. He wanted the loan to buy furniture. By April 28, he'd received the check from Columbia, was quickly congratulated by that bank, then he politely turned down their offer, investing that huge sum elsewhere in a family trust. With that trust, Savage bought years of financial security, particularly after he quit the ranks of academe in 1955.

In 1983 Savage revealed to interviewer John Scheckter that the role model for Lona Hanson was Margaret Jean (Bennett Kelley) Orr (1917–73), a granddaughter of (veterinarian) Dr. Will Orr Jr. (1873–1934): the Poindexters and Orrs ranked as the first family among Beaverhead Valley, Montana, ranchers, and the Poindexter-Orr mansion remains Dillon's most distinguished private home to this day. Savage told his interviewer, "don't tell anybody but that's who it is." By then, Margaret Orr had been dead for a decade.

Lona Hanson completes the rough portrait of Savage's West. The novel represents a negative anatomy of empire, one that suggests more baleful consequences for the Jeffersonian vision of agrarian democracy than are implied by *The Pass*. If the historical ideal of the citizen-farmer is translated, in the Intermountain West, into the rancher who controls hundreds or thousands of acres—an empire writ small—it proves untenable, a failed ideal, according to Savage. A ranch dooms those who found or perpetuate it: it destroys people rather than sustains them in the top socioeconomic class. *Lona* figures as a ranch precursor to novelist Jane Smiley's Pulitzer Prize-winning *A Thousand Acres* (1991) minus the *King Lear* plot. Instead, Savage has the mismatched couple, the title character and her "soft" husband, writer Clyde Barrows, discussing Theodore Dreiser's famous novel, *An American Tragedy* (1925), which the cultured Barrows describes as "a good study of what blood and background can do." (Barrows and Dreiser's protagonist, Clyde Griffiths, share their first name.) The gloss of Dreiser accurately defines Savage's adaptation as though a ranch dynasty—something "spoiled" in *The Pass*—becomes the American tragedy of the American West. Instead of the gold standard, the best rural life, a ranch guarantees division if not disaster. At times overheated, *Lona* ends with a flourish and faceoff, but that doesn't lessen the meaning of Savage's grim anatomy lesson.

Lona, great-granddaughter of forbidding ranch patriarch, Bert Bart, appears as avatar of Bert, a chip off the old block. Bert Bart's character is contained in his name, two explosive monosyllables. Lona remains fundamentally torn between the (literal) pants she wears and the dresses she occasionally desires and dons. She embodies an uneasy alliance of masculine and feminine traits and, enslaved by the legacy of the Bart Ranch's 20,000 acres in "Lost Horse Valley"—i.e., Horse Prairie, Montana—she destroys her family if not herself to keep the ranch intact in the teeth of the Depression. She has nothing and is nothing apart from the ranch. The descendants feel paralyzed by Bart's legacy: his stern portrait in the hallway, his heavy black walnut bedroom suite, even the "Bart Block" in distant "Sentinel" (Savage's first name for Dillon, Montana). Lona; her weak grandfather, Tom (who dies halfway through); her mother, Ruth; as well as Clyde, who eventually leaves with Ruth, his natural partner; and others: all feel prisoners in the silent, cold, big house suffused with "the breath of decay," "a shabby, tottering kingdom" whose "walls were rotten."

If the Depression tightens belts on the giant Bart spread, Tom Bart (named for Thomas Yearian), "a good fellow," fails as a businessman and turns to dude ranching as an alternative (*"Come to a real ranch,"* chap. 15), just as young Tom tried "dude-ing" one season after giving up on sheep ranching. That fails as well, excepting the arrival of Clyde Barrows—Savage's version of an Owen Wister, arrived in the Old West to regain his health and focus as a writer. The glance into dude ranching matches the plot turn in Mildred Walker's *Curlew's Cry* (1955) published less than a decade later: in both cases, the working family ranches get turned to a familiar version of western recreational tourism to survive. Savage wrote the dude ranching plot based on his time in Skookum-chuck, B.C.

Lona's marriage, intended in part to refinance the failing ranch, fails, and Barrows eventually links up with Lona's mother, Ruth—a beautiful, alcoholic woman, a pianist and ranch misfit, all but the last trait taken from Savage's mother, Beth Brenner—who together quit the place. Savage satirizes, through Barrows, young novelists such as himself who come from money but don't make much. Yet Barrows "becomes" western, learns ranch chores as his skin toughens and his writer's block disappears, as though he closes such distance with Savage the ranch son.

In addition, with Clyde Barrows, Savage not only satirizes the Owen Wisters of the American literary canon and underlines his link with Dreiser's novel, but sardonically glances at Clyde Barrow, male half of the notorious Bonnie and Clyde gang of the early 1930s. When the novel's couple takes off, they're not going on a rampage, robbing banks and turning themselves into legend. But they're outlaws of convention, Barrows divorcing a daughter (Lona) to marry her mother (Ruth).

In many regards, *Lona* serves as a rough draft for later novels, especially *The Power of the Dog*, several characters introduced in this novel later reappearing in elaborated versions. In the novel's second half, Lona's acts of cruelty increase along with her single-minded resolve and desperation. She'll cut off whomever necessary to preserve the 20,000-acre legacy. In her world there is no room for French composers Ernest Chausson and César Franck, both of whom are mentioned: nineteenth-century composers with modest oeuvre whose music Savage knew and loved.

Lona imperfectly suppresses her divided sexuality in her clenched hold of every acre. In the opening chapters, for example, she wins her rodeo event but in front of famous rodeoer Bonnie Earl, she's branded a "cowgirl" who thinks herself a "cowboy." (p. 20) A tough tomboy, Lona grows terminally hard in her heart even as her repressed femininity is awakened around her lover and natural mate (Eddie Rohn), but the hostile, manipulative foreman, Joe Martin (first use of William Brenner), exploits her vulnerability. Lona, both male and female, bends genders at considerable cost: Lon-a ends essentially a-lon[e].

She signifies, on a far larger scale than *The Pass's* Billy Blair, the ways in which Savage characters push against gender stereotypes and occupy fluid, fused positions in terms of contemporary notions of masculine vs. feminine behaviors and roles. Lona represents a first draft of the Sheep Queen: an undisputed female boss who always "mans up." Savage's foregrounding these fused positions such as the female boss reflects his own status, split at the root, and protest against a

West (i.e., ranch culture) that perpetuates gender boxes wherein, for example, women usually don't own or manage ranches. Or men cannot pursue cosmopolitan interests: Mozart or interior design, for instance.

Savage balances our attention on Lona's decline and fall with lyrical evocations of the "Lost Horse Valley" across the seasons, which reflect the abiding grip of southwest Montana on him. The painterly details underline the hold the acreage has upon the protagonist. Savage also balances the valley views with a panoptic gaze over "Sentinel"—his first, harsh evocation of Dillon, Montana. He focuses upon whores and whorehouses ("the Dixie Rooms"), for example, with the same sympathetic understanding he expressed in mid-1930s letters and that Henri de Toulouse-Lautrec, a favorite painter of Savage's, demonstrated in Paris less than two generations earlier. And he sardonically notes the decline of local piano culture in the ranching community (chap. 15), where such attention to classical music seems only frippery. Here sounds again Savage's critique of anti-cosmopolitan provincialism.

In *Lona* Savage creates a baleful allegory of wealth to suggest that a ranch a priori dooms its owners, and this narrative exists at cross-purposes to the usual (and almost always) white ranching genesis so consistently enshrined in popular culture as well as more literary images of the rural Intermountain West. In *The Pass*, death strips Jess Bentley of his family; in *Lona*, the title character drives everyone away except for the scheming Martin, who has raped her and effectively controls her. Midway through the novel, Lona discovers the $15,000 "chattel mortgage" accrued by her weak grandfather who had repurchased a "piece of wasteland from a wild-cat mining company. Where the gold camp was"—this novel's originary scene, which Savage invokes three times. The scene rewinds the family tragedy to its fairy tale genesis in the act of extracting gold.

In a lurid chiaroscuro storm scene at the gold camp (chap. VIII), we watch Lona watching her grandfather mumbling to his father' spirit— the patriarch—inside an old cabin: "His lips moved slowly, but his voice was flat and sank into the rotten logs. He said, 'I wish you'd never bought the God-damned ranch.' Her eyes followed his voice across the room to the corner, vague in a thin pool of light. He said, 'We're all afraid. Afraid of everything. And afraid to leave.'" (p. 69) In this recognition scene,

Lona cannot fathom its meaning: "in his face she saw what her mother saw in hers, what she saw in her mother's: loneliness that sickened and twisted. She turned away, began to walk away, afraid. Afraid of deformity." (p. 70)

Savage's use of the genesis scene differs markedly from family history as portrayed in *The Sheep Queen*, wherein his maternal great-grandparent's first names remain unchanged. Family members gather ceremonially to celebrate the patriarch, the gold site in Jefferson Davis Gulch (just north, and below, Bannock Pass), and their dynasty:

> We picnicked annually, sometimes as many as fifty of us, on the very spot where George Sweringen [Yearian] had discovered gold and we ate what he had eaten: beans and bacon and trout fried over the fire, and dried apple pies. We felt we could reach out and touch him and his wife Lizzie who had often sung hymns. We were proud of them and felt they would be proud of us. (p. 140)

Again Savage captures family history: his grandmother, the Sheep Queen, recorded at least one such visit in her day journal ("Later drove to our diggings where I went when first married. All cabins gone." (May 11, 1941)

There is more at stake than that site and story. Though gay, Savage absolutely believed in the family he made with Betty; he felt deep loyalty and affection for the Yearians, and most of the Brenners, he grew up among. As I shall discuss later, *The Sheep Queen*'s primary theme concerns the centrality of family even as new members are discovered and new identities negotiated. In that novel the narrator suggests that identity endures beyond death because of family memory, and Savage writes the scene of memory as a picnic, thus linking it with the originary scene of the founding great-grandparents quoted above:

> If you leave a family, you do not really die ... You appear at picnics because the lunch in the basket and the contents of the thermos bottle are the foods you ate and the liquid you drank. You chose the sites because the cold spring wind couldn't find you there, and the pretty shells were in greater variety for the children ... They remembered how you laughed. What was weak in you, or selfish, is often forgotten. Time has burned the dross out of you. (p. 201)

The foundational act—mining gold then buying and growing a ranch—becomes indistinguishable from the act of affirming family membership; of belonging. The site of origins represents the best site for renewing identity. In this instance, the contrast between Savage's biography and fictive definitions of ranch life could not be starker. In the contest between centripetal (i.e., the Yearian Ranch) and centrifugal (i.e., the Brenner Ranch) forces, queer men or women might find a place in the former but not the latter.

The antithetical use of a piece of family tradition underlines his intent in his negative anatomy of empire, wherein a ranch signifies an ideal miniature in the national imaginary. In his American Tragedy, the curse of gold dooms a ranch and destroys its people. The novel's closing chapter begins implying that Lona has come to understand her "insane" grandfather's repurchase of that "bad land" which enabled the 20,000 acres: "When you lost a part of you you were crippled, deformed. You had lost something that wouldn't grow back. Or in its place grew something strange and ugly that you had to hide. She was glad, fiercely glad that he had bought it back." (pp. 290–91) But she's understood nothing of this homily offered the reader (i.e., the second-person appeal), which glosses her progressive deformity. She effectively earns her name, Lon-a / a-lone, with vicious Joe Martin parodying any supportive human community still available to *The Pass*'s Jess Bentley at that novel's end.

The *New York Herald Tribune Weekly Book Review* reviewer claimed it "is chiefly rewarding in its atmosphere and its vivid descriptions of life," but significantly commented, "Mr. Savage does not believe in happy endings." (October 17, 1948) In old age, Savage disparaged his second novel, which can be classified a naturalistic fiction wherein the big ranch serves as protagonist and owns its owners. It poses one baleful version of settler colonialism, a negative example of that American legacy that erases indigenous cultures captured in the concluding lines of Robert Frost's "The Gift Outright": "Such as we were we gave ourselves outright. . . / To the land vaguely realizing westward, / But still unstoried, artless, unenhanced, / Such as she was, such as she would become."

In the opening paragraph of *The Sheep Queen,* he answers the charge about happy endings. There's not only no pot of gold at the rainbow's end, "There is no ending, happy or otherwise, only a pause." Once again, Savage affirms his aesthetic that has no truck with genre westerns. *The Pass*'s harsh verdict against *The Virginian* (chaps. VIII, XX) declares this writer's independence from any formulae, just as many in his cast of characters, major and minor, occupy fluid positions of sexuality and gender. In his western fiction as well as his other (five) novels, he writes a more grounded and authentic set of landscapes, one he knew acutely. His Savage West bears little resemblance to any species of wish fulfillment endemic in local histories and popular cultural production. Yet Savage insistently returns to Horse Prairie, to its wide vistas and sagebrush: staples of the mid-twentieth-century Hollywood western.

Lona sold approximately 750,000 copies in a pocketbook (pb) edition. This young novelist showed great promise.

□　□　□

Having defined his West in the period spanning 1911–33, Savage turned away from his home region to his adopted New England in his next two novels. By the time *Lona Hanson* was published, he'd turned to teaching. After his year at Suffolk University, he joined the School of Arts and Sciences faculty at Brandeis University (1949) in nearby Waltham, Massachusetts, then in its second year of operation. That same year Savage's daughter, Betsy, was born, and from infancy she developed an extraordinarily close relationship with her father, one sustained until his death more than a half a century later. She later attested to this closeness, saying "I have never loved a person as I loved him": her father "was the most important man in my life."

Hired on the basis of his two novels, Savage would work at Brandeis for the next seven years. By his third year (1951–52), he'd been promoted to assistant professor. Savage also worked as a fundraiser. In a phone conversation decades later with professor Sue Hart, he recounted, "On Fridays, I'd take a plane to somewhere in the country to talk to Brandeis supporters. I'd meet with them and they'd give a cocktail party or something—and make contributions." He would play his guitar, sing with his Gene Autry voice, the ol' westerner from the predominately Jewish university by Boston. Savage, a social chameleon, shifted effortlessly. This chapter of his life becomes the opening scene in *For Mary,* in which the unnamed narrator—Savage—addresses a group of Congregationalists as a Brandeis ambassador. Savage's son, Russell, has remarked that he was the only "goy" on the faculty and gladly wore the yarmulke given him by a colleague. Savage was happy at Brandeis, where he taught both creative writing and literature courses. Yet he admitted, much later, "I hated faculty meetings, the whole business. The only position I ever held of any importance . . . was the Chairman of Protocol . . . And the question was, 'Should the marshal's baton be made of Cedar of Lebanon?'"

Russell refers to these years as his father's "golden years." Savage counted as friends faculty members such as Ludwig Lewisohn, a Goethe expert—"my closest friend," according to a later newspaper profile— and Milton Hindus, a Proust scholar and leading New Critic. Savage paid tribute to Hindus, "probably America's foremost authority on Proust," by citing him twice in *Her Side of It* (1981), his eleventh novel. The Savages lived nearby, occupying a comfortable old brick home on Florence Road, in the Cedarwood neighborhood of Waltham, Massachusetts— though Savage, in old age, recalled it as a "ticky-tacky" house.

Betty Savage still wrote, in between sewing and mothering three young children. Just ten days before her death at age eighty-five, Big Mama—the Sheep Queen—noted in her final entry in her day journals, which she'd kept for decades: "Heard that Betty, Tom Savage['s] wife, sold her story to Sat. [*Saturday Evening*] Post for $850—I'm just thrilled." (December 15, 1951) The matriarch was particularly proud of her oldest grandson and his wife who worked worlds away from sheep or cattle ranching.

Savage oversaw the interior decoration work in the Cedarwood "front" room—according to the rest of the family, the living room. He acquired an enormous Persian carpet from the basement of Boston's St. John the Evangelist Church: the same Bowdoin Street neighborhood, on the "wrong" side of Beacon Hill, that became the setting of *A Bargain With God.* According to Russell, "It was the pillar and cornerstone of his philosophy of interior decoration, from which all ancillary corollaries of interior decoration would proceed: first, you get your rug. Then . . . you continue to embellish your salon with Russian samovars, brass student lamps, Lautrec prints, and epergnes, from the antique shops on Charles St., in Boston." He remembers, "the Waltham house smelt of stale cigarette smoke, brass polish, and typing paper."

Even as his young family rooted themselves in Waltham, Savage drove them across country in the summers to visit relatives and old haunts. In what turned out to be the final summer of her life (1951), the Sheep Queen noted, in her day journal, at least ten visits with some or all of Savage's family between late June and early September. Savage wanted his children to know his grandmother as he had. Until her death "Big Mama" adhered to her role as matriarch, and the Yearian Ranch remained a gravitational center for children, in-laws, grandchildren, and beyond.

While Savage advanced in his career at Brandeis and worked on his third novel, Beth and Charlie Brenner, his mother and stepfather, retired from the Brenner Ranch (1952), moving to Missoula, Montana, and occupying a sixth-floor apartment in the historic Wilma building (overlooking Higgins Avenue); thereafter, half the Brenner Ranch was run by Tom's cousin, Jack Brenner, and the other half, by his sister and brother-in-law, Isabel and Bob James.

A Bargain With God (1953)

While at Brandeis, Savage wrote and published *A Bargain With God* (1953), his most sentimental and lucrative novel, dedicated to Brassil Fitzgerald, writing mentor and father-in-law. As he recounted to Sue Hart, *Bargain* appeared in several translations, was optioned, condensed, and republished by *Reader's Digest,* and even televised as a *Studio One* production. (*Thomas and Elizabeth Savage,* p. 11) It aired on Studio One's Channel 7 to a national audience on November 16, 1953. In a *New Bedford* (Sunday) *Standard-Times* profile a few months later, Savage complimented the *Reader's Digest Illustrated* condensation but criticized the televised version: "They did a terrible job on it, as a picture. The spoken lines, however, were all right." (February 7, 1954)

He made more money from it than any other novel, at least $65,000, but judged it his worst. He generally turned his back upon "happily ever after": the easy lure of commercial copy, the pop western, the thumbs up. But not with *Bargain,* Savage's first fictive departure from his home ground. *Lona* spikes into melodrama at moments; *Bargain,* confined to a Boston neighborhood—Savage's adopted city—reads as a sentimental parable. Savage would never write another parable.

That *New York Herald* reviewer of *Lona Hanson* would swallow his words, as *Bargain* delivers a feel-good climax enhanced by the sentimental setting of a poor Boston parish church, just like a commercial feature film. The final paragraph of the promotional copy on the dust jacket reads, "The story is a simple one. But its emotional impact is deep and lasting. In these days of strain and tension [read, Korean War and McCarthyism] it is a rewarding experience to read a book so uplifting to the spirit. It makes one feel good, and fills the heart with hope as well as compassion." One reviewer, James Kelly, concluded *Bargain* "is a refreshing change from novels of despair and Freudian fogs." I imagine this sappy homily and intended praise turned the novelist's stomach. His aesthetic undoubtedly tended toward "novels of despair" and, sometimes at least, Freudian psychology.

Certainly in *The Sheep Queen*, Savage's narrator-avatar takes a sardonic view of it:

> I had written a novel about God and a miracle in a church in Boston where were—and are—gathered together a mixed bag of Harvard professors, blacks, Cabots, reformed alcoholics, paupers, millionaires and jailbirds, artists and writers. A sentimental book, readers wept through it and a thousand wrote me, among them two admirals and a United States senator. It was my worst book and it made me the most money because people need to believe in miracles. What but miracles can save them? Is there another answer? Love? You may have seen that book on television, but who now remembers Studio One? (pp. 148–49)

Savage again blends fact within fiction, since, as noted, old Studio One had televised *A Bargain*. In a Maine newspaper profile published many years later, he added "[A Bargain] was a selection of the *Reader's Digest* of books in English and three other languages, and there was a complete translation into Italian last year. Readers wrote me a thousand letters and I answered every one of them."

In *A Bargain*, a tale of bald wish fulfillment, he cannily satisfies that need for miracles or belief—contrary to his aesthetic defined in *The*

Sheep Queen's opening—that chasing a rainbow yields a pot of gold or at least a happy ending. Savage links the novel's neighborhood residents with naïve readers in his second paragraph as he announces its subject: "Their hopes were like the hopes of children: suddenly, as if by magic, everything would change." Yet on some level, Savage's attraction to this fundamental desire mirrors his own queer yearnings in which he would not feel split down the middle, divided between his sexuality and his family. "Somewhere Over the Rainbow" is, after all, a queer anthem.

Far from fraught western ranches, this novel sticks to the grainy poverty of Boston's Bowdoin Street: a poor Beacon Hill neighborhood defined, in part, by St. Mark's, a decrepit (Catholic) "Mission Church" with a threadbare playground immediately adjacent, the only safe space for the neighborhood urchins. St. Mark's, held together by irregular wiring and plumbing, leaks and develops a large crack in a wall. Its decrepit condition is matched by protagonist Father Raymond T. Ferris: old, impractical, shabby, and with the clichéd heart of gold. The opening pages define the impoverished character of Bowdoin Street—a real street and unchanged name—as though Savage borrowed a piece of Dickens's London.

The first miracle occurs when Father Ferris discovers a $100 bill left in the St. Anthony's box with a pinned note that just reads, "*For the church.*" He uses it to pay the back rent for the Longs, a Dickensian couple, inept and pathetic. The second miracle occurs when the young couple, Jebby and Johnny Moss, whose baby has died from smoke inhalation in an apartment fire, announce Jebby is pregnant again. The third miracle, the novel's climax, softens the heart of the Scroogian Miss Lydia Brumell, a stereotypical New England spinster who lives in the large, affluent family home across the churchyard. Miss Brumell manages the family fortunes while dying from loneliness until her rescue of a neighborhood urchin, who tells her of the threat to tear down the playground if not the church. Attending Mass in the final chapter, Miss Brumell calculates how much she'll gift the church and priest, enlarging her estimate as she inspects from her pew. Meanwhile, Father Ferris, ignorant of what we know, is willing to throw in the towel, admit his failure to save the church. We know better.

Perhaps Savage borrowed parts of his playbook not only from Dickens's *A Christmas Carol* (1843) but Leo McCarey's popular film from eight years' earlier, *The Bells of St. Mary's,* which proved the highest grossing movie of 1945. At St. Mary's, an inner-city parochial school deteriorating to the point of condemnation, Sister Mary Benedict (Ingrid Bergman), the headmistress, and other nuns hope that the new adjacent building, owned by wealthy businessman Horace P. Bogardus (Henry Travers), will be donated; the newly arrived Father "Chuck" O'Malley (Bing Crosby), wants to try another strategy. There's more than a little resemblance between the setting, plot elements, and above all, maudlin tone, though Savage's *Bargain* lacks the tunes and, above all, Crosby's legendary soft croon.

With this novel, Savage ignored the homily he utters when his young couple, the Mosses, are at their nadir: "The question is not, then, that there was no miracle, but how to live with things the way they *are*." (ital. original, p. 208) That homily matches his acerbic view of the West and harsh dismissal of genre fiction. The Savage West has no truck with romantic conventions. Yet he implicitly critiques "the way they *are*" because that suppresses queer desire—for example, the "miracle" of overt acceptance of sexual minorities in the world in which Savage grew up.

But with the successes of his second and third novels, and his position secure at Brandeis, he seemed poised, at age thirty-eight, to make a big name for himself in American letters. He'd published three novels in nine years. Despite this success, he published only one more novel in the next fourteen years, his largest gap until old age, and relentlessly walked his own path. Why did he apparently turn away from commercial success if not a high critical reputation? And why did he unswervingly make his imaginative way back home, again and again? Part of the answer, both in his personal life and his fiction, consists in the safe path of his third novel he roundly rejected. In a way, life had become too easy: he needed to take more risks, live and work closer to edges he didn't entirely understand or foresee.

CHAPTER THREE

Gay Family Man, 1953–1967

ART OF THE BACK dust jacket cover of Savage's *A Bargain With God* reads, "His principal hobby is motor cars—he is a member of the Veteran Motor Car Club of America—and personally drives a 1922 Franklin." This club represented a key component of Savage's identity for many years. The club (subsequently called "The Vintage Motor Car Club of America") was founded by twelve enthusiasts in a Boston hotel in December 1938, according to its website. They issued their first publication three months later and held their first meet at a Framingham, Massachusetts, estate the following September. The club incorporated as a nonprofit organization in May 1940, and in 1946, commenced its annual "Glidden Tours." In 1954 and 1957, the club joined with a comparable club in Great Britain in staging rallies (i.e., tours).

In *Daddy's Girl* Savage, via his autobiographical narrator, Chris, ironically recounts a typical club meeting: "Each Wednesday now I met with other old car buffs in a barn that had sheltered old cars ever since the passing of the horse, and there we talked and argued about Stearns-Knights and vacuum tanks, ending up with coffee in tin cups— another salute to the past—and soggy jelly doughnuts." (p. 137) In a later retrospective moment, that narrator recalls a different genealogy of cars than Savage himself bought and traded, and Chris reaches his apex with a Jaguar, which he "drove well enough by now . . . I had the guts to join the Sports Car Club, and felt pretty grand driving around with the insignia bolted up there on the front bumper." (p. 225)

Savage couldn't have been better positioned in Boston to indulge his love of older cars, especially exotic, luxury sports cars. By the time *Bargain* was published, he'd been driving an old Franklin manufactured midway through the generation of Franklins (1906-34), which were distinguished by their air-cooled engines and quick responsiveness. Particularly in the 1950s and early 1960s, exotic cars became a mode of self-definition, even a visible suggestion of his homosexuality, as he calculatedly separated himself from the mainstream status of Cadillacs and Lincolns. His personal brand demanded elegant, imported luxury or sports cars that he judged superior to Cadillacs. The stream of cars served as a primary language through which Savage distanced himself from heteronormativity, precisely during the years when his three children grew from childhood into adulthood. Savage declared his identity as a gay man during the mostly happy family years on the Maine coast.

Savage flaunted his gay desires through his luxury sports cars, as the bright luster of their finish and purr of their engines proclaimed his sexiness and desired upper-class European heritage. For many years they proved his favorite self-representation. The oiled leather and tooled hardwood enabled Savage to fancy himself an aristocrat, one who could declare and observe his own sexual mores. If cars define their owners, Savage advertised himself as exotically different and superior to those who drove American cars. His cars flashed like his colorful scarves.

Savage changed vehicles with some speed during this period, a sign of his restlessness and ambition. He traded out the Franklin for a huge gray 1939 Packard Twelve (i.e., twelve-cylinder), the size of which left a permanent impression on his sons. He wanted big and fancy and patrician, like the Brenner grandparents (the elder Burbanks in *Power*). Russell Savage remembers it as the biggest car he's ever seen anywhere, claiming, with a child's hyperbole, that its tires were taller than he and that the rear seats could hold a football team. This Packard Twelve makes a cameo appearance in *Trust in Chariots* (1961), serving as the Esposito Funeral Home flower car. (p. 47) But Savage wanted the best, not merely the biggest, luxury car.

In 1952 he traded out the giant Packard for a 1939 Rolls-Royce Phantom III Silver Cloud, which he bought from a Massachusetts bishop. This particular Rolls (also twelve-cylinder), featured in the 1939 New

York World's Fair, had carried President Franklin Roosevelt, and Savage expressed his fondness for FDR via his cigarette holder. This Rolls displayed a "glossy, coal-black finish," the result of twelve coats of hand-lacquered paint. Though he only owned it a couple of years, he twice drove it out to Montana, snaking up the Beaverhead River canyon highway south of Dillon and reaching Horse Prairie. He wanted everyone to know he was doing quite well a long ways from the ranch he left behind. From the driver's seat he could scorn the ranchers who measured their wealth through their Cadillacs parked in front of Dillon's premier hotel, the Hotel Andrus. He declared queer independence through the glamorous international car market.

A photo survives of Savage, wearing a white shirt, necktie, and fashionable overcoat, casually standing next to the passenger seat, left leg on the running board and left hand gripping a door handle. The license reads "58 474 MASS 51" and the car's glossy sheen matches the easy wide smile of its handsome, young owner. He's thirty-seven, assured and ambitious. In later years he fondly recalled his seasons with the Rolls, always describing it as the best of the best, spoiling a car enthusiast for anything else. He also claimed that his time with the Rolls, more than anything else, precipitated his fourth novel, *Trust in Chariots*, which he ultimately called "a very strange book." He later told interviewer John Scheckter that he "wrote a novel about [the Rolls]" several years after driving it cross country.

After its dedication page and before the "Contents," the book displays a series of nine testimonials about Rolls-Royces including three advertisements and references to a British novel (Michael Arlen's *The Green Hat*, 1927) and an "American song of 1916." This page distills his earlier love affair. Why didn't he hold onto it? Looking back, he stated that the first time he started it and "could hear [the engine]," he sold it—to Peter Paul Luce, son of American magazine giant, Henry Luce, publisher of *Life, Time*, and *Sports Illustrated*, among others. If Savage spent any time with the Luces, there is no record of it. This sale yielded no contracts or publicity. Selling the Rolls, more than anything, marked his restlessness.

His period of ownership, though, marked him. In the climax of *A Strange God* (1974), his eighth novel, protagonist Jack Reed, whose problems are marked, in part, by his owning a series of Cadillacs, turns his thoughts to Rolls-Royces. Savage contrasts "The Standard of the World" (Cadillacs) with "The Best Car in the World": "Just as 'Cadillac' projected images of Wall Street, Michigan Avenue and the cottages at Newport, 'Rolls-Royce' prompts thoughts of potentates, Fauberge, and the Ascot races." (p. 285) European high culture and queerness trump American wealth and the heterosexual majority. Savage's sports cars—a set of international credentials—measure, in part, his scorn for his native region and sense that he's risen far above its stifling provincialism.

From its sale, though, he bought three cars: a four-door silver gray 1955 Mercedes-Benz 300-S sedan; a British racing blue Porsche Speedster Coupe; and a drab olive Volkswagen Beetle for Betty, who had finally learned to drive. He also owned, however briefly, a Riley and a Jaguar Mark VII. With his last fancy car, a Morgan two-seater (a "+4"), he drove across the country back home, to Horse Prairie and Salmon, in the summer of 1961.

In *The Sheep Queen,* Savage reviews this chapter of his life:

As a boy, I was fascinated by automobiles and longed one day to own a Rolls-Royce. Eventually I did, secondhand. I bought it in 195[2] on Long Island from a fellow who collected all the fabled cars—Rolls, Isotta-Fraschini, Hispano-Suiza, Invicta, Lagonda, and Bugatti—and lay in wait for eccentrics like me. My car had been the Rolls exhibited at the New York World's Fair, a jet black *sedanca de ville* with a price tag of thirty-six thousand dollars in 1939. It figured in a novel I wrote about a ruined man's search for perfection." (p. 155)

Russell Savage remembers a memorable road trip with his father in that blue Porsche, cited in my introduction, when they scouted a house location. He recalls, "In those days land in Maine, even shore-front property, could still be had, and a few tiny, spruce-sharp islets, made so by the rising tide, might still be for sale, cheaper than you might think, but the word was getting out, which was how we wound up where we were." For this son, growing up in this rural locale before the open Atlantic Ocean was paradise.

□   □   □

Savage's cars were fancier than his day job. After eight years in academe
he was tired of teaching and wanted to write full-time, even though
his Brandeis position was secure. Savage's status was confirmed by
the honorary master's degree he received from Colby College, his alma
mater, in 1954. In the group photo of fourteen recipients, Savage stands
in the back row, second from left, a restrained smile on his face. He
looks the youngest recipient among more than a few oldies.

He moved the family north to the ocean's edge in the summer of
1955. He would teach one year, 1958–59, as a lecturer at Vassar College
(Poughkeepsie, New York); thereafter, he taught an occasional course at
Franconia College (New Hampshire). In old age, he saluted teachers and
stated he couldn't teach and write well simultaneously, even claiming
that teaching cracked his hands. He believed he suffered from "excessive hornification" [i.e., dried, callused skin], liberally applied Mentho-
latum, and wore out dozens of pairs of white gloves. He feared many
thought he wanted to be grand with those gloves, but instead, he or at
least his hands "went all to pieces." As one who has taught for decades,
I find this rationale for quitting improbably funny. In an interview
many years later he conceded, "if I wanted to be a good teacher. . . I
would have to stop writing," and there was never any question about
his priorities.

He had bought four lots near the end of Indian Point Road, just
south of Georgetown, Maine, for $4,500, from a Dr. John Nelson; in
1956, he purchased two more lots for $2,100 (and, in the usual story of
waterfront land appreciation, he sold them, twenty-one years later, for
$30,000). It's hard to imagine a setting farther removed than Savage's
first geography: two high mountain valleys in the northern Rockies. Yet
he'd dreamed of living by the ocean since childhood. He would sit beside
the pond behind the Brenner barn and bunkhouse (an ice pond where
they'd chop ice by New Year's), insert a stick by its edge, and pretend
he awaited the tide.

Like many a traveler and writer, Savage moved far away to more
easily return home in his imagination. He claimed the openness of
sagebrush flats reminded him of the open sea facing their home to

the southeast and defended this affinity between "prairie" and ocean: a familiar affinity in Great Plains literature. Savage put 2,000 miles between his Intermountain West and the Maine coast, their adopted home, to clarify and write his Savage West. He claims in one novel that one must hate in order to write clearly, but that overstates his hostility to Montana. He straddled two literary regions, belonging wholeheartedly to neither. As a gay family man, Savage sought another rural landscape just he bought imported sports cars—twin tales of separation—but Boston was just a couple of hours south. Savage needed and used southern Maine's rocky coast as the platform for his family life and his sustained project of writing his highly idiosyncratic version of the American West.

After those years in and around Boston, he moved the family to a rural corner, though one not as remote as Horse Prairie, Montana or Lemhi, Idaho. Tom had been scouting several properties, told real estate agents that he was looking for isolation, and eventually bought a shack near road's end, three miles beyond Georgetown village. Betty had reservations about the location because on that early June day (1955), "it had begun to rain and waves were high out here and it was foggy and terrible." (Georgetown Historical Society interview, July 16, 1981)

They added onto the shack piecemeal, and the windows all faced the ocean; none faced the road, in the middle of which tall grass grew. The living room, unsurprisingly, featured big windows that provided a panoramic view of water. Their house was "gray shingled with white-trim and a brown old garage," as Savage described it to friends. And as it turned out, they dodged the waves for twenty-three years, until a February 8, 1978, Nor'easter. Indian Point Road, often deep in snow or sheathed in ice, proved an obstacle course in Maine winters, sometimes stranding Tom or Betty at or away from home. They battled the road with a series of Jeeps and, eventually, a front-wheel-drive Saab: in the 1960s, another unusual European import though no luxury sports car.

Georgetown, principal settlement on Georgetown Island, was incorporated in 1716 but never grew much. When the Savages moved a few miles southeast of the village, it numbered less than 500 inhabitants, and in 1970, it counted only 464 residents. The Savages were the first year-round residents on Indian Point. For the first several years

there were no neighbors. As he remembered much later, "it was absolute isolation...We had no social life whatsoever. We're just not social
beings...I grew up in isolation...This is what I wanted...Living as
we do, we're still isolated." (Georgetown Historical Society interview,
1981) Tom and Betty were social beings when they chose to be, but that
fact in no way lessened their need for solitude nor the quiet remoteness
of their Maine coast home of thirty years (1955–85). As a queer man, he
separated his family from any town, thereby exerting more control over
their lives with others.

Georgetown Island lies southeast of Bath, Maine, and US Highway
1, and is reached via State Highway 127. Approximately nine miles long
(north-south) and two miles wide (east-west), it forms the eastern
border of the Kennebec River's mouth. Nearly bisected by a long inlet
running north-south—the Susanoa River, but quaintly known in the
nineteenth century as "Robinhood's Cove"—Georgetown straddles
the (south) head of the cove. Indian Point Road runs south-southeast
from the village; Indian Point forms the easternmost of three points—
prongs—that mark the island's south side. To the east and south of it,
open ocean. Reid State Park, Maine's first state-owned saltwater beach,
stretches about a mile northeast of Indian Point, and, rare in Maine,
includes long wide sand beaches and dunes. The Savages commanded
a sweeping view of this beach. Across the mouth of the Kennebec River
to the southwest, Popham Beach State Park also draws people because
of its broad sand beaches.

In earlier generations, islanders had subsisted through commercial
fishing, including a local herring fishery, and in the nineteenth century,
haying. On and near the Savage's property, they found old barbed wire
and stone walls—a local reminder of New England's vast land clear-
ing in the nineteenth century, after which forests regrew. The island
includes salt marshes, four ponds, "Great Pond" in the southeast, and
a string of islets dotting the head of the Susanoa River and the jagged
north, northeast, south, and southwest coastline. Four islets jut offshore of Indian Point, with Salter Island lying farther south. In short,
classic Maine coastal country, a rich ecotone of fresh and salt water, of
conifer stands offset by salt marshes, and below the vegetation, jagged
rock, fingers of which reach into the sea. Everywhere, the sound of tide

and waves, and the endless rhythms of ocean, the fundamental heart-beat of the place.

The Savages had a bathing cove, or rock strand, just below their small house (approximately 1,000 square feet), and they swam in the cold North Atlantic in summer. Much later Savage recalled the water is "colder than hell" year round, but that they swam and picnicked daily in summer. Savage liked to swim nude or to wear a small tight suit. One surviving photo shows a naked Savage, salt water glistening on his skin, a festooned braid of seaweed serving as his G-string.

Betty Savage used their Maine home as primary setting in two of her novels. In her final novel, *Toward the End* (1980), her characters—summer residents, mostly—decide to winter over: "Maine was the good place, Jacataqua [Georgetown] Island the good part of Maine and Crow [Indian] Point the good part of Jacataqua Island." That sentiment reflects the Savage's conviction. A few pages later, she sketches a fast-forward geologic and human history:

> First and for eons the ancient seas rained down shells. Then earth-quakes and volcanoes pushed the new land high; twelve times the ranges rose and weathered and the seas rose and fell. Glaciers, like cold bulldozers, pushed rock to the water's edge until the weak ground sank beneath the weight and the sea rushed in, leaving the drowned peaks islanded. Storms shook the shore. Then came the Red Paint People and then the Indians and after them the farmers and fighters and fishermen. (p. 6)

Like her husband, Betty Savage willingly adapted to a remote spot fronting the ocean: she loved it as deeply as he did.

Betty wrote and published her nine novels on Indian Point, and Tom, nine of his thirteen novels. Yet as late as 1981 he declared he wouldn't write about Maine or Mainers—contrary to Betty—because he "doesn't understand them." Savage remained as detached from Mainers as he was from his Montana ranch culture. He kept his literary focus primarily on the northern Rockies, his physical distance enabling his invention and, later, productive output.

In both cars and choice of home, Savage moved into the exotic, as his family members were never summer residents only. With a four-wheel drive Jeep, he drove his kids to school those first five years, as the road was unplowed. The family did without a telephone, later by choice: they could make or receive calls from the village post office. For anything more than basic necessities, they drove off-island to Bath, Maine's old shipbuilding center, or Brunswick, ten or eighteen miles, respectively, northwest.

For Savage, the ocean replaced the northern Rockies as an elemental setting, a visual promise of eternity. He worked in the living room, his view not unlike poet Robinson Jeffers's from his Tor House near Carmel, California. One of the four autobiographical statements Savage supplied for the dust jacket of *Trust in Chariots* reads, in part, "The surf is loud today; there is fog, and spray on the windows, and nobody is within four miles of me. In a few minutes the tide will turn, and go out; there will be rocks again." For a man who grew up far from any large body of water, and who first saw Lake Erie from a bus seat at age twenty-two, Savage went whole hog. And the view out took him home.

In *A Strange God* (1974), Savage explains our Whitmanian longing for the seashore as an instinctual homecoming:

> Beside the sea again, a man assumes the primitive, sheds his clothes as the law allows, eats what is at hand, digs holes, shouts and leaps and swims for the day or a week or the summer. He returns inland with shells, starfish and kelp, precious souvenirs of the mystical experience of having been once more at the very spot where man and beast, fish, reptile and fowl were once all one. There, one time, a wave broke over a hidden ledge; the new sun was caught in the spray, and all fates were settled. (pp. 92–93)

A profile, "They live and write in a house by the sea" (*Maine Sunday Telegram*, Sec. C, February 12, 1961), includes four photos and captions, three focused upon the living room. The story cites their Sarouk (Persian) rug, about which Savage was extremely proud and which covers his largest room. It took four men to carry it in and unfurl it. Betty always thought Tom wanted the Indian Point place because the big floor could accommodate the carpet. The story also salutes their idyllic life—at least that was their public face.

He tried one stint of civic involvement, serving as president of the local PTA a few years after their arrival. He avoided town and "association" meetings. Yet they attended church "religiously" until about 1970, when they abruptly ceased attendance. Savage stated, "What in the name of God am I doing this all the time? I'm too old for it."

Savage marked his unusual personality by not only his cars and home, but his work routine. He had developed the nocturnal writing habit back in Missoula. Many writers, of course, work at night, but not so many prime themselves so obsessively with classical music. Reminiscing in old age, he described his unusual diurnal rhythm he supposedly followed every day. He would drink cocktails by 2:00 p.m., taking notes with pencil and paper while listening to Haydn. He would eat something then retire to bed by 5:00 or 6:00, sleep until 1:00 a.m., rise and drink coffee while listening to a bit more Haydn, then write for three hours before going for a walk before or during sunrise.

Russell Savage remembers the routine in more detail. He describes his father's "afternoon ritual" of "sitting in the living room listening to the symphonies of Bruckner and Mahler, a cigarette in his left hand and a glass of gin in his right, while he 'took notes,' writing down his thoughts on a wad of paper with a number two pencil." Martinis were consumed after noon; Betty Savage usually didn't start drinking until later. While he loved the broad, late Romantic symphonic canvases of Bruckner and Mahler in the afternoons, Savage most of all loved the classical period of classical music. He variably judged Haydn or Mozart the greatest composer. Savage built up an enormous record collection and in letters, eagerly discussed new acquisitions and particular conductors or soloists. He voted for Mozart in another autobiographical statement on *Trust in Chariots'* (inside back) dust jacket: "I think better when I listen to Mozart's music. Mozart is the only artist who never fell on his face. Somebody said that nothing much can be wrong with the world, when there is Mozart's music."

Classical music clearly primed his pump, and he played more than the phonograph. According to Russell,

> Well before sun-up...I could hear him hammering away at the old upright Baldwin in the living room, as was his custom before he began to type. The smell of coffee and cigarettes seeped through the cracks in the knotty pine boards of my bedroom wall which, since

it was contiguous to the living room, was not insulated, and reso-
nated nicely as a soundboard for my father's tiniest movements. I
could lie there in the dark and guess exactly where he was by what
I heard—the sound of his favorite egg-shell-thin china cup placed
with finality on its saucer and then the whap whap whap of the
keys of his huge, old, glossy black, Remington typewriter.

Though Savage claimed perfect pitch and tuned pianos just with a
tuning fork, he never learned to read music. Nonetheless, he worked
hard on "Ah, je vous dirai-je, Maman," a French folk song on which
Mozart composed Twelve Variations and which we know as "Twinkle,
Twinkle, Little Star."

Savage "was ordinarily sound asleep before the seagulls gathered
around sunset and headed for their rookery, out by the black rocks in
Sheepscot Bay." The three hours of early percussion from the big black
Remington measured his workday and drummed through the family's
life. Later Savage replaced this typewriter with a tangerine orange typewriter, vividly recalled by a young cousin-once-removed who spent college breaks with the Savages: a pastel choice that matched, in a sense,
that series of classic sports cars. Savage wrote on a family heirloom converted desk, which he describes in *The Sheep Queen*: "at this desk I wrote
my last six novels [i.e., from *Trust in Chariots* through *Midnight Line*,
1976]. It was once a square piano that belonged to my great-aunt Nora
[Yearian Whitwell, Tom Yearian's sister—another unchanged name].
My great-grandmother had it hauled all the way out West and I had it
hauled all the way back East." (p. 181)

In *The Sheep Queen* Savage lovingly inventories the heirlooms or
gifts surrounding his writing desk, each thick with meaning, and he
concludes,

> Nothing valuable, everything invaluable. This room looks like the
> Old Curiosity Shop, but the curiosities are dear curiosities and
> when I sit here in the evening with a drink in my hand and the
> hi-fi belts out Schumann and Chopin—the very things my mother
> played so well—I know exactly what we were and exactly what I
> am. I think a man with such a family is all but invulnerable. (p. 183)

"Invulnerable" "family" includes the suite of artifacts and, above all, the

Romantic world represented by Chopin and Schumann. His declaration also insinuates the sharp feeling of vulnerability exposed in his novels.

As critic John Scheckter claims in the only scholarly article devoted to Savage before the twenty-first century, Savage's fiction hinges upon "a single situation—the discovery, in middle age, of a deep and painful need to re-examine the entire process of becoming an adult. Such concentration, perhaps obsessive, mirrors an autobiographical crisis." ("Thomas Savage and the West: Roots of Compulsion," p. 36) That crisis, the root of vulnerability, measures Savage's fears about being outed in the context of his family life and the historical period during which his queer identity would damage his career and sales.

During the late 1950s and early 1960s, Savage published much less than in the preceding decade. At the same time he gradually came out, exacting a toll on his wife, particularly, and his children. His midlife crisis, if it can be called that, presented his long closeted gay self. Both Russell Savage and Eleanor ("Ellie") M. Savage Quigley, Savage's former daughter-in-law, attest to slight shifts in his manners and clothes. Because of his psychic need after age forty—while his three kids hurried through childhood into adolescence—to allow his gay self to surface, Betty Savage's drinking increased. She never overtly criticized the husband she deeply loved, even during his seasons of infidelity. Betty knew he was first attracted to men, not her. Though he always relied upon her as editor and though they were close, theirs was also a violent relationship at times, the drinking leading to vicious verbal fighting and, occasionally, more. In one drunk, Tom supposedly threw Betty into nearby blackberry brambles. Their family life, apart from Tom's temporary desertion, veered from riches to rags and back.

One relative describes the children, once in a while, walking the remaining miles home from Georgetown village only to find both parents drunk and fighting, and no food. More than once the children scoured the tidal pools, gathering mussels that became the base of a wine-infused soup: they lived off the land more than they wished at times.

The tensions in no way lessened their drive to write novels. Betty signed with Little, Brown before Tom and published *Summer of Pride*, her first novel, in 1960. After the 1960s, during which she weathered her husband's temporary desertion, her sons' undergraduate crises, and all three children's launches into adulthood, she published her second novel, *But Not For Love* (1970): thereafter, remarkably, she published seven more novels in the next decade. She remained Tom's editor and willingly played second fiddle to his achievement. She self-deprecatingly called her novels "mere entertainments." Ironically, "Mrs. S.," as she was known to some, was the natural "brainiac" of the family, and Brassil (Bob) inherited her natural intellectual ability; Tom had to work harder to display the aristocratic erudition that came naturally to wife and firstborn.

Savage's increasing identification as a gay man, evident to his daughter, sons, and after 1964, his first daughter-in-law, did not slight his dedication to his family (cf. German novelist, Thomas Mann). As his sons stretched beyond childhood he enforced a serious reading diet: according to Russell Savage, "Thomas Hardy's *Jude The Obscure,* Dostoyevsky's [*The*] *Idiot,* and a lot of other fun kid reads." He would quiz them about their homework and if they "performed" sufficiently, they were released into the neighborhood and their playmates. The regimen resembles the Reverend Maclean's home schooling in writing for the young Norman Maclean, lovingly recounted in *A River Runs Through It.* (1976): severe lessons in revision via compression in the mornings, then free afternoons.

Regarding the children, both parents were extremely permissive, doling out second-hand cars and generous allowances into adulthood, and giving them free reign. Savage felt a need to protect and provide well into their adulthoods, and the sense of dependency helped create rocky roads, subsequently, for all three. In letters he'd ruefully speculate about earning far more money so that he could indefinitely bankroll and care for everyone. Savage felt this need to provide financial care through old age, which reinforced his Caesarian self-image and likely eased his guilt as a gay father, particularly regarding his sons. And for Brassil and Russell, at least, he harbored top-drawer, Ivy League ambitions: no surprise from a former Rolls owner.

In *The Sheep Queen* (chap. 14's beginning), Savage writes an apologia for permissive parenting, conceding his sons, "are gentle, talented liberal arts majors and the business world is alien to them": "My sons sometimes need help and I am happy to help them, since I didn't teach them to be aggressive. I have sometimes needed help. . .In my view, fathers are supposed to help. I believe that is what fathers are for." (pp. 168-69) Savage never wavered in his sense of responsibility for his sons and daughter, no matter their age. He believed being patriarch always meant being the bank as well.

The oldest, Robert Brassil, favored his mother's Irish side and proved a talented high school track star and student council president. Robert—Bobby as a youngster, then Bob, and in later life, Brassil—became a serious drinker and indulged in drugs, washing out of Harvard. His ex-wife, Ellie, described him as a "beatnik-hippie guy, smarter than both his parents," but he presented bipolar behavior the rest of his life. Her unpublished memoir contains many harrowing episodes. He'd read the entire Proust À *La Recherche du Temps Perdu* unprompted, and recommended Tolstoy's *War and Peace* to his equally young wife. Savage's relationship with his firstborn remained tumultuous, according to Ellie, who loved both husband and father-in-law. Betsy Savage Main, his sister, remarked his life proved "an odyssey of tragedy." Another relative stated, "Brassil was so bright that he couldn't live on this earth," and remembered his abilities as a writer and painter. According to his father, some years later (i.e., mid-1970s), he completed a master's degree in English. His mood swings were destructive and his life led him down a wandering, unstable path.

In *The Sheep Queen* narrator (and protagonist) Tom Burton, essentially Savage, describes the Indian Point living room beyond his writing desk, remarking, "Paintings by my elder son are on one wall and over the mantle, and it is he who gave me the two-volume 1870 edition of Zell's *Encyclopedia and Dictionary*." (p. 182)

Both sons worked as summer lifeguards at those nearby state park sand beaches. Russell, taller and shyer than his older brother, also drank a lot and, a few years later, washed out of Princeton. Both sons ultimately received their bachelor's degrees from Colby College, their parents' alma mater (in 1968 and 1970, respectively). Four years in the us Navy provided Russ the self-discipline he lacked earlier. He went on to a career as a German teacher in a regional high school in Maine, and, very briefly, as a policeman. His first marriage, however, proved a fatal disaster.

Daughter Betsy, six years younger than Russell, felt almost unnaturally close with her father, always her idol. He treated her like a princess and spoiled her. She recalls that she bought her first bra herself, at age eleven—one example of her mother's hands-off approach to parenting. Betty, uninterested in cosmetics and makeup, never judged or guided her, and Betsy believes she learned how to be a woman on her own. She thought she and her mother were "asexual friends," but she remained closer to her father. As a young adult, she was particularly drawn to art history as she was to Nicholas Main, Bob Savage's brother-in-law. Betsy attended Kent Prep School (Kent, Connecticut), and later, the Parsons School of Design (New York City). She had sold her first designs before marrying Nicholas Main, Ellie Savage Quigley's younger brother and a career Naval officer, in 1967. Thus two of the three Savages married into the Main family of Bath, Maine.

Perhaps unsurprisingly, all three children later suffered, variously, from alcoholism; Russell stopped drinking by the mid-1990s, thanks in part to AA and his own will. Perhaps also unsurprisingly, both sons evidenced literary talent, Russell for example becoming a short story writer (though his stories remain unpublished).

After three years away from teaching, Savage moved back and forth to Poughkeepsie, New York, in 1958–59, teaching at Vassar College, which would not become co-ed for another decade (1969). Recalling his Vassar year some years later, Savage stated, "the girls rode about on squeaky bicycles and wore old fur coats."

The only surviving evidence of his year there is an article, "Review: 215," published in The Miscellany News (Vassar, October 15, 1958). In it Savage critiques an issue of 215, the "new campus [literary] magazine." He tartly asserts, "English 215 is not an advanced course in writing," then praises four stories after stating, "a good deal of [the content] shows what people do insist on calling great promise. One wishes to live long enough to see what will eventually become of these writers, barring the professional tragedy of marriage." Despite his own intimate, fraught marriage with a fellow novelist, that final fillip seems vintage Savage in its ironic bite. The comment may carry, as well, a hint of regret in Savage's long-ago decision with Betty, to the extent he felt untrue to himself. But the real bite occurs in his opening paragraph in which he variably chastises Melville, Dostoyevsky, Steinbeck, Hemingway, Stowe, and Joyce as flawed novelists, and even questions Shakespeare's motives about Hamlet, to set up his claim, "No piece of writing is perfect."

Trust in Chariots (1961)

Certainly he illustrates his own statement in the only novel he published during the first decade in Maine. *Trust in Chariots* (1961), Savage's only Random House novel, distills his infatuation with luxury sports cars, as already said, particularly his brief seasons with the '39 black Rolls-Royce, which casts its long shadow across the plot. The novel distills Savage's cross-country trips to Montana, though in the plot the two protagonists, Sheldon Owens and Pal Forbes, only reach Nebraska before claims of responsibility turn them around. Savage later glossed this novel as "a ruined man's search for perfection," and in Sheldon's case, marital infidelity and cuckoldry launch his purchase of the same car Savage had owned.

For his fourth novel, Savage took his title from an Old Testament verse: a pattern he continued in his next two novels, *The Power of the Dog* (1967) and *The Liar* (1969). With *Trust in Chariots*, the Biblical verse ironically depicts Sheldon, a well-meaning, soft-hearted man: "Some put their trust in chariots, / and some in horses: / but we will remember / the Name of the Lord our God." (Psalms 20:7) The consolations of Christianity—the thick atmosphere swirling through *A Bargain With God*—are unavailable to Sheldon, a decorated World War II vet with a limp. Midway through the novel, the narrator states, "Sheldon was not a smart man; only a kind one" (p. 149), and this Walter Mitty shifts his faith in marriage to faith in the Rolls.

It's hard not to read *Trust*'s plot as an implicit protest against Savage's sense of his marriage as a ruin, and Sheldon's developing relationship with Pal, some years younger, as an expression of Savage's liaison with Tomie dePaola, the lover with the same first name, twenty years younger, for whom he deserted his family for a few seasons. After all,

Savage, in his mid-forties, had repressed his desires most of his life up to that point. Not a shred of surviving evidence indicates he'd sought out men earlier. His unusual midlife crisis slammed him and his family, and its baleful influence tinctured his wife and children for decades.

The gruesome climax of *Trust* derived from an accident Savage and family witnessed, according to a cousin, Janet Moore, who accompanied the Savages back East (summer 1952) in the Rolls-Royce. Father and sons rode in the front; Betty, young Betsy, and Janet (then twenty-nine) rode in back. Their second day out, they saw a horrendous accident, after which Tom said, "that deserves a story."

In *Trust*'s braided plot a betrayed man, Sheldon, crosses paths with a hitchhiking teenager, Pal, a product of Chicago poverty who's essentially raised his younger sister, Janey, and who temporarily abandons her, believing her prospects better without him. Pal displays a natural "passion for cars" and, as a young mechanic, a particular interest in "down-draft carburetors of the Zenith type, and fuel injection" (p. 43), ultimately winning an auto race because of his expertise. When he is a kid his bumbling father, poor Dick, wants to buy him a Rolls-Royce model but the fifty-dollar price tag precludes that. Savage gives to Pal his loathing of Cadillacs: "Pal hated Cadillacs, because Cadillacs had somehow usurped, in the minds of fools, the place of better automobiles." (p. 47) In Savage's satire, status trumped the superior knowledge of car cognoscenti—a condition as despicable as inevitable. Most people are "fools," at least about cars. The whole sentimental Pal-Janey plot derives from Savage's wartime experience in the Windy City as a claims adjustor: the abject poverty in the city left a permanent impression.

Savage sprinkles loving details about the '39 Rolls throughout the novel. It sits in a basement corner of Boston's "Continental Motors," and Sheldon, a moth to its black flame, slips inside and fantasizes:

> He only sensed its mechanical excellence, the fabulous acceleration, the girderlike frame under the rakish body that made it a little less stout than a Pullman car and about as safe in an accident...when he stood near that car, with its eighteen coats of jet-black paint, its tulip wood and astrakhan interior, he stood straighter. (p. 25)

After exposing his shiftless wife in bed with another man, he spends $37,000 for this "ultimate perfection, ultimate possession":

> Very few in the world know the feel, the heft, the balance on the hinges of a Rolls-Royce door. Like the door of a safe.
>
> He climbed in, and shut the door. You don't slam Rolls-Royce doors. You can tell who is used to a Rolls by how he closes the car door.
>
> Click.
>
> Inside, it was quiet, and safe. No sound of Massachusetts slipped inside, no chirping of Massachusetts birds; in the first pale light the gleaming mahogany of the dash glowed like a smile. (pp. 144–45)

Savage returns his readers to the same luxurious "Continental Motors" showroom, evoked in loving detail, late in *A Strange God* when protagonist Jack Reed, facing an identity crisis as deep as Sheldon's, test-drives a "maroon Rolls demonstrator." His ride, like Sheldon's trip, proves brief, incomplete: "Now he was feeling the road telegraphed through the marvelous steering gear of the best car in the world, savoring the silence of the engine, sniffing the aroma of the leather. The feel was that of riding in a Pullman." (p. 288) Neither protagonist sustains the perfection of a Rolls. No one can.

In a familiar story, Sheldon, a hurt little man, magically reaches the top through his wild purchase and, in his case, wild plan for a road trip to California and some vague new life. With "the awesome silence that enclosed like a womb," he rides west reborn, mightily compensating for the radical disillusionment of marriage: "The only way you'd know the engine was running was to see the red warning light blink out. There was the faintest murmur of the exhaust; the enormous engine of over seven liters turned evenly at three hundred r.p.m." Sheldon speculates about a brotherhood of craftsmen who make the ultimate car: "he considered the shape of the steering wheel, the contours of the knob on the shift, the odor of the leather seats, the grain of the wood on the dash, the instruments." (p. 147)

Just before Pal stumbles into Sheldon's roadside dilemma—a blinking red light on the dash, which he easily solves for the unmechanical owner—Savage again compares the car to that symbol of luxurious train travel:

> Long after midnight the Rolls was sweeping through the dark with the feel, Sheldon thought, of a Pullman train. The weight and suspension of a Rolls have a curious ability to absorb road shock in a sort of purposeful silence—as if it ate it. You feel that should a Rolls strike something, nothing particular would happen; it would simply sweep on. (p. 204)

The Rolls survives with unbent frame and undamaged doors the accident that kills Sheldon on the novel's final page, his resolution to return to his pathetic wife unfulfilled. In his brush with perfection, this "ruined man" decides to return to her—a decision most readers would reject, given her tawdry character.

In an undated 1962 letter to Ernest Cummings Marriner, dean of Colby College, Savage wrote, "My last book was a great critical success, especially in England, but really the only money I got out of it was the money the [*Saturday Evening Post*] gave me for the first chapter which they published as a short-story, probably the grimmest story they ever published."

In a newspaper profile published half a dozen years later, Savage strongly endorsed his fourth novel: "I think it was by far my best book until *The Power of the Dog,* but I don't think anyone else does." In a later letter he calls *Trust* "my wife's favorite" and "my most difficult and metaphysical book": a judgment I dispute. He's right about the general assessment of it. Perhaps he held such a high opinion, at least for a while, because in its "Book Two: The Journey" he wrote the same-sex, cross-country road trip fantasy he soon lived, as though fiction slightly anticipated life.

However sentimental the arc of the novel, it distills Savage's gay separation from the mainstream through his luxury sedans and sports cars, as well as those summer trips from his adopted state to his home state. And by the time *Trust* was published, Savage uncannily enacted its older man-younger man plot in his own act of betrayal of his marriage and family. Fiction and fact blurred, as they sometimes did in Savage's career. His affair with Tomie dePaola would prove temporary just as, in *Trust*, the road trip prematurely ends just before the protagonist is killed.

□ □ □

He found a lover in the self-described "short, cute looker," whom he first met in October 1960. Savage was forty-five and a half; Tomie dePaola, who'd lived a few years with a Catholic priest in Weston, Vermont, was twenty-five—only seven and eight years older than Savage's sons. dePaola, a then-unknown set designer and painter (who'd been illustrating Christmas cards), visited the Savages in company with Gene Youngken, an assistant director at the renowned Weston Playhouse, Vermont's longest-running professional theater (1935). Youngken summered at Indian Point, as did Blanche Gregory, whose literary agency (founded 1936) represented both Tom and Betty early in their careers (both authors remained with this agency). dePaola was married to Parisian Monique Chéret but the marriage faltered, and would end during his affair with Savage. Blanche ostensibly set up the meeting, just as she'd introduced Youngken to the Savages.

dePaola would go on to become a renowned children's book author and illustrator. In his career spanning more than half a century, he's published at least 260 books and won numerous awards (e.g., the Smithsonian's Smithson Medal) and honorary doctorates. A giant in his field, he couldn't decide between a career as a children's book writer and illustrator or as a tap dancer when he was growing up. During his undergraduate career at Pratt Institute (Brooklyn, New York, bachelor of fine arts, 1956), he realized he was gay. Later dePaola separated from his wife, who departed for New York City, and took up temporary residence in an empty house near the Savages, arranged by Tom in the winter of 1961.

Savage's daughter, Betsy Savage Main, describes their passion as a "bonfire"; looking back two generations, dePaola called it a very intense, "tortured" relationship. dePaola believes there was "something hateful, something sad, something stimulating" about Savage, who took Tomie under his wing, attracted by his creativity, and taught him a lot about classical music and writing. dePaola also saw his then-lover as a very heavy drinker and smoker who needed, always, to be in charge.

That winter (1961), with Savage caught between family and lover, things spiraled out of control. On one occasion, Betty Savage, no doubt drunk, tried to stab dePaola with a kitchen knife; on another, Russell Savage wrecked dePaola's sports car in an accident driving home from school. Betsy remembers that Valentine's Day, when she found three Valentines on the table: one from each parent and one from her daddy's new friend. This friend also drew her portrait and wooed her. She believes dePaola "destroyed my childhood," but she's since forgiven him (she was eleven to twelve during the affair; her brothers, at the end of their high school careers). By springtime, dePaola returned to Youngken's house in Vermont.

According to dePaola, when *Trust in Chariots* was published that year at Random House, "they were calling him the new Truman Capote." Ironically, Random House only published Savage's fourth novel. To celebrate the publication of *Trust,* the lovers took off in Savage's blue two-seater Morgan Plus 4 across the US in the summer of 1961—surely, for Betty and the kids, the nadir of their family life. In his forty-sixth summer, Savage was enacting a version of the fantasy about which his son Russell speculated during the road trip, in the hot Porsche, north to Maine in the mid-1950s (quoted in the introduction).

The couple visited Horse Prairie, Montana, and the family of Tom's younger (half) sister, Bob and Isabel James, and the Yearian aunts in Salmon, Idaho. dePaola recalls there was "always lots of booze" and that Tom's aunts, in particular, "were so much fun," as though they stepped "out of a movie." The time in Salmon proved dePaola's favorite part of that fateful summer. The routine afternoons included numerous rounds of cocktails and eventually, dinner at the Dew Drop Inn. Savage drank "milk punch" (half gin, half milk) or gin and bitters. On one spur of the moment, they all drove to Jackpot, Nevada, to gamble for a day. The couple also spent time in San Francisco and Los Angeles, in the latter visiting Benjamin Savage, Tom's "matinee idol" father whom, dePaola speculates, likely wanted to be closer to Savage than Savage wished.

So dePaola made the family rounds as though he'd replaced Betty Savage. Apparently the Yearians kept smiles on their faces, welcoming Tom's younger "friend," and if any recognized the pair as lovers, as some likely did, they said nothing. The younger lover recognized that

Savage was "riddled with guilt," however: every two-three days during that trip, Savage would say he couldn't do this any longer and should put dePaola on a plane for New England. But he never did. After twenty-two years of marriage and his three children on their various paths to adulthood, Savage clearly felt rubbed raw by conflict between same-sex desire and family obligations. He wanted both but knew that could not work for him. His relationship with dePaola proved his only infidelity though much later, after Betty's death, Savage quickly transitioned to a gay lifestyle in San Francisco.

Savage was a devout Episcopalian, at least periodically; dePaola, a Roman Catholic who was part of Catholicism's "liturgical movement." In the fall of 1961, Savage, who favored formality and ceremony, insisted they solemnize their bond, at least in their own eyes, by exchanging rings in the Cowley Fathers Chapel, a part of Boston's (Beacon Hill) St. John the Evangelist Church. By this time, dePaola had divorced his wife.

After the lovers returned to New England in Savage's last sports car, Savage dropped dePaola off in Connecticut. dePaola took an apartment in Boston, and on one occasion, with Savage present, Brassil Savage, then a Harvard sophomore, turned up. By this time, Savage's children had figured out the affair. Brassil, either drunk or high (possibly LSD), beat up dePaola while his father sat on a mattress, watching. Savage's paralysis testifies to his deeply divided loyalties. By this time Brassil was well on his way to addictions, and Tom no longer tightly controlled him any more than he controlled his quasi-marriage to dePaola, given his much longer marriage to Betty. In *Power*, Phil Burbank's overt hostility to Peter Gordon gradually modulates to affection, even unacknowledged love. Brassil's act of homophobic violence suggests, on some level, Savage punishing himself for succumbing to this gay affair; Phil's "punishment" for acting according to his true nature is death.

Brassil stopped hurting dePaola and left when Savage asked him to. According to dePaola, Savage said, "Why do you people do this to me?" clearly displacing blame from himself about his core division. dePaola was no doubt incredulous about Brassil's violence and Tom's indifference. After dePaola cleaned himself up in the kitchen, Tom insisted on sex, which dePaola characterized as "very rough." (personal communication with author) Savage left the apartment before dawn, and the note he left read something like, "This just won't work. I have my family to take care of. You're strong, you'll be fine." He cut ties and reverted to his older loyalty.

Betsy Main, looking back, claimed her father quit dePaola "cold turkey" and returned home just as, many years later, he suddenly stopped smoking (Betty didn't). dePaola concedes that "it was probably very hard for Tom Savage to leave me." Denying his sexual orientation and desire, Savage would channel his inner conflict into the next two novels, though he tossed the manuscript of the first into the Atlantic.

But the two lovers saw one another a few more times. Sometime in 1962, at a Boston salon evening hosted by a mutual friend, Betty Beresford, dePaola met Betty Savage, whom he found "lovely and forgiving," and so kind to the younger man throughout the evening. (Beresford is cited in *The Sheep Queen*, pp. 137-38) She had long transcended her kitchen knife rage, and her generosity seems consistent with the open-armed response to her wayward husband's return to Georgetown and Indian Point. She loved Tom deeply despite his sexual orientation and premarital disclosure.

She felt on the verge of divorce more than once, but her Catholicism precluded that. She lived apart when she taught, a few years, at their alma mater, Colby College, in Waterville, Maine. At one stage she had an apartment across the street from the one occupied by the newlyweds, Brassil and Ellie Savage (married 1964), and they shared meals. On at least one occasion when Betty acted suicidal, Brassil stayed up all night with her. Her suicidality likely derived from Savage's betrayal and violation of their marriage pact, and her fear that he didn't love her enough to sustain it. However, by all accounts he remained solidly devoted to Betty even as he became verbally and, rarely, physically abusive after extended drinking. She knew how to get his goat.

After several years, the former lovers saw one another three times, briefly: twice, in 1969 and in the early 1970s, at Indian Point in the houses of mutual friends (incl. Youngken) and once, in San Francisco's Castro District in the early 1990s, where Savage was living. Visiting San Francisco, dePaola was having drinks with friends in a bar and Savage, now an old man, was buying coffee at a shop next door. The two writers shook hands and hugged, and dePaola told him that Savage had played a crucial role in his young life. By then, arguably, the prolific children's book writer and illustrator was much more famous than the novelist, who didn't yet know his career was over. dePaola regarded Savage as a really fine writer. He outlived Savage seventeen years, dying (March 30, 2020) while this book was in production.

While writing his overtly gay novel after the dePaola affair was over (1962), Tom and Betty and the now-older children continued to socialize with the Mains, of Bath, Maine. Savage felt particularly close to Beatrice Main, born the same day and year as Tom, who hailed from an aristocratic Connecticut family, and who also drank steadily. They were simpatico from the first meeting. Beatrice's oldest child, Eleanor ("Ellie"), the same age as "Bob," had known him since eighth grade and they married at age twenty-two in 1964; her younger brother, Nicholas, would later marry Betsy Savage. Ellie S. Quigley has commented that both families were naturally attracted to each other, and that drinking bonded them, particularly Beatrice (a.k.a. "Lucy") and Tom. She remembers Tom, after one particular night of drinking, brawling with his two sons in the Mains' driveway.

Bob/Brassil wanted away from his folks yet would, through marriages and addictions, occasionally show signs of deep dependency.

Though Savage loved Betty, his sons, and his daughter, their family life left a trail of emotional wreckage along with good times and expressions of fierce devotion. Ellie Quigley's unpublished memoir chronicles in excruciating detail the occasionally ugly domestic life of the Savages in the 1960s and 1970s, which occasionally reads like Eugene O'Neill's *Long Day's Journey Into Night*. For example, in her typology of drunks, Quigley defines her mother and Tom as "good drunks," Betty Savage and her father as "boring drunks," and Bob/Brassil as a "crazy drunk." Her manuscript sustains a penetrating gaze on these individuals and behaviors, and many scenes make for painful reading. After all, Tom's emerging gay identity and temporary desertion left deep traces of distrust and anger, particularly with his firstborn.

In late February 1964, Ellie Main and Brassil Savage married in Bath, in the Episcopal Church. She was already pregnant with the first of their four children. Their years together proved a wild roller coaster ride because of Brassil's addictions and mental instability. Nonetheless they had four children in six years (two daughters and two sons).

Later that year Charlie Brenner, Savage's stalwart stepfather, died in a car accident, likely from a heart attack, in Spencer, Idaho. Eighty years old, he often drove alone, and he'd outlived his wife, Beth, by seven years. He is buried in the Salmon, Idaho, cemetery next to Beth. Years before her death, the Brenner Ranch had been divided in half, with Jack Brenner (Hal's only child) running one half, and Bob and Isabel (Brenner) James, the other. Savage repeatedly revisited the ranch—which daughter Betsy fancifully called "kryptonite" because, in her view, "it destroyed a lot of people"—in his fiction in the next two decades or more.

Savage's year or two as an overtly gay man and a paterfamilias, trying to live two divergent lives, unsurprisingly proved a seminal episode in his psyche. Out of his sense of being split at the root, he turned to writing, as he always did. As he aged, he frequently attested that he felt useless unless he were writing, and he never abandoned his calling though publishers, if not readers, abandoned him. So he wrote a novel about his time with Tomie. In an undated 1962 letter, Savage wrote, "I am about to finish a book, and Betty and I are working together on a play about Butte, Montana." His agent, Blanche Gregory, who'd originally introduced Tomie to Tom, thought Savage would never get it published in the mid-1960s US, so he threw the whole manuscript into the ocean just below their house. Nothing ever came of that collaborative play, either.

At least twice in the 1980s, he crucially recalled this manuscript. During his final visit to Dillon, Montana, in April 1983, he told John Scheckter, a then-assistant professor of English at the Western Montana College of Education (i.e., University of Montana Western, my employer since 1991), that he once wrote a 400-page book about himself and then threw it into the Atlantic. He wished he'd placed it in a safety deposit box. There was no carbon copy.

Six years later, in his *Contemporary Authors* interview with Jean Ross (January 11, 1989), Savage elaborated on the subject, crucially though indirectly defining his gayness. When asked about the trickiness of working with "strongly autobiographical material," he stated,

I have never written about myself truly, except once. Twenty [actually twenty-five or more] years ago I wrote a book about myself, and it came to something like four hundred pages. It was a book that was alternately bragging and whining. I tied it up in a string and put a stone on it and dropped it in the ocean! I'm sorry I did it now, because I think it would be a lot of fun to see what I wrote—but there isn't even a copy.

Perhaps Savage felt regret, one quick generation later, because the climate about sexual minorities had thawed. After all, by the early 1970s the gay liberation movement gathered steam and recommended direct political action to end persecution. The Stonewall uprising (June 27-July 3, 1969) fueled this movement that had grown since at least the 1950s. By 1973, homosexuality was no longer a "psychopathology," according to the American Psychiatric Association. The 1970s and 1980s saw the emergence of various out and proud gay and lesbian activist movements. At the same time, there was an explosion of lesbian and gay novels, poems, plays, and films, as well as, in academic fields, the emergence and celebration of gay and lesbian studies along with, a little later, queer theory.

Savage's "a lot of fun" toss-off underscores his marginal status as a major novelist of the American West, this discarded novel posing the extreme case of his distance from any heroic, conventional white settlement narrative. It poignantly suggests, as well, his disconnect from his emergent gay self of the early 1960s. By 1989, that lost novel might have found an audience.

Even in the so-called liberated 1960s, given (anti-) sodomy statutes in almost all states, an overtly gay novel likely meant bad sales. This despite the fact that, by the mid-1960s, many distinguished writers had published gay fiction in the US. British novelist E. M. Forster drafted his overtly gay novel, *Maurice*, in 1913-14, and revised it considerably twice, decades later, but withheld publication until after his death (1970). In his last revision, he appended a note to the 1960 typescript which he gave to novelist Christopher Isherwood, who had urged his older friend to publish it for decades: "Publishable—but worth it?" In 1964 Forster, in his eighties, noted in his diary, "I should have been a more famous writer if I had written or rather published more, but sex [gay love] has prevented the latter." Great Britain decriminalized homosexuality in 1967. Forster published no fiction the last thirty-seven years of his long life; Isherwood published the novel, called by some "the love story closest to his heart," the year after Forster's death (1971). [Kate Symondson's "E M Forster's gay fiction," www.bl.uk.20th-century-literature/articles/e-m-forsters-gay-fiction]

Maurice ends happily, with Maurice and his lover, Alec, ensconced in a wooded retreat; one wonders whether Savage's lost novel would not have a darker outcome, given his personal crisis and its denouement.

The Power of the Dog (1967)

Instead, Savage imaginatively returned home and wrote what became his best novel. He channeled the psychic cost of his core conflict into this taut, harrowing fiction, which in turn launched his most productive decade as a novelist: a remarkable stream of six novels bookended by his two best. Somehow, his suppressing his outed gay self unleashed a sustained creative outpouring, one that included some of his most incisive evocations of Thomas Savage Country (i.e., Montana's southwest corner and Idaho's Lemhi River Valley). His agent sold *The Power of the Dog* (1967) to Little, Brown, which ultimately published him for many years, until he was advised to change publishers for what turned out to be his final novel (1988). Little, Brown published eight of Savage's thirteen novels including five of his eight novels about the American West and his strongest fiction.

Back in his hometown sixteen years after its publication, Savage stated in an interview that *Power* "was the book that came the easiest... probably because [he] had been thinking about the story for a long time." ("Savage Comes Home Again," *Dillon Tribune Examiner*, April 20, 1983). That final comment suggests a complex psychic merger of his long loathing of his Uncle Bill Brenner, his struggles with his own sexual identity, and his relatively recent affair with Tomie dePaola.

Though Savage repeatedly denied writing autobiographical fiction, he indisputedly wrote close to the grain of family history, often not changing, or only slightly altering, names. *Power* begins the series of family dramas in which actual Brenners and Yearians play clear roles and, perhaps most importantly, he projects himself, often without much recasting. In *Power*, several characters first drafted in *Lona Hanson* reappear. George and Phil Burbank are modeled on Savage's stepfather and step-uncle, Charlie and Bill Brenner, respectively. Rose Gordon, who becomes early on a widow and marries George, borrows many clothes from Savage's mother, Beth Y. S. Brenner. The Old Gents are drawn from John C. and Isabel Brenner, Savage's paternal step-grandparents. The ranch is easily identifiable as the Brenner Ranch.

With the Burbanks in *Power*, Savage launched a series of families in several novels whose surnames, which begin with "B," are all variations on the Brenners, as he plays close to the fluid boundary between autobiography and autobiographical fiction. He commenced the theme-and-variations form with his first two novels, with Jess and Beth Bentley (*The Pass*) and the three generations of Barts (*Lona Hanson*). And he confirms it in *The Liar* (1969), his first novel after *Power*. There Savage conflates the Beaverhead (River) Valley, within which Dillon spreads, and his Horse Prairie homeplace, making the fictitious valley far larger than either: "over half of it was owned by ranching families whose names, by coincidence, all began with the letter B. There were the Burbanks and the Barts, the Bonds and the Burks. Of course they were known as the Four Bs, but because of distance, jealousy and rivalry, they seldom met." (*The Liar*, p. 76) The "coincidence," witty authorial design, confirms Savage's theme and variations. Readers of *Power* and *Lona Hanson* already know the Burbanks and Barts, respectively; in *The Liar* Savage stretches his theme by drawing the Burks from the Yearians, while the Bonds pose as another variant of the Brenners. Good grief. In Savage's world it's no surprise that because of "jealousy and rivalry, they seldom met." The "Four Bs," thin fictionalizations of his stepfather's, mother's and father's families, meet only in his fiction as he wishes. As his career unfolded he relied upon this heavily autobiographical portrait gallery, and discerning readers recognize particular relatives, most notoriously, in the case of *The Power of the Dog*, Bill Brenner as Phil Burbank (and Ed Brewer in the later *The Sheep Queen*).

Perhaps most importantly, Savage makes his own debut in *Power*, projecting parts of himself as Peter Gordon, a teenage Hamlet who enacts the revenge plot—and who comes across as colder, emotionally remote, and calculating in ways Savage never was:

He learned early on what it is to be an outcast and looked on living with deepset, expressionless eyes that saw everything or nothing. He played no ballgames, preferred books and solitude, had an aversion to sunlight and on going out into it always paused, squinted, and shaded his eyes. (p. 31)

Textual evidence suggests Peter in fact is gay like Phil, though as a Hamlet figure he wreaks revenge rather than fulfills Phil Burbank's desired homoerotic union. The Phil-Peter relationship changes, at least for Phil, from a mutual hostility: "he and Phil had a kind of bond—a bond of hatred, maybe, but Peter felt that one kind of bond could be just as useful as another." (p. 188) He's a cold, calculating murderer, after all. Bill Brenner, misogynist, made life unpleasant for Beth so young Tom, ever her protector, kills him in his fiction.

In drawing many features of himself and Beth Brenner to create the characters of Peter and Rose Gordon, Savage once again borrowed rather than invented. The Inn at Armstead, Montana—"the Inn" at "Beech"—which opened in 1907, was sold some years later to Mary and Elmer Gordon, a well-known family in Savage's "Beech," i.e., Armstead. Savage used a local family as stand-ins for his first, realized version of his birth parents and himself, with Dr. Johnny Gordon, a heavy drinker who commits suicide, a loose sardonic comment by Savage about his shiftless birth father.

Years later Savage admitted that the novel's opening sentence— which begins, "Phil always did the castrating"—"upset a lot of people." He wanted his first paragraph to make readers squirm. He took a risk, as it foreshadows Phil Burbank's symbolic self-emasculation—which, in some respects, proclaimed his own, to the extent both character and author suppress their gay selves. That is, Phil fears his own exposure and emasculation, and projects that outward, thereby emasculating others: his steady stream of vitriol, for instance.

Writer Annie Proulx considered Savage a personal friend and literary model, and in the afterword she wrote for *Power*'s republication in 2001, she begins by succinctly defining Savage's territory: "Something aching and lonely and terrible of the west is caught forever on his pages." (p. 277) This territory, I have been arguing, runs against the grain of genre fiction, let alone prevailing settler colonialism—sunny stories of hard work but steady endurance and triumph. Add to this the fraught subject of same-sex love and its repression, and you discover some explanation for the author's story of neglect. When *Power* was published, only one anonymous reviewer in *Publishers Weekly* named its major subject, "repressed homosexuality displayed as homophobia." (p. 277)

By anyone's measure, Savage's Phil Burbank represents an impressively nasty, tragically twisted, repressed character—"a house divided against itself" (Matthew 12:25) with "the ranching world's judgment forever hounding him" (cf. title, drawn from Psalms 22:20) In the Horse Prairie and Dillon of 1924, the novel's time setting, there is little place for a gay man. In 1967, stigmas still loomed large enough that most avoided any mention, or made any place, for sexual minorities in the rural West. But by the time Proulx's afterword was included in *Power*'s republication, her own "Brokeback Mountain" (originally published in October 13, 1997, *New Yorker*), was on its way to becoming her most famous short story. Upon *Power*'s republication, *The Great Falls [Montana] Tribune* (November 12, 2001) remarked, "For a writer, it's important to be a little ahead of the curve. But three decades is exceptional."

That "curve" concerns sexual minorities and their visibility and acceptance as much as anything. By 2001 Proulx, who calls Phil "a vicious bitch"—a violent, homophobic phrase—named the novel's core subject:

> In wanting to touch and have Bronco Henry, he was forced to recognize and confront the enormous fact of his own homosexuality. His private obstacle became this thing that he knew about himself, something that in the cowboy world he inhabited was terrible and unspeakably vile. Following the code of the west, he remade himself as a manly, homophobic rancher. (pp. 288–89)

Bronco Henry Williams looms in *Power*'s background as *the* key minor character, killed in a corral in front of idolizing Phil's eyes, many years before the novel begins. Savage tellingly borrowed Williams from early twentieth-century Lemhi County, Idaho, history, as he was a "regionally famous cowboy" who briefly appears in *Images of America: Lemhi County*: "It is said that he once roped and rode a mountain goat, and that he beat a worthy challenger in a bronc-riding contest by riding his horse backwards in a rear-facing saddle." (2006, p. 59) The accompanying photograph (1915) shows a cocky buck sporting a big handlebar mustache, broad confident smile, and exotic animal skin leggings. Williams was well known at the Yearians', as he makes several appearances in The Sheep Queen's day journals (e.g., December 1915, December 1920).

Bronco Henry reappears in *For Mary* as the stalwart senior "hand" at the Cummings Ranch, "tall and gaunt, said to have broken every bone in his body breaking horses when he was young." A relentlessly hard worker, "all business," he's lived a tough life and ends up with very little, surviving his wife's desertion and his son's death. (pp. 85, 87) He's effectively become *The Pass*'s Jess Bentley in old age: alone like Lona Hanson at her end. Savage has "straightened" Bronco Henry out in the later novel, lending him a familiar ranch hand profile and plot. That shift and his solitude reflect the press of heteronormativity.

In the key revision of family (and in this case, local) history, Savage—a gay man who married and loved the family he'd created—imagines and presents this obscure cowboy, Bronco Henry, and Savage's weird Uncle Bill as gay. In fact Williams and Brenner, rough contemporaries, likely crossed paths, though there's no record that Williams worked in Horse Prairie. Out of psychic necessity, Savage links the cowboy and ranch son as a couple who impact Peter, one alter ego. In the crucial rewriting of Bill Brenner, Savage at some level denies and castigates his own gay self.

Given the dominant culture's insistence on repression and silence, if not violence, Phil can be seen as a tragic figure who fascinates because of his sustained cruelty and misanthropy, an externalization of his self-hatred. His causing Dr. Johnny Gordon's suicide serves as warm-up for his calculated hatred of Rose, the attractive young widow who becomes his sister-in-law. For example, after the piano arrives and Rose plays, Phil manifests relentless cruelty:

> Protected from his thoughts and emanations by that closed door, she sat down and began to play; but as she listened critically to her own playing, she heard another sound, that of Phil's banjo, and knew suddenly that when she practiced, he played, too... Now she

knew a crawling sensation up the back of her neck: he was playing precisely what she was playing—and better. (p. 124)

Savage himself later called Phil an "evil character," doomed by his fatal inability to realize love. Phil's destiny represents a case study of what critic Karl Olson has called "homothanaticism," the "tragic consequences of homoerotic desire" or the notion that "homosexuality inevitably leads to disaster," at least in the American West. (*All Our Stories Are Here*, p. 104) Savage subscribed to the simplified Freudian view of homosexuality as, primarily, deviance and in creating Phil, he homophobically accuses himself as a gay man.

For most of American history, the heterosexual majority has sustained that closeted "shame" of being a sexual minority, as though equivalent to weak or shameful secrets we carefully keep out of public view. When Savage turned away from his liaison with younger Tomie, he repressed his gay desires and wore a familiar cloak of self-loathing: a standard behavior among married gay men, an internalization of cultural homophobia, before changing mores eased off condemnation in some locales. While young Tom "Brenner" never felt close to the weird Bill Brenner, Bill, like Phil, was not openly gay, nor could he likely ever have been. Obviously the character's name rhymes and echoes the uncle's: Savage made them the same. He made Bill gay and transmuted him into his most notorious character. Embodied as Phil Burbank, Savage displaced his own sexual identity onto this uncle, then kept imaginatively killing him. In fact, Bill Brenner died from blackleg, a bacterial disease common in cattle but rare in humans; in the ferocious closing pages of *Power*, scheming Peter Gordon causes Phil to be infected with anthrax (cf. *Sheep Queen*, p. 229).

Savage sustains the demonization of Bill Brenner in *The Sheep Queen*'s Ed Brewer:

Ed was a bachelor by profession, a woman-hater. He was brilliant, quick at chess, puzzles and word games. . .He was lean, had a craggy profile under thick black hair he had cut no more than four times a year. He despised towns where hair was cut, where men gathered to engage in silly banter and chewed food in public. His long, sharp nose was an antenna quick to pick up the faintest

rumor and to send it on to his brain to be amplified...His laugh-
ter was an insulting bray; it crowded and pushed the air ahead of
it...He said many true words about other men. I never heard him
say a kind one. (p. 223)

In the later novel's first reference to Ed Brewer, bad manners are
linked to a loss of same-sex sibling loyalty (present in *Power*), as though
marriage constitutes an unnatural act because it interrupts an older
bond. In this remarkable and appalling portrait in which bachelorhood
is equated with misogyny, the family badass represents an ugly and
crude self, though one capable of chess and music. The power of Phil
Burbank's/Ed Brewer's viciousness stems from a corrosive inability to
accept his repressed gayness, given the heteronormative marginalizing
of sexual minorities: "But Phil knew, God knows he knew, what it was
to be a pariah, and he had loathed the world, should it loath him first."
(*Power*, p. 263) Savage's turning his back on his own gay identity and
his imaginative transformation of Uncle Bill becomes, in the fiction, a
generalizing eagerness to expose vulnerability.

In *Sheep Queen*, "Part of Ed's secret knowledge is that he knew that
almost everyone is vulnerable, that almost everyone can be destroyed."
(p. 225) And in this insistent review of family history, Ed's raison d'être
consists of destroying Beth Brewer (i.e., Brenner): "his purpose was
narrower. His purpose was to destroy my mother, and that is what he
did." (p. 228) Though few family records portray the brother- and sister-
in-law's relationship from Beth's marriage (1920) to Bill's death (1938),
there is reason to believe it was unpleasant, and that Bill contributed to
Beth's alcoholism. Young Tom, first and last his mother's defender (in
good Freudian fashion), never forgot a mean glance or hard tone, or his
mother's clandestine reach for a bottle.

In Lemhi County, Idaho, *Power*'s key background character, Bronco
Henry, is remembered. Two or three geographical features (e.g., Williams Lake) are named after Williams, who was well known to the Yearians. Savage made him gay—Phil's idol and mentor, "that best of riders,
that best of cowboys" who "learned a scorn of Death" (pp. 11, 223)—and
has him trampled to death in front of young Phil. That backstory defines
Phil as a doomed outsider.

Power builds inexorably to a climatic passage midway through the final chapter (pp. 262-64). Steady foreshadowing intimates Phil's private torture and disposition. Its infamous opening paragraph, evoking the annual castration scene, symbolically intimates Phil's lot. Homosexuality in this novel exists not in its own right, but to be exposed, ridiculed, and punished—or killed. Phil's homophobia and self-loathing sounds throughout *Power,* as he accuses the "sissies": "Why in hell didn't [the sissies, i.e., gay men] snap out of it and get human?" (p. 60) He judges Peter, and therefore himself, beyond the human pale as he brands the boy, "this little monster not boy and not girl." (p. 225) The bathing scene (end, chap. IX) exemplifies this, as though the parental judgment (i.e., the "Old Folks"), that there is "something wrong" with Phil—society's judgment—presses like an ineluctable force, inevitably distorting him.

After all, long ago critic Leslie Fiedler, in his famed essay, "Come Back to the Raft Ag'in, Huck Honey!" (1948), argued "the existence of overt homosexuality threatens to compromise an essential aspect of American sentimental life" which manifests itself as "a kind of passionless passion." And in a searing analysis of homophobia published at the twentieth century's end, one which suggests we've not made much progress, Beth Loffreda reminds us that "homophobia works not just through the viciousness of physical violence but also through the daily erosion of selfhood by the friction of widespread, casually expressed hatred." (*Losing Matt Shepard: Life and Politics in the Aftermath of Anti-Gay Murder,* 2000, p. x) We see that erosion in Phil's tragic isolation, as he behaves according to the dominant culture's negative judgment (i.e., a "pariah"): he internalizes that.

Savage, I am suggesting, performed a sustained act of self-denial in his best novel's protest against the usually virulent stigmatization of sexual minorities. After all, the hobby Phil teaches Peter, braiding rawhide rope, symbolically hints at the idealized union of their bodies—except that the rope Peter gives Phil is fatally infected and, because of his filthy, horny hands, it kills him. Peter, having discovered and cut down his father's hanging body, uses Johnny's medical textbooks to study up on anthrax, and he plans his moves carefully, using his attraction to Phil—and importantly, Phil's attraction to him—to move in close for the kill, "hands on." Savage was proud of *Power's* horrific ending, which he wrote eleven times by his own admission.

In *For Mary* Savage writes, "It was Dostoyevsky, [Mary] thought, who had written that hell is the inability to love... But it was, perhaps, not the inability to love that was hell, but not having found someone to love." (p. 220) Citing that definition in Dillon (April 1983), Savage claimed that Phil/Ed's fatally unfulfilled love of Bronco Henry and then Peter, his failure to secure a gay partner, kills him.

Power's primary plot suggests an analogy with German novelist Thomas Mann's famed novella, *Death in Venice* (1912), with the aging Gustav von Aschenbach fatally attracted to Tadzio, the bright youth on the beach. Like Savage, Mann covered his gayness through marriage and children, and channeled it into some of his fiction (e.g., Hanno in *Buddenbrooks,* 1901). Of course, there is less of an age gap between Phil and Peter, a natural gay pairing not unlike Tom and Tomie a few years earlier, and Mann's Tadzio does not actively kill the much older man.

Yet the story of tortured Phil and young Peter the Avenger is not the only focus in *Power.* He names his hometown—called "Sentinel" in *Lona Hanson*—"Herndon," a "near name" to Dillon, in *Power* and his next novel, *The Liar* (1969). As was his custom, he took the name from a local source: local couple Edith D. and Roy Herndon held various positions in Armstead and Dillon, Montana, in the early twentieth century. The composite town portrait turns increasingly satiric. Until his last novel, Savage took his cue from Sinclair Lewis's savage satire of his hometown (Sauk Centre, Minnesota), the "Gopher Prairie" of *Main Street* (1920).

With his photographic memory, Savage never conducted research for any of his "near-historical" novels, as I've called them; instead, he opened the floodgates of his past, his uncanny memory for faces and voices, for façades and odors and personal quirks. For instance, over half a century later he recounted the "tank traps" (long gone concrete posts) at the main entrance to the "normal school" (University of Montana Western) campus, where every morning an enterprising woman, one Frankie Lewis, sold freshly baked fudge to incoming students.

Occasionally he blended Salmon, Idaho, locations into his barely veiled versions of his hometown. *Power,* for example, opens and closes with quick sketches of Herndon (Dillon), as though the town frames the other setting, the Brenner Ranch, and the novel. Savage shifts his gaze back and forth from the Burbanks and Gordons to the town, presenting Herndon in several close-ups: the downtown (chap. VI), and the town in early summer (chap. IX), on the Fourth of July (chap. XII), and at night ("a different Herndon," chap. XIII), where the wandering Peter meets lowlife Herndon: a theme Savage gleefully pursues in several novels.

Savage, in *Power* and later novels, assembles townsfolk in "Herndon House" (Dillon's Andrus Hotel) to ridicule them. *Power* sets the pattern:

> And out drifted the men, talking, making points with their good cigars; these who had been asked to represent the City of Herndon, to swell the progress, were local Society. They were not bright people; as such, they would not have settled in Herndon, but they were the best Herndon had, the storekeepers, the undertaker, the doctors, the dentists; the more ambitious of them had had at least a brush with the state university [Missoula] and were now hot after their first fifty or one hundred thousand dollars. (p. 115)

Savage's scorn, his blunt puncturing of pretension, also explains, most likely, his marginal position in the ranks of novelists of the American West, let alone in the Montana letters hall of fame. His darkly comic satire and flair for ridicule swerved too far away from the typically naïve self-congratulation of local histories or more popular regional literary production. Again, he would have none of that.

Savage's best novel also reviews the plight of local tribes: a presence already absent, for the most part, in *The Pass* and *Lona Hanson*. He contrasts the narrator's ironic criticism of the settler-colonial plot with Phil's mainstream racist condemnation, as Phil subscribes to the prevailing mindset of the noble vanishing race ("The worst of it, they couldn't face the fact that their day was over, over and done." p. 180) Chapter X opens,

> When the last of the Indians were herded off their lands and sent packing to the reservation, the government no longer even pretended to believe in treaties. Land was too valuable for bargains, and there was no reason now to fear violence from the Indians and every reason to fear the wrath of the white voters. (p. 172)

The narrator's protest, Savage's truthful summary, offsets his character's stereotypical racism: "Phil had no romantic ideas about Indians.
He left that stuff to professors and dudes from back East with their
fancy cameras. [e.g., Edward S. Curtis and his epic photography project, *The North American Indian*] Children of nature, my foot. That crap.
Actually, the Indians were lazy and thieving." (p. 179)

These diametrically opposed perspectives frame *Power*'s brief story
of Edward Nappo and his son, son and grandson of a Bannock Shoshone chief, respectively, and their 200-mile journey with an old horse
and cart to their home country, the Burbank Ranch. This hot journey
north from Fort Hall Reservation across eastern Idaho's sagebrush flats
beyond the Snake River, and over the Continental Divide into Montana,
geographically reverses the tribe's forced removal. Edward wants to
show his son "their" mountains but Phil cruelly denies them camping
access and deeply embarrasses Edward in front of his son. Phil actually
believes the arrowheads he's knapped himself "superior in craft to what
the Indians did. You can look at their handicraft all you want!" (p. 180)
He's rejected the five pairs of gloves with beaded handwork sewn by
Edward's wife—her rationale for this "business trip": "You've picked
the wrong customer, old-timer." (p. 186)

The episode recapitulates the commonplace, late-nineteenth-century
and early twentieth-century American practice of near-genocide and
removal of Native Americans, Phil cast as the usual white standard-
bearer. He even feels a twinge of sympathy ("In a way, he felt for the
poor devils," p. 186) but flicks it away as he stands resolute at the gate,
master agent of usurpation and denial.

Savage uses Edward, a minor character, to place racist ranchers and
others who believed "they've got to go" in historical context—a context
that included the Yearians with their Lemhi Shoshone friends:

> In all truth there were some in that old land, some whites who
> championed the Indians, took Indians' troubles as their own to the
> capital of the United States of America, far to the East, where no
> Indians that Edward had even known had been. There had been
> whites at his father's funeral, whites in honored places watching
> the burning of his father's blankets, moccasins, headdress, hacka-
> more, wickiup. (pp. 183–84)

Tragically for Edward and his unnamed son, Phil does not prove "one of those." Tribal peoples, in fact, become merely another object of contempt for lone Phil. In his final novel, Savage enlarges the sympathetic portrait of local tribal peoples through a main character, Anne Chapman Metlen, as well as satirically presented local historical pageantry.

Power stayed on the *New York Times'* "New and Recommended" list for almost two months. *Times* critic Marshall Sprague stated "those [characters'] destinies have a classic inevitability...the author has a magic hand with his characters," and concludes, "the story, the people, the scene, the sense of doom combine to quicken our imagining of what happened on the Beaverhead in the 1920s." (April 9, 1967) In the *Hudson Review*, critic Roger Sale called it "the year's best novel," "the finest single book I know about the modern west." The *San Francisco Chronicle* called it "the year's best novel." In a review-essay (also published in the *Hudson Review*, Summer 1968), William H. Pritchard remarks, "there is so much contempt, hostility, failure of communication built into the exchanges among [the characters]. His narrative strength is felt particularly through the oblique, highly stylized beginnings of chapters that move slowly but daringly into the presentations of sequential actions."

That perceptive comment overlaps with novelist Frederick Manfred's enthusiasm about *Power*. In his *Chicago Daily News* review, Manfred gushed as though directly addressing his fellow western writer: "please don't let this turn into the usual Wyoming cowboy love story. You've got the right horse this time, stay on it and ride it out to the end...You didn't disappoint me. Your dramatic, shocking, soul-burning ending is utterly convincing." An apt figure for Savage the one-time bronc stomper. But given its low sales, most readers disliked this ride, squeamish or hostile to his Savage West.

Power continues to be reviewed (e.g., *The Montana Standard*, July 7, 2013, and the [London] *Times Literary Supplement*, February 5, 2016). In its 2001 republication, novelist Proulx ends her trenchant analysis of Savage, *Power*, and more particularly, Phil Burbank, by oversimplifying the analogy between uncle and nephew and their fictional counterparts, Phil and Peter: "In a curious way he has realized his childhood wish to see the man dead, for every time a new reader catches his breath at Phil Burbank's satisfyingly ghastly end, the child that was Thomas Savage re-kills him as surely as the fictional Peter Gordon removed his moth-er's nemesis." (*Power*, p. 293)

It has been optioned ten times to date, but no film has yet reached completion, even many years after Ang Lee's sensitive, celebrated *Brokeback Mountain* (2005), based on Proulx's celebrated short story first published eight years earlier. In one past option, Paul Newman was to be cast as Phil Burbank, but there was ostensibly a problem given the small size of Newman's hands; in a later option, Randy Quaid visited Horse Prairie. In 1983 Savage stated he'd received $35,000 from options though he doubted Hollywood could make a graphic scene of the novel's climax. In a later letter to cousin Janet Moore (April 17, 1992), he wrote, "An option has been taken on THE POWER OF THE DOG for the sixth time. The movie has never been made, but I've received over seventy-five thousand dollars in options. The man who has the option now thinks Fay[e] Dunaway wants to play Rose, but I don't know."

Currently, though, internationally acclaimed director Jane Campion is filming her own adaptation. Campion's attraction to *Power* signals, as much as anything, a Thomas Savage revival. She wrote the screenplay herself, Benedict Cumberbatch and Kirsten Dunst have been cast as Phil Burbank and Rose Gordon, respectively, and shooting occurred in 2020. Netflix is backing the film. Best known for her prize-winning *The Piano* (1993), Campion, who adapted Henry James's *A Portrait of a Lady* (1996), believes Phil Burbank's tragic story will find a big audience. I hope so.

Though Savage seemed unclear about its stature, critics and other writers since *Power's* publication have deemed it his best novel. Yet Emily Salkin Takoudes, who oversaw its republication thirty-four years after initial publication, estimates *Power* sold no more than 1,000 copies in 1967. Savage uncannily surmised its very low sales in a later novel, *Her Side of It* (1981), when the narrator describes this novelist-protagonist's similar neglect: "I doubt her novel, *Masquerade*, sold a thousand copies." (p. 24)

Power set the pattern of superior fiction and superior reviews, yet feeble sales, inadequate recognition, and a stalled reputation, at least among the mainstream. In 1968 critic Pritchard saluted Savage's quality and simultaneously lamented his coterie reputation—a protest subse-quently taken up by other critics, notably Jonathan Yardley. Regarding

Power's climax, he states, "I know few American novelists, perhaps none so neglected as Thomas Savage (he is 53) who give satisfying expression to both claims," that is, that "theme alone" can articulate "pure wildness."

▫   ▫   ▫

While Tom Savage wrote *Power*, Bob (Brassil) Savage, holding down dishwasher jobs and in between binges, attended enough classes at Colby to not be dropped and imitated his parents, writing "Twenty," a novel, as his undergraduate thesis (1966), and finally graduating from Colby in 1968. "Twenty," a self-indulgent self-portrait (though young Savage altered a few details), reveals Alex Shiva—fraught surname— failing at Harvard, spending most of his time drinking or painting or experimenting with drugs (via the "Claverly Dart Club," an underground drug club at Harvard). The Oedipal father-son conflict between Alex and his father harshly paints Tom Savage, "who chose more often around Alex to be a father image rather than a father." (p. 4) Parental love fuels the usual need to break away for independence: "their protective, compassionate shield was freezing him, his secret mind, like Perseus' shield reflecting his own *id* back onto him, congealing his life into a safe static pattern with no snakes." (p. 9) Brassil never lacked for "snakes" in his life. "Twenty" provides one New England snapshot into the early 1960s culture of sex, drugs, and rock 'n' roll.

But Brassil's declaration of independence felt more pronounced than the usual. This unpublished novel also evidences early signs of his bipolarity. Back in 1960–61, he wanted out of the house, and his competition with and combativeness about Tom was unusually acute, driven as it was in part by the sibling discovery of Tom's affair with Tomie dePaola. Nonetheless, Savage, who admitted to Ellie Savage Quigley he thought the novel "shit," recommended it to Little, Brown, his own publisher. One press reader out of three disliked it, recommending extensive revision. Brassil abandoned it.

The year after *Power* was published, Brassil had voluntarily committed himself to Eastern Maine Insane Hospital (or the "Nut House," as it was informally known; now the Dorothea Dix Psychiatric Center), in Bangor. For a while he sobered up and religiously attended AA. The attending psychiatrists diagnosed paranoid schizophrenia: a diagnosis Tom would not accept, instead blaming the alcoholism that ran in Betty's Irish-American family (e.g., both parents). According to Ellie, Tom tragically believed, "It's simply nonsense, my dear! It's just the booze." Within six years, the younger Savage family would move to Montana, their marriage in shambles.

Reviewing the fourteen years between *Bargain* (1953) and *Power* (1967), a period that yielded one novel, Savage recognized he would never match the sales of his *Lona Hanson* and *Bargain* even as he entered his most productive period as a novelist. For the rest of his career and life, Savage would be haunted by his small audience and poor sales, having resolutely turned his back on the kind of novel he judged his most immature work. Savage's West denied the pot of gold at rainbow's end (*Bargain*), instead anatomizing family life, whether in ranch culture or Boston. His anatomy usually yielded grim disillusionment, though without *Lona*'s occasional fanfare and alarum. He kept writing, refusing to stop telling his version of the West. He never gave up because he couldn't.

The Dutch colonial Yearian home (1911), Lemhi, Idaho, where Tom always felt he belonged with his extended family. Reproduced by permission of the Savage family estate.

Savage's mother, Beth Y. S. Brenner, inside a canvas tent pitched next to the Brenner ranch house. Beth loved camping, hunting, and fishing when not busy on the ranch. Reproduced by permission of the Savage family estate.

Young Tom Savage (here, still Tom Brenner) in a contemplative moment just below Lemhi Pass. Reproduced by permission of the Savage family estate.

An attractive young couple with their futures as novelists in front of them. Reproduced by permission of the Savage family estate.

Tom Yearian as great-grandfather holding baby Robert (Brassil) Savage, with Tom Savage (*left*) and Beth Brenner (*right*) looking on. Reproduced by permission of the Savage family estate.

As an assistant professor of English, Savage conducts a class in his living room in Waltham, Massachusetts (March 1951). Reproduced by permission of the Savage family estate.

Left to right, Betsy, Russell, and Bob (Brassil) Savage in the Waltham, Massachusetts living room (mid-1950s). Reproduced by permission of the Savage family estate.

The proud owner of a 1939 Rolls Royce, ready to show the world. Courtesy Elizabeth S. Main.

The Andrus Hotel lobby, Dillon, Montana, which Savage invoked repeatedly in his fiction. Courtesy Great Plains Quarterly.

Emma (the Sheep Queen) and Russell Yearian in old age. Reproduced by permission of the Savage family estate.

Left to right, Emma R. Yearian (the Sheep Queen) in old age, seated next to Helen Y. Hamner (youngest daughter), Gladys Whitwell (a niece), and Nora Y. Whitwell (sister-in-law and beloved great aunt of Savage's); behind them stands Thomas Yearian, Savage's maternal grandfather after whom he was named. Reproduced by permission of the Savage family estate.

As assured writer, age fifty-nine, at the top of his game (1974). Reproduced by permission of the Savage family estate.

Despite Tom's homosexuality and despite occasionally bitter fights, Tom and Betty remained extremely devoted to one another. Reproduced by permission of the Savage family estate.

CHAPTER FOUR

The High Tide Years, 1968–1975

T HE POWER OF THE DOG unleashed the most productive section of Savage's career, as he wrote and published six novels in a dozen years (1969-81). The psychic pressures released in *Power* created a surge, a continual rewriting of family history, as though the overtly gay novel he could not publish a few years earlier inspired a related series he could. Meanwhile, Betty Savage cranked up her own production, remarkably publishing eight of her nine novels in one decade (1970-80). Brassil, Russell, and Betsy had entered their adult lives, each marked by occasionally serious problems and each, in various seasons, circling back around their parents. Tom savored his patriarchal role, and his chronic need to be the banker likely challenged his adult children's independence.

What was he like in his prime?

According to his daughter, Savage acted tightly about small matters, reusing dental floss for example, but always behaved magnanimously about larger matters. A perfectionist, he sought after exactitude and always wanted an atomic clock. By the late 1970s he and Betty had removed their telephones, which had finally been installed years earlier; thereafter they walked or rode to Georgetown for the pay phone. In fact Savage begins *Daddy's Girl* (1970) discussing the absence of phones on "Crow Point" (i.e., the actual Indian Point):

> The nearest telephone is at the store, four miles out of the woods, a pay phone in a booth brightly lighted at night against hanky-panky and so close to two private houses that you feel compelled to

deposit at once your overtime money when the phone screams for it, should anybody hear, and be watching. (p. 3)

Again, this reads as fact. The Savages preferred the absence of phones characterizing their first years on the coast. (cf. "'And the best thing,' I said, 'is that there are no telephones,'" p. 195)

In literary matters, though Savage claimed to never be a steady reader, he held clear opinions about American literary giants of the preceding generation. He preferred Fitzgerald to Hemingway as a stylist, but thought both of them less interested in what mattered most to him: family and family relationships. (He mocks, via his protagonist, Robert Jordan of Hemingway's *For Whom The Bell Tolls* in *Daddy's Girl*, p. 221)

Family demands piled up during the Savages' busiest time as novelists. In the summer of 1972, one of Tom's favorite aunts, "Winnie" (Edwina Yearian Nichol), was dying and he flew out for a final visit. Older and younger generations needed support. Betty looked after the bedridden Dottie Savage, Tom's stepmother, as well as Brassil and Ellie Savage's four children. By the end of 1973, they had divorced though they remained together for a brief while. Tom likely savored his local reputation as outsider/eccentric. A Christmastime letter (December 19, 1973) from Tom's Aunt Mary, whom he'd later write a novel about, to her granddaughter comments, "Mrs. C. [?] reports that Tom is nuttier than ever, at least that is the gossip in Bath [Maine]." She stated soon after (January 6, 1974), "By the way [Tom's] son Bob divorced—I imagine wife and *four* children back in Maine [from Montana]. What a life they have had." Russell Savage's marriage was also in trouble because, in large part, of his then-wife's alcoholism and promiscuity. That wife, Tressie, described by her sister-in-law as "vapid, meek, and pathetic," was also very pretty: some believed she resembled Greta Garbo. Married before, she'd had three children; she and Russell had three more. According to her sister-in-law, she remained an incorrigible flirt.

Tom and Betty both wrote and published at a fast pace despite the daily presence of extended family.

Their pace of production in the 1970s, in the ramshackle house above the ocean, seems all the more impressive given the chronic presence of these relatives. Dottie Savage lived with them for most of eight years (1971–78) after the death of Tom's father, Ben Savage (September 1,

1971). She was followed by Betty's mother, Mildred Fitzgerald, for four years (1978–82), followed by three grandchildren (Russell's three kids, 1982–88) who moved with them to Langley, Washington (Whidbey Island) in 1985 when they finally quit the Maine coast.

The biggest external challenge during the second half of their decades on Georgetown Island's southern tip occurred in early February 1978, when a pair of blizzards with hurricane-force winds crashed their house and unmoored it. In a *Times Record* (Brunswick, Maine) profile (December 1, 1978), Savage stated, "We were next door. . . because we were in danger of being inundated by the sea. This whole room [the living room] was filled with water and rocks and glass. . . I've been refinishing furniture ever since, but [Betty] got a book out of it." Betty Savage's final novel, *Toward the End,* climaxes with these huge blows. For an extended period after the blizzard they had no running water. The Savages moved their foundation thirty-five feet back and rebuilt.

After seven more years, they moved cross-country to Washington's Puget Sound for family reasons.

In a letter to his longtime agent, Blanche Gregory, he stated, "After having got [*Her Side of It*] off my hands I feel that the winter of 1978 is at last over. No one will ever understand what that storm did to us. How on earth did we continue to write? It was a great pleasure, with the house in its new position, to look down last week and see waves again that would have destroyed this place had it still been down there." (March 22, 1980)

Ironically, the year that Savage published *The Liar* (1969), a more insistent rewriting of family history than *Power,* he discovered, at age fifty-four, his full-blood sister: a far more consequential event than those 1978 blizzards. Through her (deceased) father's confidential files and her attorney's work in Seattle, Patricia ("Pat") McClure Hemenway contacted the Yearians in Salmon, Idaho, as well as the Savages in Maine. This shocking discovery, and readjustment of his understanding of family, led directly to *I Heard My Sister Speak My Name* (1977; rpt. *The Sheep Queen*), an autobiography cum novel. In a letter written to the Hagenses, close friends, late in the decade, Savage commented how well Pat fit into his family: "one of the best things about having found a sister is that she and Betty get along so well, that she is so fond of my children and grandchildren, and that she is not penniless." (July 17, 1979) Pat occasionally flew out to Maine, and her places in Seattle and Whidbey Island guided the Savages' eventual (1985) move to the Northwest.

In a letter to Gregory just before *Sheep Queen* was published, Savage declared, "what I really want to do is sell the whole place and move to the San Juan Islands, one [of] them without ferry service. I'm serious about this. It's ridiculous, after having found a sister, to live 3000 miles from her, especially at our age." (April 2, 1977) He still wanted rural isolation. Eight years later, the Savages would move to southern Whidbey Island: "closer in" than the San Juans, and boasting a quick ferry crossing.

Savage's quality and quantity should have led to greater sales to match the laudatory reviews each new title commanded. For example, *The Liar* was published in paperback (Dell) within a year of its release; a few months later (September 1970), *Daddy's Girl*, his seventh novel, was released. Influential *Washington Post* book critic, Jonathan Yardley, long a Savage champion, marked his growing critical reputation. Savage's fabulous 1970s were capped by his receiving a Guggenheim Fellowship in 1980. Yet partway through his run, critic Roger Sale, in *The American Scholar*, singled out Savage as his most dramatic example of a gifted novelist being virtually unknown (quoted in the introduction). The wrenching combination of strong talent and lingering obscurity dogged him even in his most prolific phase. His plots of rural life in the West are too critical of settler-colonial mythology for popular consumption. His versions of ranch or family life, derived from the perspective of an outed gay man, proved too tough to swallow for most readers.

□   □   □

Given the preponderance of work in his middle age, Savage's literary credo—his comments about the craft of fiction—should be reviewed. Savage, particularly in his near-historical novels, did not do the kind of research that became, for example, novelist Ivan Doig's hallmark. Instead, he fixed his gaze on the past: his own, his family's, his town's. Those never left him, remaining in sharp focus. He references himself when introducing Jack Reed, troubled protagonist of *A Strange God* (1974), his eighth novel: "His ability to match a face to a name and a name to a face never failed to flatter. He could remember the most casual conversation. He possessed almost total recall, knew where things were, who had said what. He never missed the inflection in a voice. Once he had written down a telephone number it was his forever." (p. 7) Nor did Savage forget neighborhoods, façades, interiors, nooks and crannies.

Some of Savage's writing habits might seem old-fashioned. He regularly asserted that he never wrote without knowing the opening and closing sentences of the novel-in-progress: the drama occurred along the way, as characters led him. He also self-consciously phrased his sentences and revised quickly according to his ear, because he proudly asserted that he never wrote a novel that shouldn't be read aloud. His narrator's commentary about novelist Liz C. Phillips's gifts as a stylist, manifested in her first novel, Masquerade (1945)—the primary narrative within Savage's Her Side of It (1981), his eleventh novel—describes, to some extent, Savage's own self-regard.

Savage also favors essayistic interludes, remarking in 1983 that some readers took him to task for these "little essays." He recognized that "a few paragraphs about death or love" interrupted narrative flow, and that "ordinary" readers complain because they resent an author's ruminations. Yet these witty commentaries, tangential and unpredictable yet always plausible, became a Savage hallmark, as expected as his shapely prose rhythms and his sardonic irony.

In that same 1983 interview, he asserted that he was unhappy with his work, claiming that out of (then) twelve novels, only a few paragraphs pleased him. Yet he often repeated that he knew his calling by high school and had never wavered. Looking back from his sixty-eighth year, he told interviewer John Scheckter that he'd had about six editors, three of whom contracted ulcers. On the one hand, he remarked that he never had an editor who actually edits; on the other, tongue in cheek, he defined a good editor as one who praises wholeheartedly, never edits, and "takes you to lunch at the Ritz [Boston]," where more than one martini was swallowed. His favorite editor, Llewellyn "Louie" Howland III, worked with him during his high tide years. Savage stayed in touch with Howland in his old age. In a letter to his daughter, Betsy, he wrote, "[Howland] told me that he considered me the finest writer he'd ever dealt with in his long career at Little, Brown. That did please me." (December 27, 1995)

His primary editor remained, however, his novelist wife, Betty, who reviewed every page of every novel. Writing was always the foundation of their relationship.

More disingenuous than his statement commending the oral basis of his style is Savage's claim that he never wrote the same book twice. He also stated that none of his characters "are real, of course." Savage deftly played whatever part best suited him, and these Twainian "stretchers" served to cover the deeply autobiographical story he repeatedly drew on. His fictitious returns derived from an acute psychic necessity, as Schechter remarks: "the return to the West came out of psychological necessity, as the distance between his self-image and his fiction collapsed." ("Thomas Savage and the Roots of Compulsion," *Western American Literature*, Spring 1985, p. 39) Savage never imaginatively left his home country though he rarely (literally) returned for the bulk of his life. His West fiercely gripped him.

Scheckter argues that Savage's plots force the protagonist to revise his self-understanding because unexpected turns of events demand he overhaul his prior identity. While this claim does not describe all his middle novels, it certainly offers a powerful interpretive lens for *Midnight Line* (1976), his ninth novel, and *The Sheep Queen*, for instance, which hinge upon the protagonist's discovering a son and a sister, respectively. Those unforeseen claims demand the protagonist, if not others, revise his conception of family and reconceive his past, however fraught: "Savage forces his autobiographical characters to face the new revisions of adolescent crisis, geographical displacement, and mature identity which their discoveries thrust upon them." (Scheckter, p. 46)

In an interview with Scheckter (1983), Savage conceded that naturalism or even determinism infuses his fiction, with one powerful character—sometimes one of several strong women he wrote—arranging events if not fates. He saw his later fiction differing markedly from the early novels.

Yet across his career Savage doggedly rewrites his own and his family's past, thereby suggesting that the autobiographical project is central and unavoidable, and suggesting as well that, as Norman

Maclean observed, the problem of identity is not solely a problem of youth. Much of Savage's power comes from the drama of main characters' destabilized and expanded sense of self; from their valiant accommodation of disjunction and reconciliation with a more complex and contingent identity, one impossible to imagine earlier. Writing in *The American Scholar* (1973-74), critic Roger Sale salutes Savage's energetic treatment of a very old idea—fate—in a comment quoted on the dust jacket of *A Strange God*:

> Thomas Savage is superb at destinies, at creating a sense that this life had to end up as it did. Start with almost any set of details, and you can see in their fixity the way people will strain against them. But they must yield to their destinies, and at his best, Savage's stories about these people are truly mysterious.

In this conception, the psychological drama consists in the tilt from characters' resistance to an acceptance of their fates: an arc curving from opposition to embrace. In light of his oeuvre, likely the most compelling, and most tragic, manifestation of this drama consists in Phil Burbank's surrender to his gay desire, which precipitates his death in *Power*. Savage's fiction echoes, in some respects, the determinism of classical Greek tragedy.

Even as Savage protagonists, usually autobiographical surrogates, are forced to redefine their adult identity, Savage continued to declare his literary independence announced in his first two novels. Whatever the cost, he insisted upon his own West (or occasionally, Savage New England), which couldn't be further distant from the celebratory West of genre fiction or local history. In *Her Side of It*, Savage employs Liz Phillips's biography as an indirect frame of reference for himself. Phillips's coterie appeal precisely limns Savage's own: "She knew...that she'd never be a popular entertainer. The vast public would reject her complicated images; their own lives were complicated enough. They did not wish to read the unpleasant truths about human relationships...they preferred belief to truth." (p. 183)

Savage sang a harsher song in a minor key, scrupulously avoiding the sentimental pieties or hard-earned victories characteristic in settler-colonial literature. As with other "regionalist" writers such as Willa

Cather, William Faulkner, and Flannery O'Connor, Savage comprehensively understood his native region. He skewers notions of "western" that distort and simplify the "unpleasant truths" of the Intermountain West he knew firsthand: a West that includes, however problematically, sexual minorities like himself.

The arc across these half dozen novels of Savage's high tide years makes itself evident through a range of links, one of which concerns occupation. Gerry Sawyer, protagonist of *The Liar*, is an up-and-coming novelist; Tom Westbrook, *Midnight Line's* protagonist, ranks among the senior and most respected radio talk show hosts; *The Sheep Queen's* Tom Burton is a middle-aged, moderately successful novelist; and Bill Reese, English professor and narrator of *Her Side of It*, frames the story of (novelist) Liz Phillips. These writers (or radio personality), usually foreground and expose a grim Intermountain West, a dark counter-narrative.

In *The Liar* Savage defines, at least in part, his credo in the form of advice young Sawyer receives from one Miss Eastman—a favorite Beaverhead County High School teacher of Savage's and mentor who appears in cameo (unchanged name) in several novels as well as his essay, "Why a Pilgrim Traveled to Boston" (1980): "You must hate it where you live, she said. People write better about what they hate and whom they hate. . . . And thus, in a few words, she told him a more practical thing about writing than anybody else ever did." (p. 179) Though hyperbolic, there is more than a grain of truth in this position for Savage who, after all, aligns himself with the Sinclair Lewis of *Main Street* (1920): a template of scorching satire about small-town provinciality and stultification. Savage's set piece excoriation of the pretentious rubes in "Herndon" (Dillon) in *Power*, quoted earlier, sets the pattern.

Savage liked to assemble Dillon's so-called elite in the Andrus Hotel's dining room, for example, to ridicule them, his group portraits resembling Daumier caricatures. In *Midnight Line* Old Pete limps with an express wagon to a baggage car: "Sometimes he loaded on it cartons of sour-smelling, peeping baby chicks, sometimes a coffin containing what remained of someone whose beginnings in Grayling [Dillon], Montana, had at last overcome his hatred of them." (p. 78) In *Her Side of It* narrator Bill Reese's cold evokes tactile memories of Grayling: "Again

I wait for the dusk and the shriek of the Union Pacific travelling west or east, bearing lucky passengers. At last I was one of the lucky ones." (p. 6) Caricature exposes some fundamental truths about what's missing in small-town life supported by cattle ranch culture. These comments clarify Savage's feeling of good fortune getting the hell out of Dodge at an early age, because he felt there was neither position nor audience for him in the home ground.

Yet part of him always honored his origins. His regard proved a not uncommon blend of hate tinctured with residual love.

Savage satirically pictures the local reception of his first novel, *The Pass*, in *The Liar*. Neither protagonist nor author hold any illusions: "[Sawyer] could imagine [his mother, Anne] handing his letter to the postmistress who would see that the news got around, and sweeping into the Herndon House with the news, urging her friends to go to the Thomas Bookstore where Mr. and Mrs. Thomas quarreled quietly in the back of the store and sold newspapers, Hershey bars, and Zane Grey." (p. 258) Savage knows he'll never sell much because most believe Zane Grey fantasy, not a native's truths, among those: that ranches destroy families as easily as grow them; that the region shed its facile pieties and embrace its dark settler-colonial legacy; that it concede then lessen its cultural impoverishment; and that it openly make room for all, not merely the heterosexual mainstream.

Through the 1970s Savage reminded his readers of his commitment to his "truth" about the Intermountain West. In implicit reference to his growing reputation after the publication of *Lona Hanson* two decades earlier, a critic in *The Liar* calls Gerry Sawyer "a young Lochinvar come out of the West," "liken[ing]" him to North Carolina's novelist, Thomas Wolfe, after 1929 and two others: "He was compared to Faulkner and to Steinbeck (because he knew about men who lived in bunkhouses) and when he had too many drinks he felt himself greater than any of these and able to write the whole story of the ranching country." (p. 267) Despite the self-mockery, Savage imagined he defined "the ranching country" and its bunkhouses as well as, or better than, any contemporary. Repeating his final work on *The Pass*, Savage allows Sawyer to be contacted by a "Boston publishing house, impressed by a first novel about the West that was not the West that Hollywood imagined." (p. 215)

That is his defiant territory. Certainly "the whole story" characterizes his ambition and unwavering commitment to *his* American West.

Savage defines his particular territory again in *Her Side of It*, when narrator Bill Reese—a homely English professor with one brother who doesn't write, a marked opposite of Savage—confesses, early on, to an unrealized ambition:

> I had wanted to write a novel about the West I believed I under-stood—the small-town West, the social strata, winter afternoons in the Public Library and the midnight striking of the courthouse clock. Thousands, maybe millions, have wanted to write that novel, one that would lend wings to fly from the Philistines and to join ranks with other artists, for artists are judged only by themselves and are the envy of all those back home. (p. 20)

This is precisely what Savage accomplished up through his final published novel, *The Corner of Rife and Pacific* (1988), for that is the West he knew inside out: one suffused with quiet awkwardness and loneliness, with little or no place for sexual minorities. Despite the usual self-mockery ("maybe millions"), Savage followed the trope of writers (e.g., Joyce, Lewis, Cather, Wolfe) leaving their first geographies far behind precisely in order to imaginatively, obsessively reinhabit them.

Savage defined his own safe space on the southern Maine coast, with cosmopolitan Boston a couple of hours south. In some respects he followed the rural exodus of gay men portrayed, for example, in Will Fellows's oral history, *Farm Boys: Lives of Gay Men from the Rural Midwest* (1996). This pattern is tragically represented at one moment in Annie Proulx's famed "Brokeback Mountain": when Ennis del Mar asks "'This happen a other people? What the hell do they do?'" Jack Twist answers, "'It don't happen in Wyomin and if it does I don't know what they do, maybe go to Denver.'" The big cities provide safe space small towns typically lack.

Given *The Liar*'s trenchant comment about what sells in the Thomas Bookstore, Savage satirizes his local reputation (though as his final hometown appearance, a hero's return, in April 1983 proved, he enjoyed a substantial local reputation). In light of his pervasive, Lewisian scorn of what passed for culture in the provinces (i.e., Dillon, Montana), his derisive dichotomy between "Philistines" and artists, and contemptuous dismissal of the former, comes off as close to the mark.

Savage never wavered from his chosen path, whatever the potential loss of sales. In a *Publishers Weekly* interview that appeared shortly after his final novel (July 15, 1988), he closed on a defiant note: "I'm writing for rather highly educated people, and I think my writing is only going to appeal to people who have extreme sensitivity . . . And if you don't have it," he adds emphatically, "you'll never understand *me*." That coterie appeal confirmed his understanding of a self-selected audience, one who discerns and accepts his real rural West present from his first novel on. In a letter to a fan he states, "A writer like me sells almost entirely to libraries. My books seldom get into paperback," though he admits, "*Daddy's Girl* did, and *The Liar* and *Lona Hanson* and *The Pass* [did], years ago." (June 3, 1977)

In *Midnight Line* Savage captures both his own escape and his solid autobiographical base in a teasing, third-person cameo appearance—one of several Hitchcockian cameos he wrote: "in the past quite unlikely people in Grayling [Dillon] had later on made names for themselves in far places . . . Another went off and wrote books. You could tell a lot of people in his books. (p. 117)

This quiet dare, contrary to his later (1983) hometown protest against the charge of autobiography, rings true, particularly given his habit of not changing, or barely changing names. For example, "Herndon," the name of a couple who lived in Armstead, Montana, and later, Dillon, is a near-rhyme of "Dillon"; and "Herndon House," by *Midnight Line*, is called the "Hotel Andrews," a close echo of Dillon's Hotel Andrus already mentioned. Savage thus teases the reader with generous helpings of historical place. In another sense, he rewrote chapters of local history as it suited him.

□   □   □

Having studied Savage's statements about the writer and his subject, and his lagging reputation, let us return to his unusual writing desk in the home just above the open Atlantic and review the extraordinary sequence of novels that issued from it. From *The Liar* onward, Savage insistently returns to Montana, sometimes even when the plot unfolds primarily in Boston. He does so because it provided the wellsprings of his fiction, given his Wordsworthian loyalty ("the child is father of the man") to the geography of childhood and adolescence à la Cather. He does so because of his photographic memory and his project of limning his Savage West according to his hometown and county.

As will be seen, a series of intertextual conversations ensue in which one or more characters from an earlier novel, for instance, reappears—resembling, in this regard, the frequent habit of fellow Montana novelist, Ivan Doig. Among other subjects, Savage anatomizes small-town life in the Intermountain West, the obligations of family and severe challenges to family loyalty, and the dismissal of sexual minorities through marginalization or the corrosive habit of self-condemnation to open up the territory: to protest its limits and advocate for a more comprehensive, inclusive region. Clearly Savage wants to complicate the ways we understand and live rural life. After returning to wife and children in 1962, and destroying his overtly gay novel manuscript, Savage in effect continued to accuse himself through a host of minor characters in the 1970s novels.

As stated, Sinclair Lewis's blistering satire proved a model for Savage as he repeatedly rewrote his hometown. At least twice, Savage slyly glanced directly at his model. In *The Liar* Hal Sawyer, the title character, is in Los Angeles arranging his new job with a company president, Henshaw, who faces various labor problems: "The Henshaw Deal! He was proud of his handling of it, so far. Henshaw, surprisingly, was a well-read man, and they'd talked about *Main Street* . . . We don't want to get in a rut like those Gopher Prairie people, Mr. Henshaw said. Times are changing, Sawyer." (pp. 168–69) Henshaw's boosterism shows him kin to Lewis's George F. Babbitt. The "rut" of course defines all the Herndons—small towns as fishbowls with omnivorous eyes and insistent leveling pressures—not a big city like Los Angeles in the earlier twentieth century, with its huge in-migration.

In his final novel, Savage confirms the link between Lewis's Gopher Prairie, based on his hometown of Sauk Centre, Minnesota, and his Savage's Herndon/Grayling (Dillon) precisely by denying it: "Grayling was no dismal Gopher Prairie in 1913" (*Corner*, p. 55). Savage doth protest too much, as that is exactly what Dillon if not Montana in the 1920s and 1930s felt like for a gay, up-and-coming writer who had no place and who would become a habitué of Boston (cf. his essay title, "Why a Pilgrim Traveled to Boston and His Improbable Arrival There").

Savage wrote, more than a few times, what it felt like. He damns Herndon in his harsh review of sordid gossip that swiftly replaces the town's momentary, dazed glance at local boy Gerry Sawyer's first novel within *The Liar:*

> He knew there were many who would twist the knife by asking questions, and then they would stop asking questions, and there would be some new thing, a knifing in the Cabbage Patch outside of town where old people visited each other in tar-paper shacks and went blind drinking wood alcohol or Sterno, a car full of people's friends rolling off into the river, the sudden disappearance of some woman nobody believed would disappear. Or the boy bound for Harvard who ended in state prison. The suicide of yet another minister, the exposure of another gentle old doctor as an abortionist. The public quarrel between two women at a cockfight—the larger and slower had got most of her left ear bitten or eaten off. How well he knew it all, the retired old ranchers grumping and complaining, sitting in the big green leather chairs of the Herndon House, angry deposed old kings . . . (*The Liar*, pp. 258–59)

Such harsh contempt, however true, didn't likely increase his local fan base: the usual risks many famous American writers have run. The contempt underlines Savage's conviction that he knows and demands more of his native region. His Savage West critiques popular tropes about the American West in myriad ways. It serves as a dissenting opinion against the usual triumphalist narratives, insisting as it does that it's rarely any happy story. Savage repeatedly wrote that scene of angry, bored old ranchers passing their days in the big hotel lobby as a shorthand indictment of deadening life in a Montana cow town. The lobby and the Cabbage Patch were real places through which Savage gleefully exposed the town's socioeconomic strata. The passage paints a grim picture with the same relish and effect as songwriter Tom Lehrer's sardonic song, "My Home Town." (1953)

Savage was *of* southwest Montana's old ranching culture but not *in* it, at least after 1937 and after his series of luxury sports cars. He'd long abandoned his transitory infatuation with the Brenner Ranch (1935). During his final visit home he recalled with unflinching gaze the caste system of agricultural Dillon: "the who's who of a ranching community is a rigid list confined to those who 'walk in the light'—those who own the most land and who have the oldest family names." ("Savage Comes Home Again," *Dillon Tribune Examiner,* April 20, 1983) In a newspaper profile published when *Power* appeared, Savage contrasts his native region with his adopted one:

> I have often thought...how curious it is that as much as I love the State of Maine I do not understand Maine well enough to write about it. I shall probably always write about the West which I do not love but thoroughly understand. The Western mentality has changed astonishingly little in the past forty years...the people who still count out there are the people who got there first, and own the land. (March 23, 1967)

Savage's condemnation of the rural West's ranching elite is as clear as his dim view of his remote roots. His candor shows his allegiance to that credo, write what you loathe, ingested from his old high school teacher, Miss Eastman. Yet as I've been claiming, Savage didn't *merely* despise his home turf: it was always more emotionally complicated for him and included an unquestioned imaginative loyalty.

The perceived indifference or scorn from the hometown was countered by family approbation, especially from Savage's mother and grandmother. After the publication of Sawyer's first novel, which confirms his status as a writer, his mother, Anne, tells him, "Darling, do you know you're the first one of any of us to be truly independent!" (*The Liar,* p. 217) By leaving ranching far behind yet imaginatively owning and repeatedly evoking it, Savage proved a match for the matriarch—and again, his fictional paraphrase closely matches the accord with which the Sheep Queen singled out her oldest grandson. Her fictional surrogate, Adele Burk, comments, "I always told you if you let him alone he'd amount to something and now it turns out he's the only one of the lot of us that really amounts to something and I'm not likely to forget it." (p. 259)

Yet *Main Street* proved but one model, and Savage, sympathetic as he was to the credo taught by Miss Eastman, also swore allegiance to Willa Cather's example in her frequent novelistic reworking of her hometown, Red Cloud, Nebraska. Savage paraphrased her credo: "Willa Cather says somewhere that we are most sensitive between the ages of eight and fifteen." (*Daddy's Girl*, pp. 10-11) Savage's allegiance to his youth includes much besides a scornful loathing of Hicksville. Savage's and Cather's conviction, coupled with his photographic memory, explains his obsessive recircling to his small-town Montana of the 1920s and 1930s. Certainly *The Liar* extends the town portrait of Herndon in *The Power of the Dog*, and *Midnight Line* does so even more.

The Liar (1969)

With *The Liar*, Savage stylistically experimented by omitting quotation marks. In his 1983 Dillon interview, he stated that with this novel, he wanted to "get a kind of linear feeling," without impeding the pace by graphically signaling speech.

In this novel the reader inevitably supplies what the writer omits. *The Power of the Dog* clearly loosed any constraints about using his family as the primary subject of the fiction. This sixth novel represents Savage's first clearly autobiographical novel, as the plot arcs from southwest Montana to Boston. Additionally, *Power's* Peter Gordon, who in many ways reflects Savage as boy then teenager (a stepson of the Brenner Ranch), reappears as Gerald/Gerry Sawyer, whom we follow from before birth through his early success as a novelist. "Sawyer" and "Savage," both trochees, bear more than a slight resemblance, and through the pattern of unchanged or related names Savage writes close to the bone.

The title character, Harold ("Hal") Sawyer, is based on Benjamin Harrison Savage, whom Savage saw intermittently at best, and whom the Yearians regarded as "all show and no go," a dud, the handsome failure who quoted Shakespeare and never developed any sustained career or decent income. In fact the dust jacket cover of the hardcover edition displays him: the quintessential "Arrow Collar Man," an oval within a rectangular frame. The silhouetted figure looks hard left, and a giant stickpin (with an oval ivory cameo, slightly blurred, on the end) thrusts itself diagonally through the high stiff wings of his white collar, behind the knot of his red bow tie. It looks uncomfortable, as though he's nearly impaled. Perhaps Savage's father felt impaled by the fond public gaze.

Perhaps Ben was gay despite his four marriages, as he's presented as a version of Charles Beach, the life partner of illustrator Joe Leyendecker who, after 1903, became the primary Arrow Collar Man and general model in all Leyendecker's art. In November–December 2019, a play about the Leyendecker-Beach liaison, *In Love with the Arrow Collar Man*, was produced in New York City.

Hal Sawyer lies about his career and prestige throughout his sporadic communications with his son. He isn't the only liar, however, as lying infects several family members including, near the climax, his son, Gerry. And Savage complicates the theme of lying in relation to personal integrity and manners: "most people's lying was just telling the truth too soon." (p. 58) In *The Liar* Savage writes his father's life story including his parents' failed marriage. It also presents the first fictional version of the Sheep Queen, matriarch Emma Russell Yearian, as Adele Burk, and his mother, Beth Brenner, appears more clearly as Anne Burk than she does in *Power*'s Rose Gordon. In many ways *The Liar* concerns the Adele-Anne, mother-daughter clash, a subject treated as well in *The Sheep Queen*. These two novels overlap considerably. The forceful female character Savage first wrote in protagonist Lona Hanson reappears in the Burks.

Savage's use of his "four BS," as mentioned earlier, confirms his Faulknerian project in recycling characters in his chosen setting of the ranching valley and the county seat, thereby creating a network of intertextual links. Savage politically teases old and contemporary Horse Prairie, Montana, by having "the Burbanks and the Barts, the Bonds and the Burks" "all Democrats"—Savage revered FDR, and Beaverhead County, Montana, has almost always voted Republican. And he satirizes the notion of good neighbors since "jealousy and rivalry," let alone Montana geography, keep them apart (p.76) though they sometimes meet in Savage's pages. For example, *Lona Hanson*'s Ruth Bart, "the alcoholic daughter of Old Tom" Bart, and her good-timing father, periodically resurface. Anne Burk Bond, an avatar of Ruth Bart, displays her alcoholism. (p. 185) Beth Bentley (*The Pass*), Ruth Bart, Rose Gordon, and Anne Bond, all variations of Beth Yearian Savage Brenner, manifest the abiding centrality of his mother—"my beautiful angel mother"—in the novelist's psyche.

And *Power's* Burbank brothers also return to the stage: "George was dull" and "Phil Burbank hated women" (p. 79), but Savage now conflates Burbanks with Bonds and George metamorphoses into Herb Bond, whom Anne marries after unceremoniously dumping handsome Hal. Additionally, the Gordons from *Power* briefly reappear, as Anne and Hal Sawyer spend their disastrous honeymoon night at the "Red Mill" in "Beech," where Rose and Peter still work in the dining room (i.e., the Inn at Armstead, Montana, p. 109).

The Burk Ranch is run down, shabby (pp. 88-89), opposite the actual Yearian Ranch, but they drive a Locomobile, the "Best Built Car in America": in the 1900s and 1910s, "one of the most expensive and elegant automobiles manufactured in the U.S." (In Savage's final novel, *The Corner of Rife and Pacific,* John Metlen extravagantly buys a Locomobile for son, Zach, upon the latter's college graduation, and Zach holds onto it even after the family's fortunes sink.) Adele Burk should own a top car: she writes with a mannish hand (p. 96), shorthand for her domineering personality and industry.

But Adele meets her match in Anne who will have her way in love: a contest of will replayed in *The Sheep Queen.* Savage imagines his own conception in painful, disappointing detail (p.111), Hal's failure to sexually perform well foreshadowing his overall failure as a husband. (pp. 122-23) Anne's swift disillusionment with sex and marriage forecasts Mary Skoning's in *For Mary, With Love.* (pp. 130-31) In *The Liar* Savage fancies his parents' marriage—Anne's whole reason for escaping the ranch and her bossy mother's reach—lasting less than a year rather than the six years (1911-17) Beth and Ben Savage were married, and producing one child (himself) rather than the actual two.

Additionally, Savage writes, for the first time, his own marriage and imminent family, with Helen Sawyer as a sympathetic first portrait of Betty Savage. This is new ground for Savage as an acutely autobiographical novelist, since he shifts closer to the present in his plot. In several novels hereafter, he fictionalizes his own family members and his essential conflict as a gay family man. He cross-references his childhood and adulthood obsessively.

In *The Liar* Savage again alters dates a few years to suit his aesthetic purposes (e.g., preserving the claims of fiction): a pattern he'll continue through his final novel. For example, Gerry Sawyer prepares for World War II enlistment as an officer, only to receive a deferral, and suddenly it's 1948 when Sawyer/Savage's "second book" is published; in 1942–43, Savage thought himself enlisted but received a deferral because of wife and two babies. (pp. 266–67) Similarly, he conflates the publication of Gerry Sawyer's first novel—a clear echo of *The Pass*'s publication (1944)—with Savage's second, with its "Twentieth Century Artists'" option for $47,500—Savage's slight rewrite of Columbia Pictures's $50,000 option (1948) on Savage's *Lona Hanson*. (p. 260)

Equally important in *The Liar*, Gerry Sawyer's emerging identity as writer, not changing his name in his juvenile stories (pp. 158–59: cf. Savage's habit of barely altering the historical record) clashes with the stigma of being a stepson. By birth a Sawyer (the young writer) yet passing as Bond loosens the anchor of genealogy: "He felt he stood naked and instinctively dropped his hands, as if protecting his private parts." (p. 185) Savage elaborates this fear of origins both for his long-lost sister, an adoptee, and himself in *The Sheep Queen*, virtually rewriting the same high school scene. (pp. 176–77)

The sense of being unmoored, without his birth father, haunts Sawyer as though he were emasculated: "I felt as if I were castrated." (cf. *Power*'s opening and Phil Burbank's symbolic self-emasculation) Helen reassures her fiancé, Gerry, in a telling passage:

> It's a wonder, he said, with that [his father's infidelity] and my stepfather, it didn't make me a homosexual.
> Well, she said, it didn't.
> I don't mind telling you, he said, it was awful. (pp. 218–19)

Through his protagonist, Savage doth protest too much. Of course a father's infidelity or a stepfather have no causal relation to the presence or absence of homosexuality. Neither Ben Savage nor Charlie Brenner engendered Tom Savage's gay self. Yet the protagonist's disclaimer slyly reveals the author. Savage glosses the illusion that heterosexual marriage and children altered his sexual orientation. He happily married and sired three children, but this indirect (i.e., character's) denial affirms Savage's sexual identity. Of course he wasn't *made* homosexual, he *was* homosexual, and he struggled the rest of his life with the demands of heteronormative life against his own true nature. The frequent, fleeting cameos of gay or lesbian characters in the 1970s novels proves as unsurprising as his steady condemnation of them: a familiar, "saving" habit of masking his own sexuality under the cover of the vulgarized Freudian conception of the etiology of homosexuality.

The Liar fast-forwards through the stock market crash, the Depression, Sawyer's courtship and marriage to Helen, World War II, and the birth of their first son, "Bozo" (Bob/Brassil Savage) in 1942. The novel climaxes with a father-son Christmas visit and reconciliation in which the younger Sawyer family carefully preserves the elder's façade of professional respectability—that, for example, Hal Sawyer (Ben Savage) was an important Seattle businessman with an office in "Pacific Towers," a thinly veiled Smith Tower, for generations Seattle's first and most elegant skyscraper. The façade props up old Hal, a bad Victorian actor. In fact "he was the editor of a whole string of trade journals; for the painters union" and others, Savage later stated ("Tom Savage and Betty Savage" interview, July 16, 1981): unglamorous stuff. At least Ben Savage's fourth wife, Dorothy Ritchie, lasted much longer than her predecessors, outliving her husband by fourteen years, not dying until 1985 (they're buried together in a Walla Walla, Washington, cemetery).

Two additional plot elements need comment because of their autobiographical basis. In the climactic scene between husband and wife, Helen confesses her rape, as a thirteen-year-old, by one of her "drunken father's" friends (p. 285): as close as Savage ever came to writing his wife's sexual abuse as a teenager at the hands of her father, a serious alcoholic as well as the writing teacher Savage most admired.

Perhaps more importantly, Gerry Sawyer's one-year affair with "Mimi," a groupie/fan who's actually named "Lois," represents Savage's first fictionalization of his Tomie dePaola affair earlier in the same decade. Sawyer ends the affair because of his sense of betrayal to his son even more than his wife: "The bad thing about illicit sex is how the image of your son will confront you and all you can say is,

Nobody's perfect." (p. 278) That the "illicit sex" was for Savage sex with another man fueled the theme of self-accusation swirling around the use of minor gay characters in the 1970s novels. Brassil Savage, it may be recalled, as a twenty-year old played a key role in Savage ending his affair with his lover in 1962. As will be seen, the accusation and guilt intimated here receive their most elaborate treatment in *A Strange God* (1974).

Although he claimed *The Liar* "not a very good book," Rollene W. Saal conceded, in a *Saturday Review* column, that "the author can write." (September 26, 1970) *The New York Times Book Review,* however, praised unstintingly: "*The Liar* works again and again because of his keen ear, his ability to convey meaning through physical details, and his mastery of intricate statement. A first-rate exploration of inevitability and humane wisdom"—the same note critic Roger Sale would strike four years later in his review-essay of Savage's career.

Daddy's Girl (1970)

Daddy's Girl, published just one year after *The Liar,* is a lesser novel but proved the first of three "frame" narratives (the others being *Her Side of It* and *For Mary, With Love*), or character studies. The titles of each belong to the framed protagonist. In each case, a male narrator chronicles and celebrates the life of an exuberant, extraordinary woman. In *Daddy's Girl* Chris, a stockbroker from Utah who "always wanted to write a book" (p. 9), tells the story of Marty Linehan, close college friend who's fatally generous with her body and any handy bottle. Both Linehan and Liz C. Phillips, protagonist of *Her Side of It,* suffer from terminal alcoholism. We learn from *The Sheep Queen* that Savage modeled Marty upon "one friend of mine now dead of alcoholism," from his Colby College days, who became a Boston socialite and who "was interested in local theater groups and played whoever it was in *The Philadelphia Story.*" (pp. 137-38) Her real name was Betty Beresford, and she presumably played the role of Tracy Lord, who lords it over at least the three principal men in that comedy. Lord resembles another strong Savage woman.

The novel's opening scene, a version of *The Sheep Queen*'s opening scene, describes the Savage's life at Georgetown Island's southern tip, halfway through their three decades there, in domestic detail (e.g., p. 197). Chris and Jane appear thinly disguised versions of Tom and Betty Savage, and Jane's snappy repartees are as recognizable as Helen Sawyer's in *The Liar*. Such details (e.g., keepsakes of their two sons or their classical music record collection, p. 4; or their original squabble about a bathtub, p. 226) offset the tragic arc of Marty's promiscuity and drunkenness.

Though the attention stays on Marty rather than Chris, Savage inevitably paints features of himself in Chris including his deep interest in sports cars (pp. 137, 225) and his increasing alcoholism (Chris is "showing serious signs of alcoholism," p. 137). Both Marty and, later, Liz Phillips (*Her Side of It*) serve as cautionary tales not only for their male narrators and admirers, but for Savage, who was described by more than one observer as a "functioning alcoholic"—whatever sliding scale or murky definition that depicts. Certainly Russell Savage and Ellie Savage Quigley have described Tom and Betty's heavy drinking in the 1960s and beyond. Savage has Chris state, "For ten minutes or so I will seriously consider giving up drinking forever, but I never had, because it's fun and the doctor told me the other day that what I drank wasn't hurting my system at all. In fact he said that it would be a serious mistake for me to suddenly stop drinking, something about my heart or metabolism." (p. 289)

The self-mocking rationale measures a narrowing gap between narrator and protagonist and rings more true than hyperbolic regarding Savage. The novel's penultimate chapter opens with Chris's declaration of alcoholism which sounds like painful authorial confession: "I drink 'on signal' as they put it, and my signal is the clock's striking five. Drinking, I tend to think; and sometimes I write down what I have thought. Sometimes I can't read the next day what I've written." (p. 292) Savage didn't wait until five o'clock. In *Midnight Line* Savage states, "On all sides you hear it said that there is nothing, absolutely nothing, worse than being saddled with an alcoholic partner" (p. 75), and there's more than a hint of accusation (re: Betty) and, more tellingly, self-accusation in that statement.

In addition to these autobiographical references, *Daddy's Girl* glances at the Brenner Ranch and Dillon cafés and whorehouses (pp. 22–26) as well as Tom Bart (*Lona Hanson*), Adele Burk (*The Liar*), and Herndon House (e.g., p. 66). Of more significance, this novel and those that follow include more sexual scenes and vocabulary (e.g., Marty's slow, luxurious blow job on Chris, pp. 99–102, or the word, "fuck") than Savage's earlier half dozen novels. Divided at the root as Savage was, in mid-career he glances more frequently and unflinchingly at sexuality even as he sustains his imaginative self-punishment—that harsh mode of masking—initiated with Phil Burbank's tragic, repressed life and horrific death in *Power*. He also punished himself by denying himself sex with men.

In a crucial early moment, Savage has Chris confess his failure to write the book he wanted, though of course he has produced, via his author, Marty's troubled biography: "I wanted to write about Marty and me, but I got started and then all the facts got jammed up and I couldn't sort them out, and I began to lie, and not tell the truth—not the truth about Marty, I told that straight enough—but the truth about me." (pp. 9–10) *Daddy's Girl* represents "the truth about Marty," but "the truth about" Chris—in many details, yet another representation of Savage— is unavailable. Chris's confession is Savage's, which glances back to that novel manuscript dissolved in the Atlantic several years earlier. It links directly to the two occasions—during his Dillon interviews (1983) and within his *Contemporary Authors* interview (January 11, 1989), published during his mid-seventies—when he speaks directly to his sexual orientation vis-à-vis his career. Nineteen years after *Daddy's Girl*, Savage unequivocally stated, "in fact, I have never written about myself truly except once," but the ghost novel was long sunk beneath the waves. In fact Savage wrote a series of self-portraits, beginning with *Power*'s Peter Gordon. But he never wrote "truly"—"the truth about me"—but once.

Instead, Savage wrote an extensive text seemingly condemning sexual minorities in his fiction, and in mocking, rejecting, or condemning gays or lesbians such as himself, he adhered to majority mores: those primary social expectations dictating family life according to parents of the opposite sex, for instance. This indictment, an apparent bid for conformity, indicts heteronormativity insofar as the majority culture is homophobic. During Chris's senior year in college, "a revealed homosexual left the [fraternity] house and college" after a ceremonial humiliation in which he stands naked amid a circle of accusers, "his hysterical voice in stuttering staccato": "the chief accuser stepped forward and slapped him against the side of his head so hard he fell forward and covered his head with his hands. I wonder what he told his parents, and how long before I forget his voice." (p. 54) Chris will always remember. The cost of coming out is clear, and Savage asserts that suppressed voice in protest. He despised such cruelty.

Late in *Daddy's Girl* Marty's husband, John Linehan, a "Catholic lawyer of good family," is dying and he demands details of Marty's legions of lovers. He's become a prurient, sadistic confessor, a nasty man who uses her confessions to sexually relieve himself. (p. 222) Chris admits, "It crossed [Marty's] mind that all along he may have been homosexual, maybe bisexual—all this interest in men." (p. 221) The dying husband's uncharacteristic vitriol is equated with being gay or "bisexual"—the first time Savage uses this term, one which he rejected, in old age in conversation with his daughter, about himself.

Savage scorns the mindset that believes sexual minorities have no place in the Intermountain West: "In Utah the postmistress had a woman living with her, simply described as her Friend, but there were whispers even out there where lesbians were not much believed in. The idea was too absurd." Chris parrots the rejection "even out there," but Marty offers a sympathetic voice: "'Hospitals are alive with homosexuality. The male nurses?. . . I think they're in there in self-sacrifice to atone for what they feel they are— monsters.'" (p. 78) The homophobic verdict and Savage's protest against it last the remainder of his career. In this novel, a pair of "twinsies" (the term used "before it was all right to be homosexual," p. 75: I've not found this connotation in a range of dictionaries) hail "from the Players' Group" and "flew in the face of a hostile, decent world by wearing matching jackets and ties" (p. 146). They and a "carrot-topped lesbian" form a recurring motif (pp. 229, 246) through whom Marty's warm-hearted acceptance and embrace gets measured against the "hostile, decent world" symbolized by Walter (Marty's longtime boyfriend, whom she dumps after his return from the war) and the mainstream. Savage is solidly aligned with Marty's generosity.

Even in an urban center like Boston, these minorities occupy

marginal positions: a theatrical troupe or "the Rendezvous," the increasingly raucous happy hour gang centered upon Marty. Her questioning
St. Paul's "attitude toward women" (p. 146) declares her independence,
but her promiscuity and alcoholism increasingly marginalize her from
the mainstream. These paired behaviors suggest a link, in Savage,
between alcoholism and sexual (or gender) nonconformity. Against
that "hostile, decent world," Chris cites the status of the Bloomsbury
Group and Somerset Maugham. He describes his mother-in-law's literary interests in Victoriana: "She dotes on biographies of Victoria, especially that 'humanizing' horror [*Queen Victoria,* 1921] by Lytton Strachey.
If she knew what I know about Lytton Strachey—the whole Bloomsbury
Group, for that matter." (p. 175) What Savage admires in the Bloomsbury
Group, his character criticizes in a smug whisper.

The implication is that the mother-in-law, voice of the mainstream, would condemn Strachey, E. M. Forster, and others including
Maugham if she knew their gay identities: she would take the author's
sexual biography as irrevocably tainting his intellectual and aesthetic
abilities. In suddenly invoking, earlier in the novel, Maugham, Savage
indicts all those who judge sexual minorities as "monsters": "Somerset
Maugham has said somewhere that if the world knew the truth about
him, the world would call him a monster—and yet, he said, he felt he
wasn't much different from anybody else." (p. 90) "The truth about"
Maugham implicitly glosses one truth about this American novelist he
never published—the "truth about me" that Chris, married and father
of sons, failed to write. (p. 10) Strachey, Maugham, all gay writers for
that matter, serve as beacons and, however variably, incisive criticisms
of those who, out of fear, judge sexual minorities as "monsters": that old
badge for demonizing the other. The overtly homophobic condemnation
of Phil Burbank in *Power,* an implicit condemnation of homophobia,
becomes in the 1970s novels, at least in moments, a vehicle for criti-
cizing the mainstream. That essayistic aside forms both code and plea
from Savage, who knows he'll never gain the sales or reputation of a
Strachey or a Maugham and who sardonically accuses the "decent"
world "tainted" by its hostility to sexual minorities.

A Strange God (1974)

In an essayistic aside in the middle of *A Strange God*, Savage's next novel, protagonist Jack Reed expresses his discomfort with gays, cross-dressers, and female impersonators—"caricatures of women": "They couldn't help it anymore than he could help things—who in God's name would *prefer* to be that way? Nevertheless, such men made him uneasy. He didn't know what was required of him, in their company." (p. 152) Savage ironically evokes the majority's discomfort. Through Jack's unease Savage protests the imaginative and moral failure of heteronormativity to understand minority sexual desire. Reed dismisses a client, his dentist, at a lunch date: "'I'm a homosexual.' 'What can I do about that?' 'Nothing,' the man had said. 'I see that now.'" (p. 152) For that dentist, a member of Savage's tribe who wanted sympathy if not more, confession and rejection occupy the same space. "What was required," presumably, is something other that blunt dismissal; rather, acceptance from the heterosexual mainstream.

Chris and Jane of *Daddy's Girl* are friends with the Reeds, the central family grimly anatomized in *A Strange God*. In fact three of the four Reeds visit them at their Crow Point home while on a Maine coast property hunt, not unlike the Savages in the mid-1950s (pp. 90–101). Further, Chris serves as Jack's stockbroker, sounding board, and cultural advisor. For example Chris, querying Jack whether he's ever read F. Scott Fitzgerald's novels, declares "'It's un-American not to read them, like not having life insurance. Sometimes you remind me of a Fitzgerald character.'" Chris enjoins him to "'Read *The Great Gatsby* sometime,'" and Reed reads it and many of Fitzgerald's published letters to Zelda after her institutionalization. (p. 160)

Savage thus coyly advertises his protagonist and intention in his eighth novel, which reads in some respects as his adaptation of *Gatsby*. The Rocky Mountain West recedes behind the Midwest, home territory for Jack Reed (i.e., a town "just west of Chicago") and Jay Gatz. Nick Carraway is implicitly attracted to Gatsby; similarly Chris, a narrator, may be attracted to glamorous Jack. In both cases, men who hail from the provinces try to make it big in cultural and financial capitals, Boston and New York City, respectively. Reed, like Gatsby, obscures elements of his past or lies about his pedigree (e.g., his fake middle initial, "w," and a University of Chicago degree rather than the state university from which he graduated). Further, Jack drives Cadillacs: in Savage's car iconography, scornful mark of pretenders and bad symbol. He's owned a series, the latest sporting "a custom, handpainted monogram." (pp. 69–71)

These trappings mark his outer success, yet the financial success and material prosperity (e.g., "their big white house on the Wellesley line," in Boston) spell his decline and fall. Successful businessman, Jack represents "the ignorant rich" and appears as a fake, seduced by self-delusion and fatally drawing wife, daughter, and son into this preferred image of ideal nuclear family moving upward from the middle class. Jack has withheld his love from his long-suffering wife, Norma, who knows she trapped him into marriage (pp. 67, 242). Perhaps in moments, Savage felt as though heterosexual marriage had trapped him away from his real self. Additionally, Jack has been overbearing with their teenage daughter, Martha, placing her in St. Margaret's Hall prep school, and his son, Tim, whom he's placed in Harvard (p. 145)—just as Savage had steered his older son, Brassil, into Harvard, where he flunked out. Certainly Jack and Norma have their share of marital spats, usually fueled by excessive drinking (pp. 114, 181, 308), as though they're Shady Hill neighbors in John Cheever's Westchester County (New York) short stories. Or Tom and Betty Savage in Georgetown, Maine.

Jack has proven fatally directive with daughter and son, not allowing them room for their own identities to emerge. Those tendencies separate him from Gatsby and underline Savage's primary interest, family life, which he faulted Fitzgerald for not foregrounding. Certainly the novel presents a Freudian anatomy of father-daughter closeness drawn from life. After all, he and Betsy, his daughter—a Daddy's Girl and this novel's dedicatee—maintained a strong and intimate bond throughout their lives, Betsy serving as primary caretaker in his old age. The real bond was far healthier than Jack's relationship with Martha. Betrayal and a need for atonement haunt the novel. Jack's affair with Claire, "the [attractive] wife of his client," lasts one year, exactly echoing Gerry Sawyer's infidelity in *The Liar*.

Now, however, the protagonist and family are older, and son Tim, Harvard freshman, catches the "two middle-aged lovers" in the act in the family dining room, which ends the affair. (pp. 199–202) Recall that Brassil Savage had similarly discovered his father with Tomie dePaola in dePaola's Boston apartment one night in 1962, which resulted in physical violence. Thereafter Tim stays away from home, sheltering himself at Harvard. When he receives a fancy birthday cake from his father, he hurls it against the wall. In Brassil's unpublished novel manuscript, "Twenty" (1966), his autobiographical protagonist, Alex, does the same thing in his Harvard room when the birthday cake arrives. Clearly, Brassil had thrown a birthday cake delivered from his father.

Jack's affair is exactly matched by daughter Martha's affair with Vincent ("Vinnie") De Leo, a blue-collar guy who's many years older than she. Jack's intersession fails: "the pedestal from which he had once spoken as a good father and honest husband had been chipped away by deceit, self-indulgence and guilt. Even as he spoke his words rang false and hollow and stupid in his head." (p. 192) Pregnant, Martha gives up her baby in Boston for adoption, drops out of Smith College, and moves to Denver for a new job and life. Martha's liaison symbolically echoes and rebukes her father's, which of course threatened to fracture the family. In this fictive version of himself as a father, Savage construes his extramarital affair with young dePaola as no different than a heterosexual affair.

The two extramarital affairs, coupled with the horrific climax of Jack accidentally shooting and killing his son (mistaken, on a drunken Christmas Eve, as a prowler), measure the collapse of family. Having been estranged from his father and past, Tim tries to make his way back to the "big white house," this time with far more fraught consequences. In a certain sense De Leo proves an older version of dePaola. "Vinnie" and "Tomie" represent more Savage near-names: the former, more than a decade older than Martha, his girlfriend, just as the latter was two decades younger than Savage. Both affairs are not only extramarital but now equivalent.

Middle-aged Jack's affair, like the younger Gerry Sawyer's in *The Liar*, again intimates Savage's self-punishment in earlier abandoning wife and kids. After all, Brassil had intervened to end his father's

liaison with dePaola at almost the precise age that Tim Reed, another
young Harvard man, catches his father and subsequently stays away,
self-destructing at school. In *A Strange God*'s climax, an Oedipal scene,
the father eliminates the son as potential competitor or threat—except
that Jack had never pledged himself entirely to Norma. He remains
torn between family loyalties and the lure of his lover: a recapitulation
of Savage's desertion of family in 1961–62. Yet Tom and Betty Savage
expressed deep, childlike devotion to one another, as Russell Savage
describes it, but their interdependency never changed Savage's fundamental, psychic division.

So *A Strange God*, a painful excavation of betrayal and guilt, served
as well as a kind of offering, an atonement. Upon its publication, dra-
matist and memoirist Harding Lemay glossed it: "the inarticulate pain
of parenthood is dreadfully hard to convey to anyone who hasn't suffered through it, but Savage conveys that fabric of guilt, foreknowledge
of loss and failure, and sweet sadness better than I have ever found it
in any other novel" (quoted on inner dust jacket, hard-cover edition).
Parenting, of course, opens wide an unanticipated range of potential
(or actual) failure and guilt, and Savage, who knew a special kind of
betrayal and guilt, keeps the reader on the rack. In the opening chapter, Jack has concocted a suicide plan, and "No matter what his actions
had been, he had clung to his puritanical, Midwestern code of ethics
that. . .ruled out suicide as cowardly and shameful. Therefore, his
self-destruction must appear to be an accident." (p. 293) Even in his
self-destruction Jack conforms to his past, giving the lie to suicide
because of that social "code."

After the mythic son-killing, Jack beats himself up mercilessly. He
knows that "people do get punished," that "the waters of punishment,
the final offshore wave, would crash in and cover him." (p. 172) He
deems himself a "tragedy" (p. 270), the "living dead, [who] like ghosts,
have no comfortable place on earth, and there is no hiding." (p. 275)
That "code of ethics" has removed him from society: "As a man who had
destroyed a child he had become an outlaw, a kind of pervert. Nothing
normal would ever be expected of him again." (p. 273) The protagonist's
self-laceration measures, to some extent, the verdict rendered against
sexual minorities in this country. The implied castigation is severe, as if

being gay—one version of "pervert"—removes one beyond the pale, the "normal": that "hostile, decent world" governed by "puritanical, Midwestern [or Rocky Mountains] code[s]."

Ultimately a random phone call rescues Jack from the "Presence" of death (i.e., completed suicide) as, in his living room, site of betrayal and shame, he reluctantly returns to living, the props of his constructed identity still intact ("John W. Reed") though now he'll live constantly indicted by his "hale-fellow, well-met" façade. (p. 310) The whimsical irony of a ringing phone pulls Jack back from the last edge. *A Strange God* reaches a darker conclusion that Savage ever would allow himself again. Death is preferable to death-in-life,

> A pit dug by a strange god, a sink hole fetid with the stench of life, crawling with matter bent on the obscene quest for money, position and orgasm. Each creature was a threat to another, each birth an occasion for future shame or sorrow. Each death brought into question the value of life.
>
> Oh Christ! If he were God, had made God's mistakes but had the power to correct them! (p. 309)

With Savage's penchant for titles drawn from the Old Testament (*Trust in Chariots, The Power of the Dog, The Liar*), it's no surprise to discover "a strange god" comes from there, as it's used in at least four places (Psalms 44:20, Jeremiah 5:19, Daniel 11:39, Malachi 2:11), and it generally spells doom for the people of Israel who have lost their way, strayed from God's path. This horrific nadir—that life is a quivering cesspool, akin to philosopher Thomas Hobbes's famed verdict as "nasty, brutish, and short"—is matched by Jack's baleful view of human isolation: "we know we are all ultimately alone, born alone, live alone and die alone, and that all human relationships sooner or later result in a dangerous tampering with somebody's mind or heart. The most dangerous tampering of all was marriage." (p. 308)

This vision aligns with Savage's view of hell that he takes from Dostoyevsky (cited in his April 1983 Dillon, Montana, interviews): that inability to give or receive love. Jack's bleak, stripped-down assessment was not his author's, of course, except in his darkest moments. Savage's next two novels variably affirm the centrality of family even as the meaning of family is unpredictably stretched. Yet the "most dangerous tampering" Jack barely survives represents, in some respects, the "tampering" Savage forced upon Betty and the kids a dozen years earlier—and, in a broader sense, the "tampering" Savage experienced all his life from the pressures of heteronormativity.

In a July 1974 letter to friends, Savage wrote "I already have the advance reviews [of *A Strange God*]—Kirkus report and Publishers Weekly, and they're the best I've ever had." In his *Hudson Review* profile, critic Roger Sale, long a Savage champion, stated "*A Strange God* is that rare thing, a novel of domestic life that seems without extending the bounds of the ordinary to encompass deep understanding of how life is, what makes it happen as it does."

CHAPTER FIVE

Savage at Zenith, 1976–1981

THREE OF SAVAGE's half dozen novels published during his most productive period, while primarily set in Boston or Maine, reveal western roots. Chris from *Daddy's Girl* hails from Utah's Wasatch Front; Tom Westbrook (*Midnight Line*) and both Bill Reese and Liz C. Phillips (*Her Side of It*) come from Montana, Tom and Bill from Herndon (now called "Grayling," named after a nearby railroad siding); Jack Reed (*A Strange God*) is the only protagonist not from the Intermountain West: from the vantage of Boston, an exotic if not inconceivable background. As a midwesterner, however, he remains very much an outsider. All these characters recapitulate Savage's own journey, as a young man, from remote rural spaces to the cultural capital of New England. Yet in *Midnight Line* the plot arcs reverse, moving increasingly westward, from Boston back to Grayling, Montana, as Westbrook's past eclipses his present. The Intermountain West remained Savage's pole star, his primary literary region.

Savage remained surprisingly loyal to his first geography, southwest Montana, just as he consistently wrote variations of himself as outsider, as novelists often do. After all, he made a habit of simultaneously belonging and not belonging wherever he was. Gerry Sawyer (*The Liar*) is born two years after Savage, Bill Reese (*Her Side of It*) is born within a year of Savage, and both Jack Reed (*A Strange God*) and *Midnight Line*'s Tom Westbrook—Savage's first "Tom" since *Lona Hanson*'s Tom Bart—are born the same year as Savage (1915). That fact alone sustains the notion of protagonists serving, variably, as authorial surrogates, embodiments of differing versions of Savage.

While Savage kept alive a gay conversation in the corners of his novels, gay and lesbian literature burst into the open in the 1970s with such celebrated novels as *The Front Runner* (1974) and *The Fancy Dancer* (1976) by fellow Montanan, Patricia Nell Warren. Like Savage, Warren came from a ranch, the well-known Grant-Kohrs Ranch in Deer Lodge, Montana, and like Savage she'd left it long behind. William Morrow, who would become Savage's final publisher, brought out these gay love stories. In a 1994 commemorative edition of the former, Tyler St. Mark of Wildcat Press wrote, "Twenty years later *The Front Runner* has been reprinted in numerous editions, sold an estimated ten million copies, and been translated into seven languages . . . [it] continues to be one of the top-selling gay novels, and is thought by many to be the most celebrated novel about gay love ever written."

The Front Runner references the Stonewall uprising and anticipates initial legal challenges to anti-sodomy laws (with a predictable anti-gay backlash). Early in the story, protagonist Harlan Brown, who's tried and failed (heterosexual) marriage, thinks, "Sometimes I wondered if that peculiar American hatred of homosexuality isn't a result of its being so rooted, so silent and unacknowledged, yet so pervasive, in our history." (p. 34) Warren thus glosses a primary emphasis of the brilliant critic, Leslie Fiedler, who consistently argued that homoeroticism comprises the core of American literature. In this light, Savage and his fiction are mainstream, not marginal. Harlan's marriage ceremony with his protégé and lover, Billy, precisely recalls Tom Savage and Tomie dePaola exchanging rings in their private Episcopal chapel ceremony: "Few straights can comprehend the gay's hunger for dignity and stability. I can't begin to explain what that little ceremony meant to us both." (p. 192)

The real Tom-Tomie liaison was far more fragile than the fictitious Harlan and Billy's marriage. More significantly, Savage never touched Warren's popular success, only a decade separating his suppressed gay novel from her game-changing one. But his gay conversation continued in his fiction, however quietly.

Midnight Line (1976)

In a letter to his literary agent, Savage described his next novel with an earlier, working title: "My new book, TALK SHOW, will take place within the space of a few weeks, and I'll have a chance at all the drunks, insom-niacs and the desperate and the lonely who call in with their problems as a background for what I believe to be a very strong story." (June 11, 1975)

Author and protagonist share the same age and common origins in Grayling/Dillon, Montana, including a consuming desire to leave it far behind (p. 73) and a love of sports cars (e.g., Westbrook has owned an MG and a Jag, p. 9). Host of a popular midnight-6:00 a.m. talk show on WBOT heard in thirty-eight states, Westbrook stands, among the com-munity of "talkmasters," as the "greatest of them all." He becomes big just as the talk radio format, which first emerged during World War II, further spread to big cities (i.e., 1970s); in the decade following *Midnight Line* into the mid-1990s, "the number of radio stations in the U.S. fea-turing talk radio quadrupled." (www.encyclopedia.com) In retrospect, Savage/Westbrook is a bellwether. No polemicist, Westbrook serves as high priest officiating over an on-the-air confessional, anonymous yet intimate, and he regards his callers as his "children." (p. 66) After all, in the middle of the night most of us lack filters or distractions and confront, or are confronted by, parts of our past or present the day's noise masks. Such introspection or self-assessment leads some to need a voice, a helpline. On his "midnight line" Westbrook acts as sounding board, counselor, and advice columnist on top of his game.

Back in Grayling Westbrook savored, as did Savage, the (courthouse clock) strike of "the Three Ones": 12:30, 1:00, and 1:30 a.m., a recurring motif. For Westbrook, this represents "an hour when he felt most him-self" (p. 77); for Savage, after 1:30 a.m. it's soon time for Mozart, then work at the typewriter.

Soured from a two-year marriage—another negative verdict on marriage (cf. *Trust in Chariots*)—and apparently sterile (pp. 62-63), Westbrook leads a private, fastidious life, trying to take stock yet aware that his life is dull, pointless. (p. 13) Savage ironically sets up this Tom for the fall, as his too comfortable, too hermetic present is increasingly punctured by "the Voice," this novel's primary motif and enactment of guilt. Savage mocks Westbrook's notion of independence: "For more than twenty years now, Westbrook had been followed—dogged—by a shadow that insisted he was a man who had always been free to act exactly as he wished." (pp. 37–38) That "shadow" proves illusory, as *Midnight Line* opens out like an Ibsenian drama wherein the past progressively reveals itself and buffets characters in their present. In Savage's deterministic version, "the Voice," a regular caller, gradually discloses the story of Westbrook's having a son out of wedlock (cf. Martha Reed's illegitimate child in *A Strange God*) who, now adult and with no father, faces trouble. "The Voice" needles the protagonist, a steady anonymous chorus of accusation—of being found out and revealed—providing the novel's plot and tension. He pushes this confessor to face his own past.

So *Midnight Line* sustains *A Strange God*'s laser focus upon shame, this protagonist in his monkish present forced to deal, like Jack Reed, with the consequences of an affair. "Tom West," with a "Brook" running through him in Boston, is clearly an avatar of Tom Savage in northern New England. Westbrook "goes West," returns to his surname and relives his childhood and young adulthood in the small-town Intermountain West. In the process the novel's setting shifts back to Savage's Dillon. In fact *A Midnight Line,* along with his final novel, represents Savage's most detailed, most relentless portrait gallery of his hometown. As is his habit of generously fusing fiction with historical fact, Savage doesn't change or barely changes names.

Midway through *Midnight Line,* in another "little essay," the narrator concludes, as though in response to Jack Reed, "Suicide is no good, for that is death": "Eventually we come to accept things we once swore we could not accept—the drunken wife, the drugged child, homosexuality, constant pain, poverty and shame." (p. 170) Excepting "constant pain" and "poverty," this roll call variably describes the Savages: Betty's (and Tom's) excessive drinking, Brassil's alcoholism and paranoid schizophrenia, and Tom's homosexuality, about which his sons were not exactly accepting because of his betrayal over a decade earlier. Loyal to their mother, Betty, they'd watched Tom tear apart the family's fabric. The note of resigned acceptance if not shame marks another indirect confession by the author.

Westbrook—likely a repressed gay man, a middle-aged version, in his fussy habits and dress, of *Power*'s Peter Gordon— represents the apparent end of "the oldest [family] in town" whose seat was "the old Westbrook Mansion"—in fact, Dillon's Poindexter-Orr Mansion. In this light he superficially resembles Hanno Buddenbrooks from Thomas Mann's *Buddenbrooks*. His family's story weaves threads from the Yearians including "the annual trip to the ghost town" (pp. 88–92), the originary gold scene written in *Lona Hanson* and *The Sheep Queen,* and the Brenners, and it overlaps with that of the fictitious Barts (*Lona Hanson*) as well. Westbrook, who'd discovered his father a philanderer like Jack Reed (pp. 89–90), inherits an heirloom "[solid gold] watch . . . and ambition and a name." (p. 93) Savage hammers his old anti-foundational theme, as the ranch dynasty yields no land, no money, and few prospects; instead, it erodes or destroys people.

Out of the old tale of decline and fall enumerated in *Lona Hanson,* young Westbrook finds himself stuck at "the normal school" which is "a last-ditch try," a "perfectly nothing" place (and my employer for many years): "The normal school was to be a four-year college. Failing that, it now trained young women and a very few young men who could not hope to be more than teachers. Teachers were not highly thought of in Grayling; women not attractive enough to marry became teachers; men not aggressive enough to succeed in business or having no prospect of inheriting land became teachers. Both groups were unfulfilled." (p. 94) They were marginalized as though sexual minorities—the implication being that some were lesbian or gay men. But then, Grayling's "Puritan ethic" ruled out higher education for the most part: "further study was presumptuous. What more did a man need to run a ranch, what more to sell sacks of feed, what more to distribute Ford cars about the country." (p. 93) The Lewisian scorn manifest in *Power* is sustained here and in later novels.

Because of Hicksville's baleful legacy, "Westbrook could not look back on Grayling, Montana, without a desire to 'get even.'" (p. 107) That notion of revenge sustains Savage's assessment of his hometown in this novel marked by his car iconography. "Peacock Alley" displays "the Packards and the Lincolns . . . parked out front" of the Andrews Hotel—Dillon's Andrus Hotel, the town's leading hotel for generations. As such, its dining room and bar ("lounge"), a magnet, drew the town's so-called elite. Tom Westbrook didn't park the family Chevrolet in Peacock Alley: "The Andrews Hotel explained Westbrook's later affection for the Hotel Pierre in New York and his 'dinners' at the Ritz in Boston.

The old Chevrolet explained his Jaguar, and Skeet's Bar explained his parking it at fashionable curbs." (p. 105) Young Westbrook, like young Savage, wanted out and lands in Boston. Tom Savage patronized this local bar and these two luxury hotels. He likely parked his Rolls-Royce in front of the Andrus when he returned home with his family in the early 1950s. Again, the series of luxury sports cars measured his sexual and psychological separation from the majority who conform and judge with equal energy.

But that revenge motive also describes any outsider, whether a future writer or not, who feels marginalized and ridiculed in what feels like the hostile, hermetic atmosphere of small-town USA—Sinclair Lewis's Carol Kennicott, in *Main Street*, dying on the vine in "Gopher Prairie" (i.e. Sauk Centre), Minnesota.

In *Midnight Line* Maxine Gates, Westbrook's girlfriend and counter-balance to Grayling's perceived hostility, proves open-hearted in her love, and after impregnating her Westbrook lies about borrowing money (from his two-timing father) for an abortion, then suffers her accusations. (pp. 135–36) The remainder of the novel exposes West-brook's lie and cowardice: the heterosexual commonplace of the male walking away once the female is pregnant. She dies in childbirth (p. 139) and "the Voice" steadily discloses Westbrook's responsibilities to his son briefly jailed then working night shifts in a gas station, where he is shot (pp. 228, 238, 262): "It was insane that the Voice should borrow her old anger, harbor it, cherish it, make a career of it and stalk a man who had done his level best to be of use to other people." (p. 137) This "Agenbite of inwit," an externalization of guilt, tutors Westbrook in his complic-ity and responsibility, and prods him, by the end, to fly home to find his son, just as he's imaginatively traveled west through his past (incl. Maxine) left long behind. As Roger Sale observed in that review-essay quoted earlier, there is no escaping, for a Savage protagonist, the fine mesh of one's fate.

In this novel Savage confirms his unfolding oeuvre though an inter-textual conversation, above all a reuse of characters or incidents in subsequent novels, and he nods at four of his earlier books. After West-brook parked his Jaguar "in front of the old gray stone church on [Bos-ton's] Bowdoin Street," *A Bargain With God*'s Father Ferris reappears, hitting Westbrook up for a $75 donation for a parishioner in trouble. (pp. 145–47). Savage again references Dr. Johnny Gordon's suicide, fruit of his sense of inadequacy and Phil Burbank's humiliation and shaming, from *Power* (p. 80), and both Miss Eastman and "old Jerry Burk" (from *The Liar*) briefly resurface. (pp. 77–78, 105) Adele Burk (*The Liar*) and the Burbanks (*Power*) offset the Hales, lead ranch family in *Midnight Line*. (p. 256) Further, Savage briefly recapitulates *A Strange God*'s plot, as Jack Reed appears among the guests at Westbrook's first New Year's Eve party, and Westbrook later thinks about Reed's accidental homicide. Rejecting the impulse "to intrude on another's tragedy," he "wondered if sometimes pride or the horror of being pitied makes a brother wish to be his own keeper, and alone." (pp. 242–43) Savage's Jack Reed must live with killing his son; Tom Westbrook must live with finding his son and drawing him close, since "the Westbrook line" has not ended.

That intertextuality à la Faulkner or Doig marks, in some respects, Savage's self-conscious confidence in his fictive world, however slightly veiled. Of equal weight, his Savage West, even in New England, demonstrates a continuing debate about social space for sexual minorities: an important sidebar in most of the 1970s novels. Gay characters keep appearing in the corners, usually to be condemned—the measure of Savage's continued self-accusation and habit of protecting himself, as with other gay men who married, according to the dictates of the majority. But by the 1970s, of course, a nascent gay rights movement steadily gained numbers and attention and, in some circles, increasing respect.

The first of four references to homosexuality summarizes even as it advances Savage's textual debate, over several novels, about the status of sexual minorities such as himself. Through his headline caption, "TOM WESTBROOK'S TALK SHOW SLAUGHTERS A SACRED COW," Savage airs a literal conversation about gay men, thus broadcasting, in miniature, his private turmoil. If Westbrook is likely a gay man—his brief marriage having left a bad taste (cf. Harlan Brown's first marriage in P. N. Warren's *The Front Runner*)—as a popular talk show host, he'd advocate for a forum that critiques the majority position about sexual minorities. An early "Midnight Line" program focuses upon homosexuality: "for the first time in radio history the word was thrown out over the air...heard in thirty-eight states. It pried up a stone and out from underneath something pale and terrible crawled forth into the sunlight visible even to the chaste eyes of Middle America." (p. 34) This is an historic claim Savage fictionalizes. The metaphor betrays Savage's scorn and anger. He ironically chastises those "chaste eyes" even as, in the ensuing, anonymous conversation, he presents the debate about gay men and the anxieties, in the 1970s, of the "middle" class. The scene, with anonymous callers identified only by a letter, calls out and reproaches the heterosexual majority: the real "something [both] pale and terrible" who insistently polices and condemns difference.

While "Mr. A" and "Mrs. B" are homophobic, "Mr. C" challenges "Mr. A's" violence ("he would knock his teeth out") just as "Mrs. D" counters "Mrs. B's" loathing (i.e., "she'd rather see [her son] dead"). A pair of psychiatrists face off, "Mr. F" claiming he'd "successfully treated...a number of homosexuals...[who] had married. He saw no reason for people to remain homosexuals. If they did, it was perverse of them..." (p. 34) The other psychiatrist ("Mr. G") dismisses Mr. F's treatments and claim, arguing "deviants could no more be changed than the color of their eyes could be changed, that marriage was no escape and only compounded the tragedy and often led to suicide..." The heteronormative positions of these so-called professionals ("perverse," "deviant"), following the popularized distortion of Freud's analysis of homosexuality which claims it a pathology, is then challenged by "the Love that dare not speak its name [which] was itself—speaking." (p. 35)

Savage thus cites Lord Alfred Douglas's famous poem, "Two Loves" (1894), in which the "pallid youth" replies to the other youth, "Have thy will, / I am the love that dare not speak its name." Parts of this poem were quoted and discussed at Oscar Wilde's homosexuality trial (1895) in London's Old Bailey. Clearly, Savage was conversant with Wilde's case: perhaps the most famous prosecution of a gay writer in modern history. "Two Loves" exposes a feeling of shame endemic to gay men who, for example, guard their identity and desire through heterosexual marriage. Wilde, like Savage, was married and the father of two sons.

When Savage's "queers called in" to Westbrook's show, he broadbrushes the childhood and adolescence of gays whose pleasures and differences are subsumed by fear—the label of "'Sissy!'" which *Power's*

Peter Gordon is called—since "the mob recognized them before they recognized themselves in the failure at games and their running from fights, their unaccountable interest in fabrics and in flowers." (p. 35) That is, they fail to perform according to normative gender roles. Savage closes the scene by countering the gay voices, and "Mr. X's" quick testimony as a gay man, with "Mrs. S" the fearful voice of the majority who cites the Kinsey Report's finding that "one in seven was queer": "Whom could you trust to be not queer? When seven men gathered together in a room or on the subway, one of them was queer. No one could be trusted. Why, Mr. Z had been married twenty years, had three daughters and a son, and no one knew but his lover." (p. 36)

Except that "Mr. Z" has been found out, and that's the point. The quick "horrified" sketch of "Mr. Z" comes as close as Savage ever came in his fiction to acknowledging his affair with dePaola years earlier: the difference being that all his family knew about Tom's lover. The Yearians had accepted Tom's "friend." In Westbrook's TALK SHOW the testimony of gay "Love," framed as it is by persecution, is succeeded by the deep-rooted fear and anxiety of the majority captured by "Mrs. S." This almost hysterical paranoia directed against sexual difference was brilliantly theorized by gay and lesbian historians from the 1970s on. In the "majority rules" perspective of "Mrs. S," anything other than absolute heterosexual conformity, according to patriarchal culture, deserves censure or more. In this mindset, "Mr. Z" and his secret gay life—the alphabet's tag end—is inconceivable. Back in 1962 Savage had made a choice and tried to conform to the "either/or" binary code, as though gay life completely precludes family; bisexuality was not an option in his worldview and even in so-called private life, it existed only to be spied and stamped out.

Midnight Line's other references sustain the prevailing view of "Mrs. S," one that rejects the protest of "the Love that dare not speak its name." That love must be met with silence, disapprobation, and more. Westbrook doesn't worry that his Grayling, Montana, son cohabits with a man in a trailer since "the Voice" speaks of "they" and "they" doesn't mean a gay couple, "unless the Voice meant to suggest homosexuality and that was impossible because to that class from which the Voice came sexual deviation as a subject of conversation was taboo." (p. 179) "The Voice," parroting the second psychiatrist ("Mr. G"), speaks the usual chorus of accusation, the "taboo" of silence measuring the tyranny of the taboo against the minority.

In the novel's late taxonomy of "special-interest bars" in Boston, gay bars prove a rare haven:

> In the one are long glances and posings, exaggerations and compulsive superlatives. A transcript of the speech of homosexuals would reveal the underscoring of key words, but not the characteristic hiss of the sibilant. There are no social, religious or color barriers; homosexuals have little in common but their preference for the same sex, Tiffany glass and certain actresses whom they envy. (p. 245)

This foray into sociological field studies represents the first mention in Savage's fiction of a safety zone where gay men thrive. Clearly Savage knew of these "special-interest bars." Only in such rare domains can that repressed "Love" flourish without persecution. Such social space, removed from the streets, constitutes a grudging concession in a world dominated by "Mrs. S." The passage describes a style and place where fastidious Westbrook would never tread, whatever his desire.

After all, in *Midnight Line*'s penultimate chapter Westbrook turns down a gay encounter that suggests a recognition scene. A man has slipped into his bar booth, and Westbrook lights his cigarette and concedes his own loneliness: "'And I have a place to go,' the man said. For a second their eyes were locked. The man smiled faintly. Westbrook clicked the Zippo shut. Now he understood. 'I'm sorry,' he said. 'I'm waiting.' 'Yes,' the man said. 'We wait, don't we.'" (p. 255) Westbrook rebuffs the stranger's recognition as he waits the promptings of conscience and gathers his energies to fly home into his past and accept filial identity—and a possibly gay son. Savage's protagonist "belonged nowhere, neither at the Ritz nor at the Hotel Andrews in Grayling, Montana" (p. 247): another criticism of the heterosexual "norm," as if Westbrook lives in exile from both his past and his present. Similarly, he lives between celibacy and those gay bars he lacks the courage to enter. Grayling's courthouse tower bell and the "Three Ones," a Savage leitmotif, toll him home because "the bell had told him what the Voice had not." (p. 273) He gathers his resolve and acts to integrate past and present, having thrown off that shadow and rediscovered purpose in his life.

In his laudatory review in the *Washington Post*'s "Book World," Jonathan Yardley calls *Midnight Line* "a good read," as it possesses "all the elements of superior fiction." Further, he judges it "an intensely 'American' novel, with a keen sense of locations and dislocations that are uniquely American." He also praises Savage's integrity in familiar fashion: "Savage stubbornly refuses to be 'commercial'" since "There are no easy answers in his novels" (February 7, 1976). Yardley, a steady cheerleader, precisely forecasts the Savage literary credo with which he opens his next novel (quoted earlier): "There is no ending, happy or otherwise, only a slight pause." (*Sheep Queen*, p. 3)

□ □ □

Savage's "high tide" is marked by the fact that twice—in 1969 and 1970, and again in 1976 and 1977—he published novels two years in a row. Typical of his speed, in an undated 1970s letter to agent Blanche Gregory he conceded, "I write so fast now it couldn't possibly take me more than six months to finish a first draft."

I Heard My Sister Speak My Name
[The Sheep Queen] (1977)

Tom Westbrook's imaginative then (implied) literal return to his roots likely prompted Savage to imaginatively return home more acutely than he ever had. In a letter to his cousin, Ralph Nichol, written in old age, Savage remarked, "[*Sheep Queen* is] a good book for the relatives to read, to know who and what we are and were." (July 1, 2000) That confession captures the insistent portrait of extended family that comprises Savage's tenth novel: one that adheres so close to fact that it proves an endlessly rich biographical source, as I have shown.

In a letter to a fan near the time of its publication, Savage held high hopes: "This book might succeed because of all this ROOTS business and the recent interest in identities." Alex Haley's novel (1976) and the television miniseries adaptation (1977) changed television history, as is well known. More crucially, Savage admits to this admirer, "My new novel is not really a novel at all, but mostly the truth." (June 3, 1977) That claim, as though historical truth—fact—exceeds literary truth—is corroborated by Savage in a confession to his agent: "this is the first book I ever wrote that didn't have its last line before I wrote it, and that was because I was more interested in truth than in craft or art." (April 2, 1977) *Times Record* (Brunswick, Maine,) staff writer Susan Lamb's profile published more than a year later called it "a highly personal, true story." (December 1, 1978)

This novel's unusual genesis (i.e., Savage writing before knowing the ending) and status ("not really a novel") mark its special position in Savage's oeuvre. Having consistently claimed he never wrote autobiography, he appears to abandon that guise, presuming a faint line between truth (i.e., family history) and fiction rather than conceding a novelist's common practice of writing highly autobiographical fiction. Savage swerved continually across that line, with variable degrees of self-consciousness or camouflage, to write his particular literary truth. Later, in *For Mary, With Love,* the autobiographical narrator—Savage, who remains unnamed—states early on, in response to an audience question, "I said I made people up, but not really." (pp. 4–5). A novelist's standard confession, yet for one like Savage, acutely true.

The original title—which Savage's favorite editor, Llewellyn Howland III ("Louie"), proposed after receiving Savage's revised closing—focuses upon the discovery of his sister, Amy Patricia McClure Hemenway, and her incorporation into the extended family. In old age (and after Pat's death), he heartily approved of the new title for the 2001 reprint that shifts the spotlight to the family's center of gravity. At the original publication, he stated, "There are a lot of timely things in this book, including my grandmother as an early Women's Libber [*sic*]." (letter to agent, April 2, 1977) Certainly "Big Mama" Yearian was family boss who "knew long ago what her life would be, how she would manage it." (p. 101) Further, "she knew . . . that aristocracy is a local affair and that they were aristocrats" for several reasons. (p. 106) Hers proved a highly successful settler-colonial story, and the re-titling honors her pre-eminence in Idaho agricultural history.

Though the first edition title focused upon Savage's sister, the cover features a young and beautiful Beth Yearian, since "Louie," Savage's editor, "was excited about having my mother's picture on the dust-jacket" (April 2, 1977), as he "was much taken with the photograph." (May 17, 1977) That's understandable, as this photo depicts a belle of the ball. Beth wears a high-necked white collar ringed by two strands of necklace. Her hair, coiffed and piled and pinned, curves above her fore-head. She's looking down in quarter angle profile, and it does justice to her full lips and eyebrows: by all accounts, the family beauty. *The Sheep Queen* reprint cover, by contrast, shows a young Emma or Beth from the back, her hand secure on a large wood staff, eyeing a flock of sheep in the background, thus emphasizing work, not beauty.

The fact that "Elizabeth Owen," the birth mother's name according to the documents in Seattle (*Sheep Queen*, part one), shares a first name and birth year (1890) with Beth Yearian Brenner (Beth Sweringen) sug-gests another fusion of fiction with fact.

The Sheep Queen's litany of barely changed or unchanged first names attests to Savage's fealty to fact—to telling his family's actual story. For example, it includes letters from the narrator's three aunts, "Roberta," "Maude," and "Pauline" or "Polly": Savage's Yearian aunts, Edwina ("Weenie") Y. Nichol, Margaret ("Madge") Y. Wilson, and Helen ("Hellie") Y. Hanmer, respectively. These letters are closer to transcripts than fabrication. Savage, who figured until age twenty-seven as "Bren-ner," becomes "Tom Burton": another Tom and another addition to Savage's quartet of "B" surnames (announced in *The Liar*), all variations on his adopted family name and story; Yearian becomes "Sweringen," another near-name. And Savage's Great-Aunt Nora Y. Whitwell, who also writes to the narrator, appears from real life. The novel preserves first names unchanged including Pat's first name, Amy (she went by her middle name). The Sheep Queen and her husband, Emma Russell and Tom, appear unchanged as do their oldest daughter (Beth) and her first and second husbands (Ben H. and Charlie)—Savage's parents. McClure, his sister Pat's name until her marriage, becomes "McKinney," another borrowed family name: Tom's aunt, Laura Whitwell, married John ("Jack") McKinney, and the McKinneys swirled in and out of the Year-ian Ranch over the decades.

So Savage played close to the record in his usual way as though he were rewriting history according to his individual, admittedly subjective slant. The novel's opening chapter, the present that frames the novel, rewrites the opening chapter of *Daddy's Girl* with the pretense of fiction (e.g., Chris the stockbroker and "Crow Point") dropped. I have already quoted the opening paragraph, which begins, "So I will call myself Tom Burton, or Thomas Burton, as the name would appear on the novels I write." (p. 3) This choice feels both arbitrary and willful, a guise temporarily adopted, though Savage repeats it more emphatically to open the novel's part three. (p. 133) Georgetown, Maine, is named (p. 135) as is this Tom's wife, "herself a novelist." (p. 3) This opening chapter reads as nonfiction, including his hatred and distance from "the ranch in Montana" and "my beautiful, angel mother's" unhappiness. (p. 7) But that's not entirely true, as the literary device of the uncommon black-backed gull sighting (p. 8) symbolically foreshadows the unexpected arrival of a sister into their lives.

In *The Sheep Queen,* part one chronicles Amy's life up to the discovery of her birth records; part two rewrites parts of *The Liar* in foregrounding Emma's and Beth's lives; part three threads his grandmother and mother through Tom Burton, detailing his past and emergence as a novelist, and stresses his initial rejection then growing acceptance of this lost sibling's claim; and part four, a letter from brother to newly found sister, explains their mother's occasionally hard life, apologizes for Beth's original choice (i.e., of giving away her newborn for adoption), and concludes with an imagined sibling conversation. Tom Burton's phone call echoes Tom Westbrook's final phone call to the airport and imminent departure for Montana. Both novels close with Tom Savage metaphorically going home to redefine his family.

Amy McKinney's story (part one) closely recaps Pat McClure's childhood, adolescence, and adult life in Seattle. Pat was adopted at birth (February 25, 1912) by Walter and Amy McClure. He was a prominent Seattle attorney, and their son, Powell, age six, had been thrown from a horse and killed the preceding summer (July 10, 1911; *The Seattle Star*). Pat grew up in comfort, in Seattle's Leschi District, and graduated from Garfield High School in 1929 and the University of Washington (UW) in 1933. She worked for a while for a UW sorority and, for longer periods, Camp Fire Girls and the Girl Scouts. Pat married Ansel A. Hemenway

("Philip Nofzinger" in the novel, pp. 31-36) September 2, 1955, in Thurston, Washington, and "they spent time sailing up in the Canadian San Juans on his wood sloop, *Kayak*, and participating in sports car rallies." (www.Legacy.com) But the marriage ended in divorce within a decade, Pat choosing to keep his name.

During 1969, Pat having contacted Tom Savage, the two made up for lost time in Los Angeles when their father was dying: "'We got to know each other in those 3 or 4 weeks while we were living close together. And it was amazing how close we got.'" ("Tom Savage and Betty Savage" interview, July 16, 1981) According to one account, "Tom was further convinced she was his sister when they discovered they had the same feet." Relatives remarked their physical resemblance and common mannerisms, including smoking cigarettes with a holder exactly the same way. Pat also loved Mozart, Savage's favorite composer, and in the novel Amy also loves Mozart. Even more striking, Pat, according to these sources, was a lesbian, her bid in heterosexual marriage much less successful than her brother's. (cf. Sheldon's marriage in *Trust in Chariots* or Tom Westbrook's in *Midnight Line*).

The Sheep Queen swears allegiance to Savage's credo: "We are all fools for Family." (p. 133) Burton/Savage declares, "this belief I hope to pass on to my sons and my daughter because I don't know what there is to believe in except Family." (p. 150) Given this theme, the paradox of Savage as gay man married and playing the part of patriarch shines brightly—but only if one believes that being a gay man precludes having a family, a conviction Savage likely accepted. In this novel about grandparents, aunts, wife, sons, daughter, and a found sister, the textual debate about homosexuality present in the preceding (1970s) novels ends. There are no cameos or quick scenes about gay men, as Savage has left them out. In the novel affirming the centrality of family by way of his own, he omits himself in a sense. In his way of thinking, gay men or lesbians tragically cannot be integrated in extended family. Split at the root, Savage seemingly cannot throw off the heteronormative verdict.

The novel's affirmation of Family (proper noun) sets in relief Amy's and Tom's parallel anxieties as adoptees. The accusation Burton as a teenager faced, because "Burton" is not biologically his name ("The world as I wished it slid from under my feet," p. 176), precisely echoes Amy's worries after adolescence that she is no McKinney: "The knowledge that she was nobody, had no more substance than a shadow (shadow of what?)—that knowledge must have colored every aspect of her days from that moment on." (p. 179) Of course, Amy's sense of being unmoored far exceeds Tom's stigma (first articulated in *The Liar*). Savage survived one kind of dislocation, as a stepson, in childhood and young adulthood; *Sheep Queen* chronicles him revising his view of his mother and of his parents' marriage while embracing his long-lost older sister. Not until part four does he accept the fact that Beth gave up her first-born baby.

If this novel traces the successful arc of the Yearians as a white pioneer story, they endure some rough bumps in the second and third generations. More space is given Emma's story than her husband's or father-in-law's, and her matrimonial designs for her first-born are blocked by Beth's sudden love for the handsome salesman, Ben Burton. Burton (*The Liar*'s Hal Sawyer), still travels for "Everfresh Products" and succeeds in advertising on the big white Sweringen barn and in winning Beth's hand in marriage, both against the Sheep Queen's plans. In fact Ben Savage, in 1910 (age twenty-one), was living in Walla Walla, Washington, with his grandmother, Agnes Laman. Ironically, he'd been a stepson since age four, just as his son would become a stepson at age five. In the novel Beth throws off her potential well-heeled suitor (from back East) and defies her mother. It sustains *The Liar*'s mother-daughter clash though now Beth's quick disillusionment and subsequent divorce are omitted.

Chapters 7–10 (most of part two) are set in 1911: on September 25, 1911, Beth Yearian, pregnant four months, married Ben Savage in Salmon, Idaho (she gave birth to her first daughter five months to the day later). One week earlier, the worst event in Emma Russell Yearian/ Sweringen's life occurred: her favorite child, Tom-Dick (the second son—another unchanged name), died of appendicitis at age eleven in Armstead, Montana, en route with his mother to a Salt Lake City specialist (September 18, 1911). He'd been sick to his stomach only a few days and was buried in the family's "Masonic plat" days before Beth and Ben's hasty wedding. *Sheep Queen* carefully draws this mother-son bond (p. 127), just as it sketches in Beth as her father's favorite child (p. 105), whom he could never refuse. Alone among white people, for instance, father and daughter can discern "the imperious face and head of an Indian chief dressed in a warbonnet" on a hillside of slide-rock and sagebrush—the same special vision and knowledge that link Phil Burbank and Peter Gordon with the dog formation in *Power*.

In part four Tom has accepted his mother's fallibility and, in his letter to Amy, speculates that Beth, newly divorced five years after giving up her daughter for adoption, returns home out of loyalty to her past and in some sustained act of expiation: "our mother was certainly mad with grief when she gave you away." (p. 240) Her remarriage to Charlie Brenner (now "Brewer") three years later (1920) fulfills her perceived double duty: duty to her mother whom she'd earlier crossed, and duty to her son without a father. (p. 219) Her actions affirmed her loyalty to family.

Savage's tenth novel lays bare the story of the two families in which he grew up, the warmth of the Yearians offsetting the cold of the Brenners: the latter, his model of the dysfunctional ranch dynasty. If the Yearians affirmed settler-colonial mythology, their story includes its fundamental challenges (e.g., a favorite son's death, a favorite daughter's bad marriage, or differing parenting philosophies). Yet in their warm personal relations with many local Lemhi Shoshone, the Yearians proved an exceptional counter-narrative: this white family practiced integration and never sought tribal removal, let alone genocide. Savage, gay son, inherited his grandfather's and mother's generous interests in local indigenes.

Sheep Queen moves fluidly back and forth in time, the details of Beth Brewer's (i.e., Brenner's) alcoholism and painful dying (chap. 12), for example, preceding the rare and failed visit of Ben Burton, with his flashy clothes and "Roamer" convertible, decades earlier to the Horse Prairie Ranch (chap. 13). Certainly it specifies most of Savage's career, as has been seen. For example, it recaps *Power*'s Rose and Peter Gordon after Dr. Johnny Gordon's suicide (now a "Mrs. Forest," slightly disfigured with a facial scar, and her son, pp. 116–18). And as the Sheep Queen rides the Gilmore and Pittsburgh Railroad (*The Pass*) up Horse Prairie to

Bannock Pass and down to her Idaho home, Savage recaps the story of
the "Brewers"—the Burbanks of *Power*—with only two details changed.

Most importantly, in parts three and mostly four, Savage resusci-
tates Phil Burbank—weird Uncle Bill Brenner—to kill him one more
time. Compared to Phil, Ed Brewer, the later reincarnation, is handled
more briefly and bluntly. He's a real bastard. His sneering malicious-
ness coupled with his gross personal habits help destroy Beth Brewer
in this telling, and align reader with Burton-Savage:

> I often wished Ed dead. How I wished I had been older and ready
> to pit my intellect against his, to find the clue to his own weakness
> and destroy him. But when I was old enough, sure enough to speak
> out, he was dead, but too late for my mother's good. By then her
> drinking was a prison, and I watched as she moved carefully from
> chair to chair. (p. 227)

The Hamlet revenge had, of course, already been enacted by adolescent
Peter Gordon in *Power*.

Savage's hatred for long-dead Bill Brenner feels unqualified, as he
died midway through Savage's undergrad years at Colby College:

> Surely even in New England there must have been something high
> like music in the air that day, an unaccountable ripple like a smile
> on the Charles River, the sun brighter on the gold dome of the State
> House.
>
> I wish I had been in Montana to see him put on his hat for the
> last time. But it came too late for my mother. (p. 229)

Given this hatred, one wonders what had transpired between the real
Beth and Bill? Had Tom overheard some disparaging remarks? If Bill
were latently gay, did Tom detect that and turn away, attracted but
repulsed? Or did Bill just rub Beth the wrong way all along, which
her son witnessed? Certainly Bill Brenner doted on his niece, Isabel
(cf. *Sheep Queen*, pp. 227-28), carving wooden toys for her with his
"clever naked hands." Presumably in favoring her, Bill willfully drove
a wedge between mother and daughter: the kind of wedge painfully
exposed between Ruth Bart and Lona (Bart) Hanson back in *Lona*

Hanson, and precisely what Phil Burbank unsuccessfully attempts between Peter and Rose Gordon in *Power.*

Savage would not revive and kill Bill again. In this novel proclaiming the orthodoxy of heterosexual family, particularly strong women (Emma, Beth, Amy), there's no place for Ed Brewer, who threatens it— or for the gay author, who has again denied his root sexual identity.

Savage knew *I Heard My Sister/The Sheep Queen* was one of his best novels, and in a letter to a friend (undated), stated, "Little, Brown is doing some advertising in *PW* [*Publishers Weekly*], the first time they've ever done that for me, but then I'm sixty-two years old, and my teeth are dropping out, and I have vague aches and pains." In the same letter he expressed a familiar disappointment: "*Readers Digest* of Books kept [*The Sheep Queen*] for months and months and then turned it down. Book of the Month Club indicates they might take it as an alternative or some such, but not as the real thing." Meanwhile, Jonathan Yardley raved in his *Washington Post* review: "A masterful novelist writing at the peak of his form. . . It is the best of Savage's ten novels, the capstone of a distinguished and, I think, important career." And the *New Yorker* raved as well: "Mr. Savage is a writer of the first order, and he possesses in abundance the novelist's highest art—the ability to illuminate and move." The same yawning gap between high critical praise and low sales plagued him even when he worked at the top of his game. The critics sang his praises, but name recognition eluded him: those "highly educated people" he wrote for, his natural readership, missed him and missed out.

□   □   □

Less than half a year after *The Sheep Queen*'s publication, the February 1978 blizzard—the worst to hit New England in over 200 years— seriously damaged their Indian Point home. But it would take seven more years before the Savages, who after 1982 were raising Russell's three children, moved to Whidbey Island, Washington—a quick ferry crossing much closer to Seattle than the San Juan Islands Savage had envisioned. By late 1979, Savage was suffering from serious arthritis, which acupuncture treatments didn't relieve: in October he was "seeing a former head of the Arthritis Foundation" for help. (October 9, 1979, letter to agent)

The Guggenheim Fellowship (1980) confirmed Savage's stature, and he wrote his eleventh novel, *Her Side of It* (1981) without the usual financial pressures upon him. The novel includes a discussion of the politics and prestige of Guggenheims, since its protagonist, novelist Liz Chandler Phillips, also wins a Guggenheim. (pp. 243–47) That cameo scene closes the imaginative distance between narrator Bill Reese (another Savage avatar) who does not write and Phillips who does but only produces two novels.

Before the novel, however, Tom and Betty Savage were asked to contribute essays to *A Book for Boston: Jubilee 350,* a 1980 publication in commemoration of Boston's 350th anniversary. The fact that the Savages bookend the anthology, leading off and concluding the twenty-two contributors, attests to the husband's and wife's reputation as writers who were transplanted New Englanders, with Boston (setting of more than one Savage novel) their adopted city. Savage's essay, "Why a Pilgrim Traveled to Boston, and His Implausible Arrival There" (pp. 13–19), recounts his 1937 bus journey and meeting with the pen pal who became, two years later, his wife. Savage loved telling the story of the Merry-Go-Round [Bar] at the Copley Plaza [Hotel], site of their initial, comic meeting. But it includes as well a fond portrait of the Sheep Queen and shearing time at the Yearian Ranch, which Savage did not include in any novel. In a letter to Blanche Gregory (May 21, 1980) he gleefully recounted details of the May 14, 1980, book launch in Boston, with lavish food and drink and hospitality including a visit with the mayor who is "under investigation," which he characterizes as per usual in Boston.

By the time Savage was writing his eleventh novel, he complained about health problems including the occasional hernia, sounding off about the ostensible wisdom accruing in old age. In a letter to Lucie Hagens, a close friend for decades, he complained, "what [age] brings is cynicism and a stunning wonder that things turned out and are turning out as they did and do and will. I had hoped in some way to keep the lid on the family, but see!" Brassil Savage likely remained this family man's greatest anxiety. Savage sourly reviews Brassil's instability and impending second marriage, stating, "My elder son was here with us for three months during the late winter and spring, several very bad scenes when we feared for our lives, at least I did, and of course there's not a chance in the world that he'll ever change. So one has in mind jails and institutions and then a final telegram. What an awful waste, because he's brilliant, beats me at chess and writes papers on Samuel Beckett I can't understand." (August 15, 1980)

In this bleak, accurate assessment the oldest child—an avenging angel for the family when breaking up his father's affair with Tomie dePaola (1962)—continues like a moth to circle around his father's flame. It would remain thus until Brassil's untimely death. Most tragically, Savage apparently never saw through Brassil's alcoholism or drug addictions to his mental illness. As a novelist Savage understood, if he understood anything, his characters: their psychology, their quirks, their nuances. And Savage kept reinterpreting family members in his fiction. Yet about his firstborn, he remained opaque, neither understanding nor accepting Brassil's mental illness. This despite the fact that the son resembled the father in many regards, above all, his wit and his artistic promise (e.g., his unpublished novel, written in his early twenties, and his painting). Tom kept thinking if only he earned more money, that alone would take care of children or grandchildren, if not their problems, as though money could save them.

Classical music, and specifically his album (and after 1982, CD) collection, gave Savage great joy and consolation, as he repeatedly reveals in letters. He loved sharing details of new purchases and new interpretations of specific compositions (e.g., releases of pianists Walter Gieseking or Alfred Brendel). As a music nerd he loved to share listening with the occasional friend, but feared that was increasingly rare: "When I was young I thought it possible to get other people to sit down and listen to music, but then somebody thinks he ought to say something, feeling that really nobody could just sit and listen to music and perhaps it's rude not to say something. And of course it's usually too loud for most people, and anyway they'd rather visit." (August 15, 1980, letter to Lucie Hagens) Savage liked his Bruckner loud (as do I).

Her Side of It (1981)

In *Her Side of It*, second of Savage's three frame narratives centering on an extraordinary woman, the novel serves as biography: "she had chosen me her Boswell, and like Boswell I have not the gift to create, only a pedantic ability to select and to organize. . .What was she? Exquisite failure or an important stranger at the gates?" (p. 298) In an undated 1977 letter to a friend, Savage describes its genesis: "I have sixty pages of a book about a female writer I knew well whose father once taught Animal Husbandry in Bozeman, who wrote beautifully and died an alcoholic after a most untidy life." In a letter to his agent he stated, "the book is so difficult." (October 9, 1979) In an August 1980 letter he describes its more extensive (than usual) revision challenges: "The problem is, in this book I have tried to say some things that haven't been said before, and every time I wasn't absolutely clear, the copy editor stopped me. I ended up rewriting 67 pages." In fact through his protagonist, Savage chronicles his own literary fate. This novel, primarily set in New York City and New England, again features the long reach of the rural Intermountain West, one region imposed upon another.

I have not been able to identify the minor novelist upon whom Savage modeled Liz Phillips. In "say[ing] some things that haven't been said before," Savage has produced an indirect self-portrait, a laudatory profile of a very talented minor novelist who's an alcoholic like Marty in *Daddy's Girl* and like Savage himself (according to some), but who dies from it. After all, narrator Bill Reese states, "I doubt her novel, *Masquerade,* sold a thousand copies" (p. 24): very close to the original sales figures for Savage's *Power of the Dog*. Reese quotes "from one of her fine reviews" in prepping publicity posters for Phillips's campus visit arranged by Reese: "The novels of Elizabeth Phillips are perhaps America's best-kept literary secret" (p. 279): precisely the verdict on Savage rendered, a few years earlier, by critics Roger Sale and Jonathan Yardley. Savage includes other self-references (e.g., "One novelist told me he knew the last line of the book before he began it," p. 207). It's no accident that he recycles his mother's first name (though now the tough woman goes by Liz, not Beth). In many respects, Phillips's story recapitulates his own career. Savage likely borrowed some features as well from his long-suffering, hard-drinking, novelist wife, Betty Savage, in painting Liz.

Savage positions his narrator as acolyte and apologist—"I sat at her feet, as I do now" (p. 215)—precisely as he positions himself as explicit narrator in his next novel, *For Mary, With Love*. Narrator and narrated share common origins in southwest Montana, Phillips's Bozeman offsetting, to some extent, Reese's Grayling. *Her Side of It*, then, constitutes an act of self-projection and a cautionary tale: whereas Liz Phillips flames out prematurely from the booze, Savage, despite his heavy drinking, continued to publish high-quality novels at least until age seventy-three. In the oblique mirror that is this novel, Savage sustains his Lewisian satire about his hometown and region. Grayling/Dillon represents one of the "shabby, failing towns" (p. 37) of the rural West. As he's suggested since *Power*, he has no use for its severe, provincial reductivism: "success in Grayling, Montana, meant money or land, there was no other standard." (p. 23)

Through Reese, Savage voices the archetype of writers or other artists or gay men getting the hell out of "dead" Dodge and escaping to the Big Apple as the Promised Land and safe space, an archetype that's flourished for well over a century: "we meant to show Montana or Colorado or Texas a clean pair of heels and head for New York where our talents would thrive." (p. 20) But distance enhances sharp clarity and return. Savage again fondly evokes details such as Grayling's/Dillon's Sugar Bowl Café (always an unchanged name, p. 52). He physically left long ago yet he never really left. Like Bernard DeVoto in Cambridge, Massachusetts, who had hated the Odgen, Utah, of his youth but who defended Utah against the ignorant judgments of Boston Brahmins or Harvard elites, Reese speaks for Savage in his defensiveness and deep ambivalences: "When I lived in Montana, I hated it. Now, having left it, I was as defensive of it as I was of myself." (p. 22) Savage maintained a deep psychic loyalty to his first geography.

Her Side of It is set in 1951 at a fictitious version of Colby College, and includes some tasty academic satire (e.g., generous colleague and gossip, Etta Murphy). Similarly, it includes satirical portraits of Iowa (via "New Hoosic," hometown of Liz's maternal grandparents) and some New England now-seedy-but-once-patrician lineages (i.e., Liz's mother-in-law, "Mammy" Phillips). More importantly, the novel returns to the conversation about and surface condemnation of gay men characteristic of the 1970s novels and dramatized in the resuscitation and blunt criticism and death of *Sheep Queen's* Ed Burbank. Again, Savage, who cast his lot with heteronormativity, punishes himself.

For example, a volume of Shakespeare's *Sonnets* and the insinuation that they address a young man rather than woman leads some to brand Shakespeare "a degenerate" who "must be forgiven if only because of his art." (p. 262) Earlier, when Hal Phillips considers ways to avoid the World War II draft, gay men are targeted (in fact, intake interviewers were trained to spot gay men trying to hide as well as those passing as gay to avoid induction). Reese offers, "'You could pretend you're queer.' 'And me married? They'd check.' 'Queers marry.' It would kill Mammy P. [his mother] . . . She's never believed in what she calls 'homosexualists.'" (p. 187). "Mammy" Phillips, however satirically regarded, embodies the majority voice of condemnation: "Homosexuals are condemned and rightly so because their lust is sterile." (p. 188) Reese, Savage's spokesman, defines, in passing, Savage's personal choice with Betty back in 1939. If Savage feared the charge of "sterility," his heteronormative reproduction (three children) masked his queerness and shielded him from the homophobic retribution he visits upon Phil Burbank in *Power*. If this mid-twentieth-century consensus pervaded most of that century, at least since Savage's death (2003), the early stereotype of nuclear family has broadened in several ways to include gay couples with children.

Two passages intimate the inner life of young and older Savage in ways he had not permitted himself before. "To be homosexual was to be damned," as seen "in the incidents [Bill and Liz] remembered in those little towns beyond the western horizon" because of the hoary majority accusation that sexual minorities "corrupt the innocent." (p. 263) It bears repeating that that notion fueled the migration of gay men to big cities (e.g., Tom Westbrook in *Midnight* Line). This is the precise territory memorably inscribed in Annie Proulx's most famous short story, "Brokeback Mountain" (1997), wherein Ennis del Mar's and Jack Twist's lives are characterized by ostracism, secrecy, violence, and death via suicide as likely as not. As Kath Weston states in "Get Thee to a Big City," "In most stories of the Great Gay Migration, the rural is not only the space of dead-end lives, oppression, and surveillance. It is also a landscape emptied of gay people." (p. 265) It's a none-place for sexual minorities. Yet her study of the urban migration of gay men in the 1970s concludes that, whatever their silencing in rural spaces, urban centers proved other than monolithically welcoming for them.

The profile of the "cringing boy on every playground" who's singled out and persecuted and culled, so that "he ran—he always ran" closely evokes *Power*'s Peter Gordon: as stated, Savage's first fictional projection of himself. The caustic irony of the sentiment, "Who would not wish to punish them for flying in God's face?" precisely matches the majoritarian fear expressed by "Mrs. S" in *Midnight Line*'s talk show debate.

Young Savage lived with the burden of being a stepson, not biologically a Brenner; he kept his real sexual identity under lock and key, the occasional girlfriend or fling providing the usual cover. In conversation between Bill and Liz, who "was most comfortable with the gay boys" (p. 208), Savage critiques the sorry fates of gay men in adulthood who might be "beaten bloody on Eighth Street by sailors in attractive pants" or retreat to fundamental Protestantism, as though being born again "would straighten them out" in "God's face." Or those who seek psychiatric treatment (cf. *Midnight Line*, pp. 34-35). Or those who turn to Roman Catholicism or the Episcopal Church only to discover "priests...damned like themselves." Or those who, like Savage, marry and father a family. Savage quotes one friend of Liz's: "'I thought I could learn how, I could understand,' he said, 'why my wife would blow up if I'd gone after another woman. But why did she blow up over a man?'" Liz's rejoinder—"'Because she was helpless against a man... She might compete with another woman'" (p. 209)—explains in part the emotional pain if not rage when gay sexuality abuts heterosexual marriage.

Betty Savage, by contrast, variably forgave and accepted Tom for what he was; for the two sons, particularly Brassil, it was more complicated, and at moments they presumably felt themselves avenging Furies who must, at all costs, protect their mother, though their parents became as interdependent as ever.

In this and the preceding novels, Savage dutifully follows the tragically flawed misreading of Freud on homosexuality as deviance, one that lingers at considerable psychic and social cost.

The reviews of *Her Side of It*, typically laudatory, saluted his acute understanding of female character: a hallmark of his fiction since *Lona Hanson*. The case can be made that male characters in Savage novels simply don't match up, in force or effect, with female characters. His maternal grandmother ("Big Mama"), mother, and sister, Isabel, provided him with role models for many protagonists and others. Of his eleventh novel, *The Chicago Sun-Times* wrote, "Savage is brilliant and his book sings"; *The Washington Post* praised him: "Savage is a superb writer, and his book is that extraordinary achievement in fiction, a novel about a novelist which succeeds in making the subject believable."

The *Maine Sunday Telegram* review (March 8, 1981), which opens calling the novel "yet another of his high quality, low visibility fictions," sounds a more critical note.

Reviewer Edgar Allen Beem singles out Savage's remarkable ability to "observe and pronounce," stating however, "Savage's mini-essays on the props and paraphernalia of domestic life are gems of sensitivity, but a whole necklace of them can get a little gaudy." The insinuation of "a little gaudy" misses the mark, as the "mini-essays" form the heart of his narrator persona and one excellence in his style. Beem concludes that this Savage novel, like its predecessors, represents "literature not in service of public entertainment, but rather literature in service of art itself." That coterie niche explains Savage's neglect and disappointment, which only increased in the final two decades of his life, even as his rate of production dropped then stopped.

CHAPTER SIX

Limelight and Obscurity, 1982–2003

SAVAGE OFTEN REMARKED—as do many writers—that apart from writing he felt hollow. In one interview connected with his final hometown appearance, he stated, "I have to write. . . I feel cheap if I don't." ("Accomplished Author Greets Hometown," *The Montana Standard,* April 30, 1983) He reminded a Dillon audience, "Retirement for an author is death." In old age he felt increasingly useless as his stream of fiction petered out. In the 1990s, for example, as he struggled with at least two manuscripts, he had no more luck publishing, and from his already marginal reputation he slipped into obscurity. Additionally, he spent the final fourteen years of his life as a widower. Yet Savage's final decades proved no tale of sorrow, and at least on three occasions, he stood in the limelight. While he enjoyed these moments, he had no delusions about his obscurity. Nor did they offset his deep frustration about his next novel and nonfiction book getting nowhere with a publisher.

By the time *Her Side of It*—which Savage thought, at times, his best novel—was published, he was already at work on his next one, another family portrait.

Tough family circumstances, however, distracted Savage from the process of publication. Russell Savage's chronically unfaithful, alcoholic wife, Tressie, made his life hellish enough that he'd discussed divorce with the family attorney. On Halloween 1982, in a fit of rage, he shot and killed her in Gene Youngken's Indian Point (Maine) house, where they were temporarily staying and where he found her in flagrante delicto with another man. According to more than one relative, Tom worked hard cleaning Gene's house where the murder took place, even picking brain matter out of a carpet. In some remote sense Tom felt responsible for this horror. Russell served time first in the Cumberland County (Maine) Jail, then three years in the Maine State Prison (Thomaston), then at the prison farm in Warren, Maine. He was next transferred to a halfway house in Portland, Maine, where he began coursework in radiation therapy; he completed his probation at a Seattle halfway house and completed coursework at the Virginia Mason Medical Center and Bellevue (Washington) College. The three children—two sons and a daughter—moved in with the grandparents, who raised them. In his late sixties and early seventies, Tom Savage was suddenly returned to the full-time and unexpected role of parenting grandchildren.

In his own words, "[1983] is the first year I've no income." The fact that after being a Guggenheim Fellow, he was plagued by money worries speaks volumes about the precariousness of his writing life and poor sales.

Deeply distracted by Russell's tragedy and the challenge of three grandchildren, Savage accepted an invitation to return to Dillon, Montana, as featured writer and keynote speaker at a weekend arts festival. The American Association of University Women's local chapter (which ceased to exist by the mid-1990s, my wife being one of the final members) had planned the "Inspirations of Pen and Palette" festival for a year and secured a $3,500 grant from Montana's state humanities council, in large part to fund Savage's visit. The weekend would include a play festival, local artists, readings by Savage and others, and a culminating banquet and lecture by Savage. According to one of the AAUW coordinators, the event was organized so that area residents could "consider the 'exceptional quality' of their cultural heritage." (*Dillon Tribune Examiner*, March 22, 1983) One wonders how many of those who came had read Savage's steady excoriation of his hometown.

Turns out the festival organizers had approached A. B. ("Bud") Guthrie Jr., who resided in Choteau, Montana, to come as the keynote, but he turned them down. One panelist, Western Montana College (now UMW) historian Rex C. Myers, had asserted, "[Guthrie's] been overdone. Let's try Savage." Chief organizer E. B. Rebich of the AAUW told Tom in Dillon, "everybody said you wouldn't come," but she'd defied the odds the previous year and sent the invitation. The famous Guthrie wouldn't drive four hours south to Dillon; the far less known Savage flew cross-country from Maine to come home once more.

This exchange marks the capricious waywardness of literary reputation and recapitulates Savage's story of critical success yet neglect. Guthrie, long celebrated in the northern Rockies and elsewhere, had published, the year before, *Fair Land, Fair Land* (1982), the final novel of his Montana sextet. After all, his most famous novel, *The Big Sky* (1947: first in the eventual sextet), had been adopted as Montana's unofficial slogan (Big Sky Country) and graced state license plates for many years. Savage, fourteen years younger than Guthrie, had published a different brand of white settler colonialism—indeed, had published more novels of arguably higher quality—yet remained, relatively speaking, overlooked outside Dillon and Beaverhead County, Montana. By inviting Savage back, the AAUW chapter recruited easily the best writer from southwest Montana and lured him back one last time.

The fact that Savage admitted in Dillon he'd never heard of Ivan Doig, by 1983 one of Montana's best up-and-coming writers, speaks volumes about his literary disconnect with his home region. Yet he was as consumed by it as was Doig, one generation younger. Savage gave shape to it even though he ignored his fellow Montana novelists.

Just weeks shy of sixty-eight but still strikingly handsome, Savage's steady drinking was taking a toll (though he would live another twenty years). According to one of the primary organizers, Savage seemed restless, distracted during one of the receptions. But he was still coping with the Tressie Savage killing of half a year earlier.

In addition to visiting relatives and being interviewed by professor John Scheckter of Western Montana College and *Dillon Tribune Examiner* staff writer Julie Simon, Savage was the featured attraction at a Saturday morning "Literary Panel" in the college's art gallery, and at the evening banquet when he spoke on the topic, "The Reason for Three Novels." More than 300 attended the banquet. Simon, a Savage convert and enthusiast, extensively covered his return. In one piece, "We're lucky to have 'Pen and Palette,'" she stated, regarding Savage's *The Pass*, that he was "trying to tell a more important story than the one about Horse Prairie and the Gilmore and Pittsburg[h] [Railroad]." She probed his coterie rather than mass market appeal, describing a Savage read as "the deeper pleasure in plunging into a book that seems to have been written out of need to create rather than a need to make a few dollars." (*Dillon Tribune Examiner,* April 12, 1983) In a review article Simon stated the "Arts festival was a big success," claiming that Literary Panel was "the best part of the weekend," with approximately 100 in attendance.

Savage enacted the "local boy meets success in his field in the big world then returns home" plot with gusto and charm. He basked in this limelight in his remote rural corner. As Simon and others noted, "With a thick brown cigarette poised in one hand and a glass of milk and gin waiting on the table in front of him," Savage reminisced easily and, a commanding conversationalist, charmed the socks off his interviewers and audiences. With that dash of "Imperial Caesar," he played roles effortlessly.

In letters Savage claimed his doctor recommended more milk in his diet, hence his "milk punch." In *Her Side of It,* narrator Bill Reese provides the simple recipe: "You mix equal quantities of ice-cold milk with ice-cold gin and over the first one or two you scatter a few grains of nutmeg to show you still care about the look of things." (p. 31) More than one newspaper byline read, "with gin and milk in hand." No doubt milk punch fills the Jefferson cup in the author photo discussed in the introduction and that's featured on the dust jacket of *I Heard My Sister Speak My Name.* In Dillon, heads wagged. He wouldn't have it any other way.

He signed the frontispiece of the banquet guestbook, "These last two days reinforce what I always knew was true: friendship & continuity." He meant it. Yet in "Savage comes home again," Simon cited the passage in *The Liar* where the autobiographical narrator, up-and-coming novelist Gerry Sawyer, received his best writing advice: "that people generally write well about what they hate the most." In Savage, love and hatred flowed forcefully side by side, as though two streams of differing shades joined but retained their own hue. He'd admitted to Simon his need for escape forty-six years earlier: "I didn't think this was the place for me." But as I've said, he never really left, even in his New England novels.

Savage also admitted, "I never thought I'd be back in Dillon" again.

After all, he'd repeatedly described in his novels the desperate desire to get a long ways away from the stultifying cow town slightly flavored by the presence of the "normal school"—also object of scorn (cf. *Midnight Line*, p. 94). Through his final novel he inscribed the scene of escape. In a letter to a cousin a few years later, he stated, "I feel like a ghost when I go to Salmon or to Montana. I can't believe that I was once a part of those places." (September 26, 1988) The same man who, when young, broke horses, taught riding, and flirted with a rodeo career as a bronc rider, now doubted he could mount and ride a horse.

In one key exchange, basking in the local glow, he remarked there were "so many people . . . still around here. I wish I had months to stay here." A dominating figure, he dissembled effortlessly, flattered enthusiastically. Most of those listening didn't imagine any implicit criticism concerning those who never went anywhere, geographically or otherwise. The AAUW treasurer responded, "You're very well remembered . . . There [are] lots of stories about you going around." I'll bet. Other novelists who influenced him—Sinclair Lewis, Willa Cather, Thomas Wolfe—enacted that fraught scene in their respective hometowns. Some of the Savage gossip easily slipped into criticism of the hometown boy's nasty take on Dillon, the Beaverhead Valley, and Horse Prairie. Some likely disapproved of his seeming flamboyant attire—for instance, his wearing lavender gloves into the Andrus Hotel "Lounge": Dillon's leading bar for decades. Most condemned such flaunting disregard of local proprieties. Some might even have questioned his masculinity, winked among themselves.

During his stay he unsurprisingly visited the Brenner Ranch in Horse Prairie and Bannock Pass where he drank a can of beer and shook his head in disbelief as he took in the panorama and recalled his childhood (cf. chap. 1). As he admitted to interviewer John Scheckter, the West "is a kind of touchstone for myself."

Savage also mentioned that, though they'd lived on the Maine coast for twenty-eight years, he remained an outsider. He stated he didn't write about Mainers because he didn't understand them, even after nearly three decades; Betty Savage understood, however, and wrote about local folks as well as the summer residents' scene.

Because of his sexual preference, he'd been born an outsider, of

course, and he savored that position no matter his geography even
as he yearned for heteronormativity through his family. During his
hometown triumph he spent at least a couple of hours in the company
of Scheckter, a young Jewish-American academic who'd never spent
much time in the West. Two years after the festival Scheckter, who left
Western Montana College for Long Island University, published the
only scholarly article devoted to Savage for decades (cited in chap. 4).
The aging novelist and young professor bonded over their respective
roles as outsiders, and Scheckter's recorded interviews (of the Literary
Panel, Savage's banquet talk, and informal conversation off-campus)
provide a crucial archive into Savage's views of his life and his career,
as this biography has attested.

The return to Dillon proved a happy distraction from Russell's tragedy. Through both events he completed his twelfth novel.

For Mary, With Love (1983)

For Mary, With Love represents, as the title suggests, an offering, an
extended salute to an aunt by marriage who shimmered through Savage's childhood and with whom he maintained a close friendship across
her long life (e.g., "I had a nice long letter from Tom—has a new book [*A
Strange God*] coming out," July 1, 1973, letter from Aunt Mary to granddaughter, Liz Brenner Tourtelot). Mary Skoning (unchanged name)
Brenner Kirk (b. 1887) died June 24, 1981, but Savage started writing
her story before her death. Though she divorced her first husband, Hal
Brenner, in 1925 when Savage was ten, and moved to California and
elsewhere, she remained a colorful relative and presence—and a shin-
ing example of bucking conventions governing women's roles.

In a late letter written to her granddaughter (March 17, 1979), at
nearly ninety-two, Mary waxed nostalgic about the Horse Prairie, Montana, chapter of her earlier life: "How I would love to see the old Brenner house now...I *wish* I could write a book about the old Montana
days—It is utterly stupid that I did not write up things—years ago. As
you well know 'I have lived.'" She certainly "had lived" independently
if not unconventionally, and her nephew, analogously unconventional,
happily served as her chronicler. Mary Kirk never occupied the passenger seat in her life: she drove, always. In Savage's third and final

frame narrative, all fictive pretenses are dropped, though he remains unnamed as narrator.

In a letter to agent Blanche Gregory (March 27, 1980), Savage commented, "the next day I got out the 65 pages of the book about the lady who broke up so many families and I've been pressing ahead on it." In a pre-Christmas 1981 letter, Betty Savage, who a year earlier had published what turned out to be her final novel (*Toward the End,* 1980), comments about the speed with which Tom has written: "We're betting no one remembers *To Mary With Love.* And the title's perfect. Even if the Mary on whom the character is based had not died (under gloomy circumstances) she wouldn't mind; in fact, she'd be delighted. She was after Tom for years to 'do' her."

The shift in preposition in the published title (i.e., from "To Mary" to "For Mary") opens the space around this particular title character and suggests an admiring defense of all the Marys out there in the two generations before 1960s feminism began to change American consciousness. Savage's Aunt Mary, sexual and exotic and high-spirited, proved a woman ahead of her time, at least according to early twentieth-century patriarchal traditions, not unlike Butte, Montana's famed Mary MacLane a few years earlier.

Savage had completed *For Mary, With Love* weeks before his hero's return to Dillon, and the novel was published in September 1983. It would prove the end of his run with Little, Brown and his last personal family novel. It features Savage's Uncle Hal Brenner; Hal's parents, John C. and Isabel Brenner (ranch founders displayed in several earlier novels); Hal's son, Jack (i.e., Savage's cousin); but most of all, the beautiful and liberated Aunt Mary. Old Man Brenner, Tom's step-grandfather John, whom he always disliked, emerges as the bully and villain of the piece. The Brenners are named "Bower": yet another near name (e.g., Andrus cf. "Andrews" Hotel, or "Herndon" cf. Dillon), and the final addition to the string of "B-surnames" commenced with "Bentley" back in *The Pass* and confirmed with the quartet cited in *The Liar.* All six names pose as imaginative if not phonetic variants on the Brenner family (with traces of the Yearians as well). There remains a tight family resemblance. Now, however, only two Brenner sons appear in the fiction, with Charlie Brenner, Tom's stepdad, cast as "Ed Bower." Tellingly, bad Bill Brenner—*Sheep Queen*'s Ed Brewer and loner who came to town twice a year or less and focused Savage's hatred—has been omitted.

For Mary, With Love opens, like *The Sheep Queen*, with a factual frame, the narrator now an instructor and ambassador for Brandeis University, where Savage worked for seven years. Savage has set it in the early 1950s, the same period as *Her Side of It*. In response to an audience question, the narrator—also a novelist—admits, as has Savage in sundry letters, "I made people up, but not really." (pp. 4–5) Savage's acutely autobiographical fiction depends utterly on family history. When queried about the "Bower Ranch," Savage's alter ego narrator reacts precisely as have earlier spokesmen: "At the name Bower, I felt a rush like the wind, and time converged like railroad tracks seen from the observation car. I heard coyotes crying at the moon, I felt a cold draft that had crawled in under a back door and filled the cold hall." (p. 7) The Proustian prompt instantly elicits painful memories: "I felt pursued, as in a nightmare, cornered in that huge log ranch house in Montana under a sagebrush hill where the light fell late—a tower of silence over which unspoken longings wheeled." (p. 8; cf. Phil's sense of the pursuing dog formation only he and Peter see in the distant rocks in *Power*)

The indictment perfectly captures Savage's career-long condemnation of ranch dynasties and life as he experienced them. He evidenced few happy memories of the Brenner place. In this Savage theme, the Rocky Mountains exemplum of Jeffersonian agrarian life transforms itself into "nightmare": a nemesis that forever crushes human desire, even language, inside its "tower of silence." Here's no place for Mozart or sexual minorities, among endless deprivations and exclusions. Ranches are the antithesis of the ideal, and settler colonialism represents a highly problematic if not fatal paradigm. Read psychoanalytically, the Brenner Ranch, that "tower of silence," represents the return of the repressed the writer continually casts off, only for it to crop up again.

In Aunt Mary, Savage had found a role model and common cause. As narrator he remarks, "What Mary and I had in common is that out in Montana we were misfits." (p. 14) Mary symbolizes mobility and escape as does Anne C. Metlen in the closing of Savage's final novel. In a later conversation that represents the novel's seed, Mary teases her nephew, "'Don't you think my life would make a good story?'" (p. 101) In a more serious exchange, Mary, looking back, queries him, "'You don't think that I was evil? That I am?'" Savage writes, "I laughed. 'Well, not actively evil.' If she could ask such a question of anyone, it was of me" (p. 138), her confessor.

That slight concession suggests grudging admiration for what many would judge a classic gold digger story. In the novel Mary uses husbands and lovers for personal gain, so is she more than a portrait of an aggressive beauty? Virtually every character concedes, "Mary was a cynosure, and she knew it." (p. 203) She embodies sexuality (pp. 30, 181), charisma (pp. 126, 128), and "the woman of fashion of [the 1920s]— brittle, chic, detached." (pp. 194–95) Mary's origins, as the daughter of a Danish dairy farmer in Elgin, Illinois ("Villiers, Illinois" in the novel), are presented very close to the factual record. Savage only slightly altered details—his pattern—just as he shifts Hal and Mary's marriage forward five years, to 1915, with Jack born the following year, instead of 1911, Jack's actual birth year. In fact, a great-nephew of Mary's, Charles Skoning, has closely compared family history with Savage's novel, and he concludes, "[Savage] has captured the essence of Mary Skoning in so fine a detail that I can see commonalities in character among contemporary Skonings." He diplomatically adds "she was quite progressive and would probably be very comfortable in today's society." (personal communication, February 6, 2009)

The gold digger of a century ago becomes today's independent, alluring woman: a complex, laudatory story measured by seismic social shifts. The son of ranch owners, Harlow C. ("Hal") Bower, who's infatuated with Mary, is "a tall scowling young man" (p. 108) whose "face, even in repose, was never free of an angry puzzled expression" (p. 114), and whose progressive "general awkwardness" (p. 152) after their marriage leads to the confession of her mother-in-law, Isabel ("Belle") Bower, with whom she's formed a close attachment, regarding Hal's fatal illness. Mary's indecision about marriage (pp. 130–31) and quick disillusionment about sex in marriage (which matches Ann Burk Sawyer's in *The Liar*) foreshadow the revelation that Hal has "creeping paralysis"—multiple sclerosis. Her feeling she's been tricked into marriage to produce a dynasty heir underlines her dislike of children and her independent life in Grayling/Dillon and Butte, via her car, a Stearns-Knight. With her car Mary leaves the confines of the Bower Ranch as she wishes and pursues her own life.

That itinerant life foreshadows her two-year liaison with one Mark Pollinger (1925-27) in San Francisco when, like Theodore Dreiser's Sister Carrie and Hurstwood (in *Sister Carrie*, 1900), she rises high by using Pollinger, whom she ultimately dumps. (pp. 162-64, 191-94) Eventually the Peter Edwards love story—Mary's fourth and final man, and second husband, in the novel—feels hasty as the Depression crashes their "Highland Riding Club" business. *For Mary* extends *Lona Hanson's* portrait of the Depression sinking its teeth into the houses and operations of the biggest ranches. Now, a Marin County, California, business sinks through foreclosure, auction, fire, lapsed insurance, and bankruptcy. On the final page, however, the Edwards's desperation eases as Mary discovers a huge, unexpected bequest (a deus ex machina), which firms her plans to leave the failed, aristocratic Peter.

In typical, intertextual fashion this novel glances at earlier novels, as Savage continues to integrate his oeuvre—the particular dramatis personae of his Savage West. The plot strand involving Tom with Adele Cloutier Cummings loosely recapitulates the Burks (i.e., Yearians) from *The Liar*. The profile of John C. Bower (Brenner)—his original and abiding inferiority (i.e., "in trade"), arrogant boorishness, even resemblance to Kaiser Wilhelm II (p. 121)—recaps *Lona Hanson's* patriarch, Bert Bart, and *Power's* Old Gent. More significantly, *Power's* Bronco Henry Williams, Phil Burbank's mentor and ideal lover, has now turned into a stock, pop western character: "He was tall and gaunt, said to have broken every bone in his body breaking horses when he was young. His wife had left him and his son had died. He was said to have shot a man, to have done time . . ." (p. 87) He's become so stock that a country and western song should eulogize him. But Bronco Henry, in his final appearance, stands as alone as Jess Bentley at the end of *The Pass*. Except in *The Sheep Queen*, ranches strip families.

Perhaps Savage's most famous minor character has been conventionalized, though his quick biography doesn't mute this novel's criticisms of the narrow box of masculine ranch life. Men don't make or

drink tea (p. 124), they don't bake or touch or say "beautiful" or mention
or pick wildflowers (p. 104), for instance. And men know that "riding
sidesaddle" is code for gay love: "They were awkward with the truth
that in that masculine society there were among them those who lusted
after the young man in the next bunk." (p. 105) Now Savage invokes gay
realities not in the city but in the sagebrush boondocks from which he
came. His criticisms ring as clearly as his plea for acceptance, which
culminates his ironic criticism of gay men in the 1970s novels. He brings
his castigation home to his first geography, completing what he began
with minor character, Billy Blair, in *The Pass*: recall that Blair, eccentric and questionably masculine (e.g., he keeps dairy cows and milks,
owns a cream separator and a sewing machine) is killed by the "prairie"
winter. Given his sexuality, Savage instinctively hated that narrow box
he calls out.

Through Mary, Savage unleashes his usual satire as he skewers the
silly pretentions of this hopeless cow town. (pp. 149, 158) Both character
and author have had it with "good, simple people" as Savage fires with
both barrels:

> Their inexplicable acceptance of vapid lives, the dedicated happi-
> ness of all those she knew in that land, had left her wretched, apart
> and angry. The houses in Grayling were hardly better. She swore
> she would never again accept a plate of baked ham and tomato
> aspic and, having eaten it, drive out past Mountain View Cemetery
> [another unchanged name], where she would lie one day, having
> had nothing, achieved nothing, been nothing. (pp. 188–9)

That repeated cry, "nothing," measures Savage's indictment. Mary
Skoning's disgust plainly describes Savage's polite evasion in Dillon,
Montana, that he didn't ever really fit his hometown. Both Belle Bower
and Mary Skoning Bower, like their younger relative, are "exiles" in the
boonies.

Unique in Savage's canon, in one passage he takes on the Montana
literary establishment, writing a wickedly satiric piece about Guthrie's *The Big Sky*, the ur-novel in Montana's canon of twentieth-century
fiction, historical or otherwise. The fact that, a few months earlier in
Dillon, Savage overheard the AAUW festival committee admit Guthrie

was their first choice and Savage, their second as guest-of-honor in the latter's hometown, reinforced his marginality compared to Guthrie's bright crown. It also justified this satire in his forthcoming novel.

Tom and Betty mockingly invent *The Big Sky*'s plot (p. 137), and he calls it the way he saw it: "The book was popular among professional Montanans. They saw themselves as a part of the background—folk heroes—saw themselves as they believed they were and, to a degree, as they really were. Openhanded. Loyal, true-blue. Honest to a fault." (pp. 137-38) The passage builds through six clichés to compare Montanans with Teddy Roosevelt's view of the US Navy, "ready for either a fight or a frolic. Teddy Roosevelt, he dead." (p. 140; cf. T. S. Eliot's "Mistah Kurtz—he dead," epigraph of "The Hollow Men") It's not that Savage despised "Open and breezy" or "Firm handclasp," for instance, as values; it is to suggest that he believed human identity far more complex and nuanced—and ugly—than these traits, which in rural spaces have a way of thwarting or condemning anything other than themselves.

Savage isn't over. Late in his career, he matches the notoriety of critic Leslie Fielder's infamous judgment about "the Montana face" in his essay, "Montana; Or the End of Jean-Jacques Rousseau." (1949) Savage riffs on that subversive piety, "good simple people":

> Belle Bower had described her neighbors under the Big Sky as "good simple people."
>
> A kind woman's way of saying they were somewhat stupid.
>
> "I suppose by good," I once said to Mary, "she meant that at the worst they were not actively evil. Harbored the wandering stranger. By simple she must have meant that they spoke basic English."
>
> Mary had smiled. "Fried foods," she said.
>
> "Simple pleasures."
>
> "Men whittling and spitting. A woman carrying a jar of homemade gooseberry jelly to a friend."
>
> "Not a sick friend?"
>
> "No. That would be a duty, not a pleasure." (p. 138)

This cruel satire, of course, can be seen as the smug judgments of a pair of self-appointed elites. Both Mary and Savage would agree—at least about the self-appointed elites. Certainly such trenchant criticism helps explain Savage's poor sales and coterie appeal. It lends credence to Savage's credo (quoted in the *Dillon Tribune Examiner*) that "people generally write well about what they hate the most." For many readers, whether "professional Montanans" or others, such a bracing tonic proves unpalatable. This isn't funny. But the Savage West contains no space for commonplace, self-congratulating pieties that reify any sort of herd behavior.

Perhaps the greatest accusation against Mary in the novel, that she largely deserted her son, Jack, is belied by family history. Mary and Hal Brenner divorced in 1925 and their son, Jack, largely lived with Charlie and Beth Brenner's family thereafter: the future novelist was around cousin Jack, four years older, quite a bit. A letter to Butte, Montana, attorney Henry Hopkins (March 21, 1926) suggests that Mary and Hal, though divorced, were allies about the care and welfare of their son, and that Hal's parents, especially his father, proved the enemy in this power struggle. She quotes her ex-husband, "Sis, you don't have to stand their bossing; you can get out and make your living; I can't, I'm nearly fifty, broke and sick." Hal had spent the preceding summer [1925] in a Butte, Montana, care facility; he would linger another eighteen years, dying in 1943 (in Walla Walla, Washington), just as his niece (and Savage's younger sister), Isabel Brenner James, lingered for at least seven years, bedridden with the same disease, before her death (1978).

Mary's accusations about the Old Man likely confirmed Savage's low opinion: "I must know that in case of [Hal's] death or incapacity to care for Jack, I am the one to assume it, and *not* his grandfather," she wrote, adding "[Hal's] life has been so crushed and warped by his father; his very absolute and utter dependence upon him [h]as aided greatly in putting Hal in his present physical condition." Patriarch John C. Brenner emerges badly in each of Savage's fictional treatments of him, but nowhere as badly as the bachelor son, Bill Brenner.

□   □   □

In its Spring 1985 issue, the journal *Western American Literature* published John Scheckter's "Thomas Savage and the Roots of Compulsion."

They'd become friends during Savage's final Montana visit two years earlier, and in a letter (September 23, 1985) to Scheckter, Savage expressed his thanks for a copy: "reading it I understand a little better the stranger I am to myself." Savage also feared he was washed up: "I even supposed that my creative days were over and was obsessed with the spectre of failing Powers, a ghost that hovers over all of us." Family circumstances had distracted him, but he'd actually returned to his typewriter already.

In July 1985, when Savage reached his Biblical allotment of three-score and ten years, he, Betty, and the three grandkids packed up and moved across the country, to the village of Langley, along the southeast shores of Puget Sound's (Washington) Whidbey Island—one of the largest islands in the lower forty-eight states. In leaving Indian Point and Georgetown Island, the Savages bid farewell to thirty years' residency, many of those as pioneering "year rounders." As it turned out, he wrote most of his fiction (nine of thirteen novels) on the Maine coast. Russell Savage's temporary location in Seattle helped prompt the move, as did Pat Hemenway's lifelong residency. They had a nondescript house built for them (429 Third Ave.) near the corner of Third and Park Avenue, across the street from Visser Funeral Home (out of business in 2017), on a lot owned by Tom's sister. The funeral home's parking lot (on the corner) bordered the Savage's house on the north. A low wood fence lines the lot on its north and south borders. Now painted a federal blue, it features a big carport in front and faces east.

On a gentle hill a few blocks above First Street and the beach, the Savages commanded views of the southern reaches of Saratoga Passage and the southern peninsula of Camano Island (incl. Camano Head, i.e., the island's rounded, southern point). Prominent among the Cascade Mountains' "front range" (i.e., western edge), Mount Pilchuck rises from its broad base to a point. A gorgeous foreground and background, but far different than the open Atlantic. And more folks closer by. But the Savages still smelled salt water as soon as they opened their front door. The shoreline couldn't differ more from the rough rock shelves and rare sand beaches of Maine's Georgetown Island.

In a letter to cousin Janet Moore, Savage sounded enthusiastic about both house and location: "this house is large enough so that people can get away from other people." He "can see Mt. Baker from the north windows. Hardly ever use the car. I walk down the hill to the only grocery store in four minutes and to the beach in four minutes. Five minutes away and I'm in deep and silent woods where the picnicking is good." (September 26, 1988)

What was Langley, Washington—"the Village by the Sea"—like in the 1980s? Perhaps the most vibrant of South Whidbey's small towns, it spreads along Saratoga Passage not too many miles north of the short Columbia Beach-Mukilteo, Washington, ferry crossing, and just beyond Mukilteo rise the cities of Everett and, farther south, Seattle. Langley had incorporated as a city in 1975, sixty-two years after first incorporating (as a fourth-class town), by which time it had attracted a couple of hundred former hippies and alternative lifestylers who created a new retail energy (e.g., a women's clinic and alternative foods stores) in town, according to local historian, Robert E. ("Bob") Waterman.

The newly designated city completed a number of infrastructural improvements (e.g., a seawall and Seawall Park, 1976). In *Langley* (*Images of America*, 2012), Waterman and co-author Frances L. Wood mark the artistic and touristic changes, citing "a series of live extravaganzas called 'Fools' Productions," as well as an artists' street fair named "Choochokam, a Hopi word meaning 'a gathering of stars.'" (p. 111) By 1989, the first of three fancy inns, the five-star Inn at Langley, opened as the town re-dressed in tourist clothes: "The prosperity of the 1980s and 1990s brought many visitors to South Whidbey. Langley's hardware stores and garages retreated out to the main highway, replaced by businesses catering to tourism." (p. 111) Today Langley numbers about 1,200 residents.

The Savages would live here only a few years because of Betty's death. One local resident, Peggy Kimball, knew them a bit because her son befriended George Savage, oldest of Russell's three children. George spent a lot of time at the Kimballs' house. Kimball reports that the Savages largely kept to themselves. She commented, "They wanted the children to have a fresh start but unfortunately Thomas was too old to raise these kids." (personal communication, July 2018)

Ensconced at "the Village by the Sea," Savage wrote what would be his final novel. He'd kept up his steady production despite the constant presence of grandchildren or other relatives for many years. In a letter (September 23, 1985), Savage described it: "the story is laid in 1922 and among other things concerns the novelty of Radio. I was seven years old in 1922 so the story has nothing to do with me or anybody like me except as a child perceives a Time when he writes about it sixty-three years later. So much becomes clear when you sort through sheet-music stored in the piano-bench and shuffle snap-shots of ladies alighting from the tonneau of a Locomobile." In fact the novel is set before 1922 and has everything to do with Savage's photographic memory and imaginative ownership of his native town.

The Corner of Rife and Pacific (1988)

Savage matches his old age against his hometown's in *The Corner of Rife and Pacific* (1988), his only novel published by William Morrow. He adopts the guise of town chronicler and casts a nostalgic glow over the 1890–1920 decades the novel covers. That glow doesn't efface the satire, however, particularly in the novel's climax. In his thirteenth novel Savage self-consciously assumed the mantle of novelist-as-historian, providing more overt clues about historical dates and using a number of real names of individuals (above all, the Metlens) and businesses. Once again he wants readers to recognize "Grayling" as Dillon (e.g., the gossipy reportage from the "Grayling Examiner," pp. 66–67: the *Dillon Examiner* was one of the town's two newspapers in the early twentieth century). Salmon, Idaho, appears unchanged as this novel's second town and is also provided an historical sketch. (pp. 116–17)

This novel rewrites the opening of Nathaniel Hawthorne's *The Scarlet Letter* by claiming that a bank and a hotel, not a cemetery and a prison, best mark a town's genesis. Savage thus sets up the rival dynasties of the Connards, the rapacious family who own the former and rise to the top; and the Metlens, ranchers who own the latter and whose fortunes plummet, as John Metlen has overextended himself in building and running the hotel. Savage loosely adapted Martin Connard from pioneer rancher-then-banker Martin Barrett (with the characteristic unchanged first name). Indeed, at one moment Savage slipped and failed to change the name from Barrett to Connard. (p. 36)

Metlen, a "poet" according to his wife with his "head in the clouds," is repeatedly drawn as a kind man who ranches well but cannot profitably run another business. The hotel runs "in the red" and ultimately the Metlens lose both hotel and ranch (to Connard). The elder Metlen represents the final avatar of *Lona Hanson*'s Tom Bart, the kind, generous, improvident grandfather who bankrupts the ranch. Metlen sees himself as an outcast as he fails the American wealth plot. Savage sardonically comments on that plot since an earlier act of kindness by the Metlens (pp. 14–15) results in the shuttered hotel reopening as Lucy Talcott, former whore now turned proprietress, plies a brisk business in Prohibition liquor and flesh and pays Metlen $500/month in cash. (pp. 141–44)

Savage tweaks dates as is his wont: "Grayling" incorporates in 1890 (Dillon incorporated in 1885); the Metlen Hotel opened in 1893 in the novel but 1898 in fact; and the rival, Andrus Hotel opened not in 1920 (as is implied by the climax) but in 1918. Additionally, Zack Metlen as early radio guru is borrowed, in large measure, from a member of the Andrus family, Harry Colfer, who built and operated (for five years) Dillon's first radio station, W7CYN, from a transmitting tower on the hotel roof. (cf. pp. 196–99) For Zach's triumphant radio debut, he plays "Jada" or "Ja-Da," a popular 1918 New Orleans-style jazz standard. As always, Savage appropriates local history for his own, idiosyncratic version of the historical novel.

The title shows Savage again teasing us with local facts, this time geographical. No such "corner"—fictional site of the Andrus/Andrews Hotel, the "Herndon House" of earlier novels—exists, as Dillon's Rife and Pacific Streets run parallel four blocks apart, with the Union Pacific tracks a wide band in the middle.

John Metlen represents a loose adaptation of Joseph Custer Metlen (1834–1906), actually the older brother (rather than castoff younger brother, as presented in the novel's opening pages) of Horse Prairie rancher David Evans Metlen (1837–1919). According to local historical sources, the elder Metlen had already run hotels in Corrine, Utah, and Glendive, Montana, before building Dillon's first big hotel: a grand architectural monument (Second Empire) to this day.

Of more import, protagonist Anne Chapman (yet another unchanged name) Metlen, a dark beauty, grew out of a story Savage had heard in his youth and that he twice foreshadowed in earlier novels. In *The Liar*, "there was a story that for a price [Tom Bart, *Lona Hanson's* partying grandfather] got a woman to undress and walk nude among his guests." (p. 76) In the "Herndon House's" dining room—for Savage, a primary site for town satire—"it was said a nude woman had once passed among the guests, an odd thing to think of." (p. 105) Just a bit of titillation. In *Midnight Line* this figure is named and condemned: "'Wasn't it awful about Helen Chapman?' Mrs. Chapman had danced nude on a table in the Andrews Hotel dining room." (p. 108) Savage wanted much more than a tablespoon of slanderous gossip since he develops her as a protagonist in *Corner*. "Helen" slides into Anne Chapman who ultimately poses rather than dances in the novel's climax.

In a letter to cousin Janet Moore a few months after publication, Savage admitted again using a real person and conflating two stories: "When I was about 17 I used to watch Anne Chapman drive down town. What a beauty she was. Then there was a story about a woman in town, wife of a judge who shed her clothes and danced on a table in the Andrus Hotel." (September 26, 1988) The adolescent admirer—Savage's final cameo—appears on the novel's final page.

In his *Publishers Weekly* interview published weeks after *Corner* was released, Savage glossed it, stating it "combines two themes that have fascinated me for years . . . absolute beauty and utter revenge." (July 15, 1988) When Anne accepts crass Harry Connard's (her disappointed suitor's) wager—$25,000 in exchange for her naked pose atop a dining room table—the revenge of beauty, the closing pages imply, prevails. Anne as "absolute beauty" requires no protection (e.g., p. 176) and freely chooses her husband and destiny as though she's a sister to liberated Mary Skoning.

The fact that Anne is racialized (her grandmother was Lemhi Shoshone) lends Savage's final novel an unusual flavor and compensates, at least to some extent, for the infrequent appearance of tribal peoples—Lemhi or Bannock Shoshone in particular—in his fiction. In *Corner* they figure as an important presence, even though it's mostly a vanishing presence, in conformity with the early twentieth-century racist ethos governing the noble but "justly" vanishing race. In *The Pass*, we might remember, local Indians are present only in their absence, as they deem

"the prairie" "bad medicine," thus paving the way for the first install-
ment of Savage's harsh settler-colonial tale. Indians barely figure in
Lona Hanson, focusing as it does on the desperate grip of the consolidated ranch empire two generations after Indian removal. Bannock
Shoshone return to the Horse Prairie setting of *The Power of the Dog*, as
two intend to summer camp but racist Phil Burbank denies them access
to their home of long centuries. His cruelty is offset by the narrator's
sympathy. Savage's fiction rarely includes Native Americans but when
they appear, they are presented with deep understanding, and nowhere
more so than in this final novel.

Recall that Beth Brenner, all her life, was deeply devoted to the
Lemhi Shoshone band: Savage grew up around Indians who were well
treated by family. The time setting of *Corner* (1890-1920) both overlaps
and precedes that of *The Pass* (1911-24), so it's historically accurate that
Lemhi Shoshone reappear in its first half even as they disappear onto
the Fort Hall, Idaho, Reservation.

For example, Savage uses the historical Lemhi Chief Tendoy (1834-
1907) and his son, John (1865-1929: known as "Eagle Foot" then "Jack" in
the novel), in the plot. Thomas Yearian and his oldest daughter, Beth,
were personal friends of Chief Tendoy; in *Corner* young Jack Tendoy,
the only tribal child enrolled in a county school, becomes loner Zack
Metlen's sole childhood friend. Chief Tendoy prophesizes Zach's chal-
lenging marriage (e.g., their infant John as a "damaged child" with a
serious "bone deficiency," pp. 17-18). Elizabeth ("Lizzie") Metlen, John's
wife, represents the final avatar of Savage's beloved mother, Beth:
both women felt a deep instinctual sympathy for and interest in the
local tribe, including its language and customs; both posed as amateur
ethnographers.

As though recapitulating the white master narrative of settler colonialism, in an incident involving a burned haystack, Martin Connard—
along with his son, Harry, chief villain of the piece—falsely accuses a
Lemhi teenager, who's removed to the Leavenworth, Kansas, federal
penitentiary. Savage writes the tribe's *Götterdämmerung* scene when
they move in a straggling line far south to the Fort Hall rez: "that was
the end of the halcyon days, the Days of the Indians." (pp. 44-45) In fact
Chief Tendoy, reputed as a peacemaker, was able to keep his band in

their native (Lemhi River) valley for more than forty years, up through
his death, despite varying instances of federal pressure to herd and
remove them. By 1909, however, federal troops had escorted almost all
the tribe to the rez, home to several other tribes. In a further example of typical white domination, the Fort Hall Reservation, established
in 1868, had been reduced in size almost 70 percent by 1934. Same old
story.

To complete Savage's recapitulation of nineteenth-century
near-genocide and removal, he features select Lemhi Shoshone in his
adaptation of Buffalo Bill Cody's "Wild West Show." As part of Grayling's thirtieth anniversary hoopla, "Indians had been hired from the
reservation in southern Idaho to dress up in buckskin, put on their war
bonnets, and 'attack' a troop of white settlers lounging around three
covered wagons." We always know who loses in this eternal western
pageant. The hired help need help with their props, though: "As for the
Indians, whose transportation was to be paid for by the city of Grayling, they had to reconstruct war bonnets and bows and arrows. Their
own, the real ones, they had long since sold to tourists and to the state
museum." (p. 202) This final novel thus satirizes the historical plot
wherein tribal decimation and disappearance is momentarily reversed
and ironically enshrined in endless loops of what counted for popular
entertainment. In their fast riding and war whoops, they eternally stage
their losing fight and nadir. The fleeting Lemhi reappearance situates
Corner, at least this facet of it, between D'Arcy McNickle's *Wind from an
Enemy Sky* (1978) and James Welch's *The Heartsong of Charging Elk* (2001).

The local beauty, Anne Chapman, is related to Chief Tendoy and
a quarter Lemhi Shoshone, as her white grandfather, with whom she
lives in Salmon, Idaho, had married a native. The fact that Anne racial-
izes her baby's birth defects both recapitulates the prevalent racism
of a century and more ago and at the same time, ironically protests
that racism. Savage states, "Anne blamed the Indian in her... Nature,
in creating separate races, meant to separate. Who tampered with
that ordinance did so at his own peril—Zack and she and her grandfather. But the horror was visited on a little boy now being tested in
a Utah hospital." (p. 187) Anne accepts the prevalent miscegenation
taboo as though she's subject to not only Calvinistic but Jeffersonian

determinism. In the nineteenth- and early twentieth-century South, she'd figure as a quadroon who's trying to "pass": another witness to the endless furious frenzy of race separation. Anne's darker skin tone seals her beauty but marks her as an outsider who, like Mary Skoning, defies custom (regarding women's roles) through her indifference to local patriarchy and through her mobility.

In *Corner*'s social scenes the satire at times feels less savage than usual, as though the author shines it with a milder light. Chapter 14, the novel's longest (about two-thirds through), chronicles Salmon, Idaho's Fourth of July (1919) "Pioneer Days" celebration. In Savage's career the big canvas symmetrically matches the scene celebrating the railroad's arrival in "Salmon City" midway through *The Pass* (which Savage placed in 1916—just three years earlier). Only the first and final novels focus in part on Salmon. The occasion commemorates another technology: the completion of a new bridge across the Salmon River. The festive scene, an example of the business of white reenactment and self-congratulation, recalls comparable scenes in Mildred Walker's *The Curlew's Cry* (1955) and Ivan Doig's *English Creek* (1983).

The fact that the local tableau vivant is devoted to the Lewis and Clark expedition unintentionally anticipated the endless Lewis and Clark cultural tourism production of the bicentennial years (2003-09). Both tableau and town omit natives except for Sacajawea with Anne Chapman inevitably cast as the Lemhi guide: "It seemed cruel that the girl publicly expose herself as Indian, what she might wish to be hidden. Those who had forgotten would be reminded . . ." (p. 158) Savage speculates about the affinity between Anne and that most famous early nineteenth-century indigenous woman: "For over that young woman hung an aura of remoteness that matched one that the real Sacajawea had perhaps acquired only with the passage of a century." (p. 161) But her "aura" hardly masks the ancient stigma driven by race separation.

Anne had already established her remoteness as high school valedictorian (1916), her graduation speech unsettling her audience: "she seemed to say that if a Creator did indeed exist, He was indifferent to His creatures." Her sermon matches the disillusioning credo voiced by Savage's alter ego, Thomas Burton, in *The Sheep Queen*'s opening. The town collectively condemns her: "being part Indian was hardly punishment

enough for Anne Chapman." (p. 154) This judgment foreshadows young
Harry Connard's racist remark during the tableau when Zack Metlen,
also present, immediately knocks him down and threatens him. (p. 163)
But Anne-as-Sacajawea stands at great remove from her audience: "In
Anne Chapman's stillness on the stage, even those who seldom consid-
ered eternity had intimations of the everlasting. As an image, she was
the difference between life and existence." (p. 162) Savage has writ-
ten her brains, beauty, and poise to state that though she—like Mary
Skoning or Savage himself—lives *among* community (Salmon and later,
Grayling/Dillon) she lives resolutely *apart* from them.

The Salmon "Pioneer Days" scene sets up *Corner's* final two chapters: another broad Fourth of July canvas that depicts Grayling's thirtieth anniversary as a municipal affirmation. Savage inserts comic and
dark moments into the parade and rodeo (e.g., the pissing and pooping
horses, a gored clown). He casts a wry eye over the former, commenting
on what is arguably the most essential ceremony in the rural West he
always knew:

> Like the horses themselves, some of the riders were fading into the
> past, and for this occasion they borrowed horses and so became
> for a day a part of the cowboy-western mystique, perhaps the only
> true American folk culture—careless, colorful, tragic and maybe
> brave—and the source of great profit for the moving pictures.
> (p. 205)

The "borrowed horses" mark the event's fiction and desire, and from
the vantage of 1920, Savage salutes a popular film genre already many
years old and in high production in Hollywood. Recall that Savage,
who sported cowboy hats (including a sombrero) and colorful garb as
though he were a local Gene Autry, played that "mystique" as a young
man. His cousin, Ralph Nichol, labeled him an "entertaining cowboy."
Savage knew both its artifice and endlessly powerful nostalgia (and
endless revenue stream) even as he scoffs (e.g., the conditional "maybe
brave"). The passage underlines the "mystique" as anachronism, which
matches the anachronism of the Wild West entertainment with hired
Lemhi Shoshone returned in borrowed gear. Of course, cowboys ride

off only to eternally return in endless pop cultural production; the Shoshone were supposed to remain out of white sight, on the rez.

Savage's roving camera turns up its satiric lights once it focuses upon the Andrus/Andrews Hotel dining room in the aftermath of the banquet. In Salmon Anne "public[ly] expose[d] herself as an Indian"; now she literally exposes herself in the wager that nets $25,000 (for husband's patents and baby's surgery in Paris), her striptease a solo ballet: "It was choreography—a taut, brief episode—Offenbach, but in Dorian mode." (p. 219) In this rewrite of Susanna and the Elders, a dining room serving as private garden, Anne has no fears:

> She stood before them naked as Aphrodite, and as indifferent. Some there present . . . seldom spoke of that evening. No one spoke now. In the past moments, they had observed what should not have been . . . like all those who have debauched themselves, they crept away into the lobby of the Andrews Hotel, and from there into the dark. (p. 219).

The revenge is not really spoiled, crass Harry Connard appearing defeated. Anne shames and bests each man present, and the ensuing scandal, fanned by whisper, rebounds onto each as though his attendance forever disgraces him: "in his bowels he knew that for such sacrilege the old gods struck a man blind." (p. 224) To put it in less polite terms, Anne has said both "Fuck you" and "Fuck this."

When she leaves town on the Monday morning following her exposure, "there was no magic anywhere." In what turns out to be Savage's last cameo, on the final page of his final novel he places himself on the sidewalk among "the watchers" who salute Anne's quiet departure. For an adoring admirer, Anne models the exit scene into the great world beyond the cow town frequently enacted in Savage's fiction: "Only the high school boy expected otherwise . . . he had put his future into her hands—that was the least he could do." (224) For leaving proves far healthier than staying, whether on a ranch or in a small town a long ways from any city. Savage, like many of his characters, stayed only by leaving.

Savage's swan song was very well received. In its review (January 6, 1989), *Publishers Weekly* declared *Corner* one of the best fifteen novels published in 1988. In her New York Times review ("Good Men, Beautiful Women and Cruel Bankers," August 21, 1988), Valerie Sayers saluted him as "not only an accessible writer and an elegantly lean stylist, [but] also concerned with American themes and landscapes so familiar that his readers may well find themselves comfortably recalling a John Ford western, or a high-school civics lecture on the American character." She likens *Corner* to those virtues enumerated by William Faulkner in his Nobel Prize (1950) lecture. Not bad company for Savage. She praised the mature novelist: "his plot is as tightly constructed as ever. . .his style remains graceful and economical. His voice is a wonder, walking the tightrope of omniscience," and she concludes with the usual plea Savage long knew, that "he deserves to be discovered by more readers."

Sayers had also compared character and author: "Like his character John Metlen, Mr. Savage is decent and only outwardly conventional." She was far more accurate than she surmised. The *New Yorker* review (August 15, 1989) was even more generous than Sayers's:

> His writing is as lucid as Willa Cather's; his sense of time and place, of the details of the then still vivid American dream of Progress, is both sad and sardonic; and the richness of this novel, like that of its dozen predecessors, emerges from an accumulation of moments, of splendid epiphanies. Mr. Savage is a fine novelist, and his work has received critical acclaim; it would be refreshing if he were finally recognized by the reading public.

This is high praise indeed, an apt critical summary, and its final glance to the story of gross neglect, particularly from readers and critics of Western American literature, forms a fitting summary of a long career. Though Savage, of course, didn't know it was over.

The back cover dust jacket of *Corner* (first edition) lists nine blurbs that collectively laud the very high quality of his oeuvre. This chorus of critics aptly assesses Savage, and I'll cite only a few. William H. Pritchard (*Hudson Review*): "The voice of Thomas Savage is always a pleasure to listen to. He writes as if Conrad and Ford, and those other technique-conscious storytellers from early in this century, still mattered." Thomas Fleming (*New York Times Book Review*): "A novelist's novelist. . . A serious artist at work, fascinated by the enormous influence of the past on the present." *Kirkus Reviews:* "A writer who is underrated, undersung and long overdue for some grand-scale attention, Thomas Savage has a pitch-perfect ear and writes stronger and better books each time out." Tom E. Huff (*Fort Worth Star-Telegram*): "One of the most eloquent writers practicing today." And Doris Grumbach (*Washington Post Book World*): "A superb writer...extraordinary."

This adulating chorus on the dust jacket of what became his final novel underscores Savage's success among reviewers and crystalizes their verdict of his career. Only one of the nine quoted blurbs (*Kirkus Reviews*) refers to the accompanying story of neglect and poor sales. Savage in old age described the typical publicity campaign for each new novel as consisting of one Manhattan cocktail party.

◻   ◻   ◻

By the time the *New Yorker* review of *Corner* appeared, Betty Savage had been dead one month.

The year after *Corner* was published, Savage received a $5,000 prize as one of four finalists for the 1989 PEN/Faulkner Award. The PEN/ Faulkner Foundation began the annual awards in 1981 and defines it as (according to its website) "the largest peer-juried award in the country." As one of four finalists, Savage was invited to the annual gala reading, held in the Folger Shakespeare Library's Great Hall (Washington, DC). One of the other finalists was Isaac Bashevis Singer (James Salter won that year for his collection, *Dusk and Other Stories*). In a letter to Lucie Hagens (June 16, 1989), Savage described the big event: "One of [my former students from Suffolk University] showed up at the Folger Shakespeare Library when I was there May 13th to read from my book. The library is a huge place of stone and marble. The Great Hall seated 500 and every seat was taken. I think I autographed a hundred books. Betsy came from Virginia, and a cousin of mine [Janet Y. Selway Moore] was there from Phoenix..."

Savage savored this unexpected limelight, a spurt of "grand-scale attention" though he felt it too late. Ruminating about the rave reviews of *Corner*, he remarked, again to Lucie Hagens, "What a shame these tiny triumphs come to one when it no longer matter[s]. Good things should happen to people when they are thirty-five or forty and don't

yet stop to realize that such things come about simply because of somebody's attention." (March 20, 1989)

Savage's PEN/Faulkner triumph came amid one of the gravest crises
he ever endured. By winter 1989 Betty Savage's health was failing and
the diagnosis was lung cancer. Wife and husband had been heavy
drinkers for decades, and Betty never stopped smoking; by his own
admission, Tom quit cold turkey, August 7, 1988, but the drinking never
ceased. She had had a complete workup at Seattle's Virginia Mason
Medical Center with Tom and (sister) Pat attending, and at least in mid-
March, didn't take chemo. In the same letter to Hagens, he states, "She's
able to enjoy the quiet and the order, and the ability to eat what we
want when we want it (and to drink what we want, too). This is the first
time in eighteen years that we've been able to be alone." Russell Savage's three children had moved to Iowa, to live with their rehabilitated
father. Tom resented her serious illness overtaking their quiet.

Within three months, her fragile condition deteriorated while she
weathered chemo rounds. In early June Betty was hospitalized for six
days. Tom reported to Hagens, "All food is distasteful to her, and nothing
smells right. Now of course she has to wear a kerchief because she's lost
most of her hair. She's cheerful about that, sanguine, and in spite of all
we're able to laugh and enjoy one another. I don't know how she does it."
(June 16, 1989) Together for half a century, they had endured an extraordinary marriage. Betty had accepted Tom's homosexuality, insisted
upon a family, forgiven him his desertion with Tomie dePaola, endured
his occasional drunken abuse. And she'd published nine well-reviewed
novels. They had enacted Tom's credo about the centrality of families,
having taken in old in-laws or grandchildren for years. She acutely
understood Tom's dependency on her (e.g., her literary knowledge and
her editing all his fiction) and slighted her own fiction as "mere entertainments" by comparison. Despite horrendous bumps and the chasm
opened by Tom's sexuality, they trusted one another instinctually, like
children.

When Betty died at home a month later (July 15, 1989, at 8:00 a.m.),
Tom, seventy-four, was holding her hand. They'd been together for fifty-
two years and would have celebrated their golden wedding anniversary
two months later.

With the foundation of his marriage gone, Tom sold the Langley, Washington, house by December and soon moved to San Francisco, finally living as a gay man. Savage took a small apartment on the 900 block of Pine Street, and his roommate and lover, John, was described by Betsy, his daughter, as a "rugged little runt" who adored the older man. A former alcoholic, according to Savage, "John pays half the rent, does up the dishes and makes up the futons. He used to be a boxer, has strong hands, and knows how to manipulate my back in the same way that the chiropractor did who charged me twenty-eight dollars a session." (letter to Betsy Main, September 17, 1991)

Savage periodically returned to Seattle but based himself in San Francisco until after he turned eighty. In a letter to Betsy thanking her for Christmas presents (December 27, 1995), he remarked, "John grew misty when he opened the package containing the snapshot of me in a red leather frame. It proved to him that you understand his and my relationship." Savage unsurprisingly loved San Francisco where he felt at home, particularly in its longstanding community of gay men and lesbians who were visible and supported. One day in its Castro District, as mentioned earlier, he had a brief, happy reunion with Tomie dePaola, by then a famous children's book author and illustrator. The men eagerly embraced, and Tomie thanked Tom for the role the older man had played in his life three decades earlier.

He stayed in the relationship with John until moving to Virginia Beach, Virginia, longtime home of Betsy, who could look after him there more easily. In his eighties he chronically complained about Virginia Beach, which he thought sprawling, without center—he'd write in letters, à la Gertrude Stein on her Oakland, "there is no here here." In one, to cousin Ralph Nichol, he ranted, "This place [is] similar to Los Angeles, no downtown, cars, malls, Baptists, red-necks and R[e]publicans. This is the wrong end of the Atlantic [O]cean and even that [is] ruined by people and hotels on the beach." (July 1, 2000)

In his writing, however, Savage experienced frustration and failure, despite the high water mark of the PEN/Faulkner Award. He was solicited by *Contemporary Authors* to write a 10,000-word piece, and he chose to "write an article about Dillon because the town figures in over half my novels." (letter to Betsy, November 27, 1989) Indeed. There is no

record of *Contemporary Authors* publishing this piece in the early 1990s.
Yet Savage believed his new publisher, William Morrow (who'd published *Corner*), "will want to publish a greatly expanded version." (letter
to Betsy, September 17, 1991)

In letters Savage plotted the progress of this manuscript that never
went anywhere. He's confident in 1992:

> I've finished and sent off to New York the piece on Dillon, which
> I call GRAYLING, MONTANA, which will fool nobody, and I've
> changed some of the names in case people are still living, which
> will fool nobody, except that they're still living. The ms. runs to
> only 102 pages and Morrow & Company may feel the ms. is too
> slight to publish. However, if they like it—and they may not—I can
> add material. (April 17, 1992, to Janet Moore)

In this manuscript Savage obsessively returns home, as he so often has,
using the town name he'd adopted by *Midnight Line* (1976). He admitted in another letter, to nephew Sandy James, that it "becomes more
and more fiction." (January 15, 1993) In his eighties his photographic
memory of childhood and young adulthood shone in sharp focus. As is
so often the case, memory in old age zooms back half a century or more
and seizes upon sensuous detail, which he would reshape into his own
brand of near-historical novel.

Just as often, Savage referred to his novella as "Buddies," which
remains unpublished. In the surviving manuscript, two childhood
friends in the twentieth century's first decades discover their mutual
love in high school. They'll follow one another overseas in 1917. He'd earlier told his daughter, "It's a rather shocking book. I may have to publish
it under a pseudonym." (January 22, 1991) In a later letter, Savage wrote,
"My first novel ended in 1919 [actually, 1924] and my most recent one in
1924 [actually, 1920]. The book about Dillon which I call Grayling ends
in 1932, my last year in high school although I butt in later on to finish
off the work." He added, "I should finish this book in a month, and then
we'll see what the publisher thinks." (September 21, 1993) His longtime
agent, Blanche Gregory, then her niece, Lynda Gregory, shopped the
"Buddies" manuscript for three years, approaching Henry Holt after
William Morrow declined it: the younger Gregory concluded it was "too

quiet" for the mid-1990s market. That's highly ironic, given the explosion in gay and lesbian literature during the same decade, the other notable New York publishers creating big lists. Perhaps the "remote," early twentieth-century setting dissuaded them, though Morrow had published *Corner*, with the same time frame, a few years earlier.

Savage continued to work on "Buddies" until near the end of his life. In a late letter to Lucie Hagens, he defined it: "'Buddies' is a tragedy about two men in the Great War who love each other. It's also about Hate, which we all now know much more about—I have in mind the Matt Shepard murder in Laramie, Wyoming. . .I doubt that Little, Brown will publish a novel so short as 75 pages, but maybe my agent can find a spot for it somewhere." (October 30, 2001) In three letters to cousin Janet Moore from the previous year (2000), he refers to a big manuscript titled "The Scheme of Things," of which "Buddies" figured as the first section. In one letter he declared, "I want these pages to stand alone and be published alone. I'm quite proud of them . . . It's difficult to get a novel published with only a hundred pages, but why not, if the prose is good enough?" (August 11, 2000) In a later letter to his older son, he said, "I'm within two weeks of finishing a first draft of 'The Scheme of Things.' It will be a short novel, a finished first hundred pages of a 300-page novel." (December 5, 2000) Savage had been reading the World War I poets and researching "Great War" military tactics including poison gas warfare.

With his extensive repertoire of 1920s pop songs, Savage had long been drawn to "My Buddy," a 1922 song written by Gus Kahn (lyrics) and Walter Donaldson (music). Al Jolson sang this slightly melancholy, reflective song with a moderate tempo. Late in *For Mary, With Love* "the Highlanders," a horse riding club who "had the Great War in common," cluster around the upright piano "over the carriage house" to sing, and

> They finished with "My Buddy," a maudlin expression of the need in the guts for another human being. Arms about shoulders, with long, lingering looks, pressing of hands, they let honest tears fall for the passing of youth and a world where a man might offer violets as well as roses, where there was indeed such a word as sweetheart. (p. 234)

The intensity of trench warfare and nostalgia evoke a same-sex love whose power subsequent civilian life cannot match and does not dissipate. In this vein Walt Whitman's biography, specifically his hands-on nursing career during the Civil War and the resulting poetry collection, *Drum-Taps* (1865), represents a fitting precedent.

After all, the song's chorus paints an aching loss: "Nights are long since you went away / I think about you all through the day / My Buddy, My Buddy/ nobody quite so true / Miss your voice, the touch of your hand / Just long to know that you understand." Clearly, the lyrics suggest more than that acute camaraderie created by foxhole, trench, or barracks. Or the corral, given Phil Burbank's reverie about Bronco Henry Williams in *Power* ("hot time in the old town tonight," p. 63)

In the mid-1990s he wrote, "I'm still fussing with the Dillon book, afraid to let it out of my hands... I certainly have enjoyed writing about Dillon, but would hate to be living there." (December 18, 1994) Publishers were uninterested, and Savage was losing confidence. The writer's divide between *writing* the hometown versus *living* there—a lifelong sensibility—reinforces his experience and commentary during his hero's return in the April 1983 festival, eleven years earlier. Two years later, from Virginia Beach, he admitted to "doing a second draft of the Dillon book. The first draft is shoddy and I'm ashamed of it." (October 4, 1996)

A year later he confessed, "I found myself going in the wrong direction in the Dillon book and had to backtrack and bring in new material... This will obviously be my *Schwanngesang* [sic: reference to composer Franz Schubert's final lieder cycle, D. 957]." (March 22, 1997) And some months later: "I have a novel about Dillon on a floppy disk, but parts of it don't work, and I'm thinking of using two parts of it as short stories. That will give me time to think." (October 24, 1997) Savage, eighty-two and just recovering from extended ill health, floundered. No one wanted a novella about same-sex love set in World War I, even forty years after James Baldwin's *Giovanni's Room* (1956).

In the extant manuscript, Savage has drafted four chapters that cover 1897–1915, retracing the same time setting as *Corner* years before. In the fourth chapter Brick Blynn (a name likely borrowed from Tennessee Williams) and his best friend, O'Mara, both eighteen and known

as the "Two Musketeers" by their football coach, develop a local reputation as a drums and banjo act. Late one night after football and music
practice, they speak their love:

> And then O'Mara said, "Brick, you are the best friend I ever had."
> "Shake on it, buddy?"
> They shook.
> Somebody lets go first. O'Mara began.
> "Don't," said Brick. "Don't ever let go. I love you."
> Silence.
> Then Brick was himself one of those they joked about in the
> locker room, and O'Mara with them who joked?
> . . . . . .
> Brick then knew nothing of death, supposed death the ultimate
> tribute.
> *I'd have died for him.*
> But O'Mara then said, "Don't you either, ever let go."

In this passage, Brick sees himself a part of the persecuted minority
and momentarily doubts O'Mara's equal love, fearing him part of the
homophobic majority. Where would Savage have taken their story from
this point? That locker room joking—the seemingly endless strictures
against that "love that dare not speak its name"—hadn't changed that
much in, for example, the Intermountain West since agent Blanche
Gregory told Savage his gay novel was unpublishable in the mid-1960s,
thirty years earlier. She hadn't changed her tune despite the success
of Patricia Nell Warren, for example, and many other gay and lesbian
novelists. Despite the example of Baldwin's second novel (1956) or the
posthumous example of E. M. Forster's *Maurice* (1971)—with the same
time setting as the "Buddies" manuscript—Savage's final fiction, with
its overtly gay theme and plot, remains unknown, a sad footnote to
his career. Ironically, while Savage continued to work on "Buddies," a
friend and admirer, Annie Proulx, wrote and published what became
her most famous (and infamous) short story, "Brokeback Mountain" in
the *New Yorker* (October 13, 1997) one year before the notorious Matthew
Shepard murder in Laramie, Wyoming.

In one letter to Janet Moore, Savage claimed, "And here I am, at

85, finishing a thirteenth [i.e., fourteenth] novel," one that includes "Sacajawea who comes into my new book." (March 4, 2000). I have found no other evidence of this project.

Thus in old age, Savage sank into further obscurity since earlier novels went out of print and he couldn't get anything else published. His fate is not unlike Nathaniel Hawthorne's sad story of failed writing projects in the final four years of his life, after *The Marble Faun* (1860); or Mark Twain's struggles with his *Mysterious Stranger* manuscript over the last thirteen years of his life (1897–1910). Of course compared to these two, Savage has thus far remained a footnote in American literary history.

But he wasn't entirely forgotten. Professor Sue Hart, of Montana State University Billings (formerly, Eastern Montana College), interviewed Savage over the phone on several occasions in the early 1990s. Those interviews, and her own pervasive reading and research, yielded the booklet, *Thomas and Elizabeth Savage, No. 119* (1995) in Boise State University's long-running *Western Writers Series* booklets. Established in 1971, this series has produced, since 1972, a collection of more than 160 titles, mostly focused upon individual writers. Hart's booklet includes brief biographies of both husband and wife novelists and synopses of their thirteen and nine novels, respectively, as well as a "Selected Bibliography" of their careers. This fifty-page booklet solidly introduces both Savages and, along with professor John Scheckter's scholarly article in *Western American Literature* (1985) discussed earlier, proves that neither novelist had been entirely neglected by scholars of Western American literature. Betty Savage's oeuvre has received no critical attention to date.

Though he disliked Virginia Beach, Savage settled into an easy domestic routine, dining with his daughter and son-in-law Tuesdays and Thursdays and seeing her other times of the week as well. He relishes details of cooking and protests Betsy's opposition, for example, to him preparing parsnip stew "which is very New England, where I very much would like to be . . ." (December 12, 1996) He spent three months hospitalized in 1997 for heart surgery ("a new valve on the left side of my heart"). He emerged with some dizziness and in his final years, complained of vertigo and the necessity to relearn walking. He sometimes used a treadmill. Meanwhile, sister Pat, who'd been indispensable in his and his family's life since their 1969 reunion, died in Seattle on May 26, 1997, at age eighty-five.

He still loved listening to classical music. As he turned eighty-two, he admitted, "I've gotten rid of all records except those I listen to often—all the Haydn string quartets, ditto Mozart and Beethoven, all the Schubert songs and chamber music, all of Bruckner and Chopin and very little else except Kurt Weill." (letter to Janet Moore, March 22, 1997)

One evening with his daughter, after several martinis apiece, Betsy asked Tom, "Are you bisexual?" This seemed a natural conclusion given his admitted same-sex orientation yet long marriage to a woman. However, he answered, "There's no such thing." In his refusal to recognize let alone accept bisexuality, one has to wonder, was Savage conservatively adhering to his primary sexual identity? Or was he stating that he was gay but had chosen to live married to his female friend and soul mate? With his rigid orthodoxy, he maintained the divide between gay man and heterosexual man he'd sustained for more than half a century. Savage's dismissal of bisexuality, a common "bi-phobic" response, reveals the universal pernicious obsession with categorizing. As Marjorie Garber states in her magisterial study, *Vice Versa: Bisexuality and the Eroticism of Everyday Life* (1995), that habit misconstrues sexuality itself, "which is fluid, not fixed, a narrative that changes over time rather than a fixed identity, however complex. The erotic discovery of bisexuality is the fact that it reveals sexuality to be a process of growth, transformation, and surprise, not a stable and knowable state of being." (p. 66) Savage adhered to the either-or categories, not fluid identity construction.

The psychic cost to himself can be measured, in part, by the turbulence in the lives of his sons and daughter.

Savage, the gay family man, enjoyed several great-grandchildren by his eighties. Grandchildren periodically visited. By now his son, Russell, who had converted to Roman Catholicism, had remarried and settled into stable employment in Fort Madison, Iowa; however, Brassil (Bob), like an unstable comet, swirled in and out of Tom's life. In a letter to Lucie Hagens written when he was sixty-five quoted earlier, he harbored only dark thoughts about his firstborn ("of course there's not

a chance in the world that he'll ever change . . ."). For a period Brassil
lived with a new wife (a tribal woman and former counselor named
Eileen) near Yelm, Washington, having built a cabin and developed a
subsistence life off the grid, one that included a school emphasizing
living off the land. But it didn't last; nothing lasted with Brassil except
his mental illness and addictions.

I stated earlier that Savage never accepted the diagnosis of paranoid
schizophrenia any more than he accepted bisexuality. He inhabited the
same position owned by Reverend Maclean toward Paul in Norman
Maclean's *A River Runs Through It*: helpless to aid and change those closest to us (e.g., deeply troubled sons). While Savage endured hospitaliza-
tion for three months (1997), "my elder son . . . spent a horrible year in
Sacramento sleeping under bridges and in the bushes." (letter to Janet
Moore, December 18, 1997) In a letter to Tom from the mid-1990s, Brassil
sadly admitted, "Dad, I hurt so bad all the time I try to find some relief
in this. It isn't only that I can't trust myself with money. I am never free
from anxiety and have never really had self-respect. I try to find the
courage someplace to go on, but I get very very tired sometimes too to
be so far from all whom I love."

In one of the last surviving letters to Brassil, Tom writes, "Happy to
know your troubles are not 'osteo' but 'neural.'" He comments, "Your
brother [Russell] neither drinks nor does drugs. Nor do I. I think I sur-
prised him. He keeps wondering why I don't slip. That's because I won't."
(December 5, 2000) If Savage meant Russell's example an encourage-
ment to Brassil, it failed. And Tom dissembled since he still enjoyed a
drink or several, actually. Perhaps the saddest note in this letter intimates Brassil's wasted talent: "You and I are both lucky that we write.
It makes all the rest of it secondary." While Savage repeated one of his
primary credos, the fact that he called his unpublished son also a writer
wistfully expresses wish fulfillment, not Brassil's damaged path.

Tragically but perhaps unsurprisingly, Brassil predeceased his
father. He had drifted to Virginia Beach, sometimes crashing with Tom.
One day, likely intoxicated or high, he ran out into a street just as the
heavy metal rear door of a moving van swung open and squarely caught
him. He had always acted headlong. He died June 1, 2001, just fifty-nine
years old. One obituary notice listed his father's apartment address as

his; another described him as "homeless." His ex-wife, Ellie, having been notified by Betsy, called Tom from California to deliver the fatal news. With harsh irony, Savage's son's death came just as he returned one final time to the limelight: a dozen years earlier he'd participated in the PEN/Faulkner show at the Folger Library (May 1989) while Betty was at home, dying. For in June 2001, Little, Brown republished his best novel, *The Power of the Dog*, in its Back Bay trade paper editions. Five months later Little, Brown re-published *I Heard My Sister Speak My Name* as *The Sheep Queen*, and Savage loved the new title, as it shifted the focus to the family matriarch.

Why did Little, Brown, Savage's primary publisher, return him to the limelight one last time? A brand-new editorial assistant, Emily Salkin, had discovered a shelf of Savage novels belonging to her paternal grandmother in 1999. Salkin's father, realizing Savage was completely out of print, queried his daughter to pursue republication of at least a title or two. Salkin read *Power*, was completely blown away, and successfully pitched its republication in Little, Brown's Back Bay Books (paperback) imprint series. The publisher invested considerably in the Back Bay series (e.g., cover design): imprints designed to stay in circulation indefinitely. During this process, Salkin contacted Jonathan Yardley, long a Savage champion, as well as Annie Proulx, who agreed to write an essay about Savage and *Power*. In 2000, French rights were secured, and Savage was delighted by invitations to Paris and to Missoula, Montana, which he declined for health reasons.

Salkin developed a close friendship with Savage, as did her fiancé, Greg Takoudes. Married in early October 2001, they had invited Tom though they knew he couldn't travel. For a wedding present, he gave them the Sheep Queen's silver candlesticks. The old novelist took a deep interest in the young couple, and he and Emily talked monthly (or more frequently). He'd sign his letters, "Uncle Tom." The Takoudeses visited Savage in Virginia Beach late in 2001. Emily recalls sitting on the floor in the dark talking all night, drinking and eating small sandwiches while Mozart blared in the background. The following year they visited again, sitting in a dark room with plenty of alcohol handy.

Savage was still using a treadmill, but his vertigo had gotten worse. Clearly Proulx, who'd won a Pulitzer for *The Shipping News* (1993) and who'd published "Brokeback Mountain" in the *New Yorker* (1997), felt Savage a deeply kindred spirit. She'd read *Power* upon its first publication; Savage in turn was a huge Proulx fan. She was happy to write what she called "an introductory essay," which proved "the first original piece of writing [Salkin] ever edited." In a letter to Salkin (October 24, 2000), Proulx stated, "It has been a pleasure to work on this project and I sincerely hope the book, this second time around, meets with the success it sharply deserves. Tom Savage is a most interesting and complex man and I was glad to have had the chance to talk with him. I wish I'd been able to meet him." She'd written Savage (October 18, 2000), "I hope our paths will cross one of these days, but not too likely I will be in the neighborhood of Virginia Beach in the foreseeable future. Yes, it is too bad we don't live closer. I think we could have some wonderful talks." Among other topics, they would have talked about homosexuality in the rural West. But as with professor Hart, the friendship occurred via phone only.

Proulx's afterword combines biography and criticism with great effect. She praises Savage's achievement in terms of what she calls "the golden age of American landscape fiction, a period that falls roughly in the first half of the last century." (*Power*, p. 285): the same period of Savage's near-historical novels. Proulx sensitively defines Savage's fictive territory, judging him one of the best practitioners of American landscape fiction, and aptly interprets his greatest novel. In particular, she persuasively limns his perhaps greatest character, badass Phil Burbank, concluding, "with virtuoso skill Savage created one of the most compelling and vicious characters in American literature." (p. 293)

Because of Takoudes's work, Savage's best two novels returned to print. The new cover of *Sheep Queen* displays a younger woman (certainly taller than Emma Russell Yearian), discussed earlier: the benches and hills beyond superficially resemble the narrow valley at Lemhi, Idaho, that formed Savage's first geography. In a Christmas letter to Janet Moore (December 13, 2002), Savage wrote, "THE POWER OF THE DOG is doing very well in France and Belgium. My translator has about completed translating THE SHEEP QUEEN . . . I think Big Mama will be happy to know she's in French." In a letter to another cousin, Mary Margaret Hasy, written ten days before his death (July 15, 2003), he added "Two of my novels have been translated into French, including THE POWER OF THE DOG which comes out LE POUVOIR DU CHIEN and THE SHEEP QUEEN, about Big Mama and which they have translated not LA REINE DES MOUTONS but as LA REINE D'IDAHO ["the Queen of Idaho"], which ought to tickle Big Mama because I always thought she thought she was. Both novels are being published in Italy."

The Denver Public Library set up a one-day seminar/workshop devoted to Savage in 2001; then came the invitation to the "Montana Festival of the Book," held in Missoula, Montana, in September, 2002. Savage, too infirm to return to his home state, sent the Takoudeses with his blessing. This was the third Book Festival, and Emily, professor Sue Hart, and myself served on a panel devoted to Savage's two best novels in their trade paper republication. This was the first panel anywhere in Montana devoted to Savage since his final hometown appearance nineteen years earlier. While in Big Sky Country, the Takoudeses briefly visited both Glacier and Yellowstone National Parks: Tom had earlier told them, "Remember, I'm in the back seat." He eagerly awaited news of the Missoula festival upon their return east. He generously supported Takoudes in her career moves, and two days before his death (July 23, 2003) he wrote her, "I'm always here for you."

Thus in his final two years, Savage happily realized he was being rediscovered by a new generation of readers, including non-English readers, and that fact lessened the sting of his longtime neglect, let alone the violent death of his older son.

In extreme old age, Savage was reading Edward Gibbon's *The History of the Decline and Fall of the Roman Empire* (1776–1789). In that same letter to Mary Margaret Hasy (July 15, 2003), he wrote, "I'm about to start on the third volume of the six my daughter gave me the day I turned 88 [April 25, 2003]. You see, I keep busy, for an old man." He wouldn't finish it, however, dying July 25, 2003, of natural causes exactly three months after turning eighty-eight. Despite his track record as a smoker and a drinker, he'd lived a long life.

Takoudes arranged for the *New York Times* obituary published one month later (August 25, 2003). In it, Wolfgang Saxon noted "the revival of his popularity in recent years," thanks to those two Back Bay editions reprints; every other title except *Corner* was out of print. That fact trenchantly summarizes Savage's low sales (since *A Bargain With God*) and relative obscurity despite the pair of reprints. A few other newspapers published obituaries (*Boston Herald,* August 27, 2003; the *Sunday Cape Cod Times,* August 31, 2003). In his home state, *The Missoulian* republished the *Los Angeles Times* obituary (August 30, 2003). *Los Angeles Times* staff writer Myrna Oliver provided a fitting epitaph for his career: "although Savage enjoyed universal critical acclaim for all of his novels, he never became well known and never had a best-seller." Savage despised best-sellers, in fact, but his marginal position reminds us of the endless gap between high literary talent and the utter capriciousness of literary reputation and name recognition.

Ironically, though most of his thirteen novels had disappeared and his oldest child was dead, Savage, the gay family man, had become a patriarch since he claimed nine grandchildren and eleven great-grandchildren.

Following his cremation, his ashes remain in a royal blue velvet bag in the back of his daughter's closet.

Conclusion

IN THOMAS SAVAGE's first novel, which along with his second, limns his Savage West, he satirizes Owen Wister's foundational western, *The Virginian*, and opens the space between that pop genre and his own, native version of the white settlement story (cf. chap. 2). But Savage wasn't done with his mockery. He periodically derided Wister, and by implication all Wister's descendants, to expand the conceptual space of his lonely, repressed West. Though he lives on a barely fictionalized Georgetown Island, Maine, Chris, narrator of *Daddy's Girl*, hails from a ranch out West but favors his mother's Philadelphia side of the family who "liked the idea of the West, of all the wholesome people out there," and who claimed "their own Owen Wister." (p. 62) "Wholesome" gives the criticism the vintage Savage touch—a preview of his harsh scorn of A. B. Guthrie's *The Big Sky* and "professional Montanans" in *For Mary* quoted earlier. Savage had devoted his career to defining his West, a queer-inflected one, and the endless chasm between it and "the idea of the West," repository of national wish fulfillment perpetuated by popular cultural production.

In this satiric sketch, Philadelphians don't believe "people in the West would read much or have many books" because of insufficient time—or interest: "Owen Wister, who wrote *The Virginian*, had noted that although the Virginian had not read books he wanted to, and that's why he married the schoolteacher. They felt him to be a wholesome if undeveloped person, possibly like my father. They like it how the Virginian said, 'When you call me that, smile.'" (p. 63) Note that repeated giveaway word: "wholesome." Wister's Virginian, like Chris's father, is preliterate, incomplete, though both are land rich and wealthy. If book knowledge completes the man—the traditional if not anachronistic value of being well-read, or educated—the severe pragmatism of the ranching world, at least in this dichotomy, questions that old value. Or maybe the cynical formula insists that only after wealth and thousands of acres should come literary interests because the latter are ornamental, not essential.

When Savage's family visited their relatives, the Jameses, at the Brenner Ranch in the 1950s, according to one cousin, Bob (Brassil) and Russell contemptuously sniffed at the sight of full bookshelves as though books didn't belong in Horse Prairie, Montana.

Of course the Virginian—that "natural" aristocrat, scion of the ol' South—and the schoolteacher live happily ever after, their land wealth bankrolled by those conveniently distant coal mines; by contrast, in *The Pass* and *Lona Hanson* Savage presents the opposite story of ranches and ranchers. In *The Sheep Queen*, glancing back over railroad-fueled settlement in general and *The Pass* in particular, he states,

> When the railroad came through, it was preceded by young surveyors, college men who had read Owen Wister's *Virginian* and like Wister had thoughts of big skies, tall timber and rolling prairies. Out there beyond the Mississippi, beyond even the Red River, they could test their manhood; if the test proved unfair, there was Tuxedo Park or the Berkshires. (p. 78)

Of course the trope of the West as test site for "sufficiently" male identity, a cornerstone of pop culture, remains a staple in many venues. Certainly it has received extensive scholarly attention, particularly in its articulation of the late nineteenth- and early twentieth-century national psyche. But Savage's final line explodes the alluring nexus between "the idea of the West" and hoary stereotypes of "manhood." Savage's West ridicules received formulas initiated by the Wisters and even perpetuated by Guthrie (i.e., the wink and slap, "of big skies"). If book knowledge means warhorses like such as *The Virginian* or *The Big Sky*—nothing more nuanced and realistic, nothing less heroic—then those "college men" should keep their tuxedos on at a distance, in a far more domesticated environment. If fact obtrudes on myth, better to retreat from the settler-colonial plot and adhere to the famous credo voiced in the climax of John Ford's *The Man Who Shot Liberty Valance* (1962): "when the legend becomes fact, print the legend."

In his final glance at Wister, Savage doesn't mince words. Late in *Her Side of It*, narrator Bill Reese, English professor and PR front man for failing novelist Liz C. Phillips, recalls a tough moment in his adolescence: "I knew, for instance, that Owen Wister's *The Virginian* was trash—'When you call me that, smile!'—but I had an affection for the book because it had been a comfort to me when I was fifteen and had broken my ankle skating." (p. 274) Savage mocks not only those well-heeled Philadelphians (*Daddy's Girl*) for whom Wister produces "the idea of the West" but anyone who believes rural westerners could or should use, primarily, tough-guy talk like the Virginian in his memorable line. This linguistic world belongs to periods before adulthood, where such juvenile fare might provide momentary comfort. Savage's fiction always demands that we grow up, accept adult realities in all their diversity and disappointment. He creates realistic rather than sentimental portraits of ranch and small-town life and presumes we'll adjust our understandings and actions accordingly. His West demands we shed our usual lens of self-aggrandizing heroism and swallow a legacy of provincialism, racism, claustrophobia, and loneliness, among other things.

Through Phil Burbank's rant about lousy cowboys in *Power*, Savage, who after all shares some affinities with his smartest and nastiest character, chastises the legacy of all the Ned Buntlines who'd been busy inventing a myth out of whole cloth since the 1870s. Recent studies such as Tim Lehman's *Up the Trail: How Texas Cowboys Herded Longhorns and Became an American Icon* (2018) define in painful detail the actual 1870s Texas cowboy, who bears no resemblance to the myth (e.g., Wyoming's license plate). Silent film directors, John Ford prominent among them, exuberantly celebrated and perpetuated the myth. From the vantage of 1924—*Power's* time setting—reliable ranch hands have disappeared beneath the cowboy: "It was all playacting, like they saw in the moving pictures, and that accounted for the silver-mounted spurs and headstalls that kept them broke, for the records of cowboy songs they bought from Monkey Ward and played on their photographs." (p. 181)

A bronc stomper, horse trainer, and cowboy balladeer in his youth, Savage knew all along the gap between romantic and realistic life in the saddle and on the ranch. He knew the power of the former even as he rejected it out of hand in his career. He demands we discard our rose-colored glasses and see his West for what it was, not what we desire.

His canon consistently calls out bullshit on not only pop westerns but many literary representations of life in the Intermountain West in the twentieth century's first half. He castigates the silly seduction of "the pot at the end of the rainbow, even as the rainbow retreats and those who follow are footsore." To assert "There is no ending, happy or otherwise, only a pause" (*The Sheep Queen*, p. 3), is to demand far more of writers and readers, as Savage implied in his (1988) *Publishers Weekly* interview defining his coterie audience. His credo insists we embrace steady disillusionment, even disillusionment governing the shape of novels whose endings are in fact "pause[s]" only. To do so means avoiding the perpetuation of destructive myths: happy endings, the hard-won settler-colonial triumph. To do so means accepting a sophisticated view of the formal artifice of fiction whose endings, like those in life, are arbitrary. It also means endorsing the reality that the rural West sometimes destroys rather than fosters people, particularly sexual minorities. It figures as a death trap as well as some venerable agrarian ideal.

The roll call sustains the reality of Savage's often grim fiction. At the end of *The Pass*, Jess Bentley stands alone with his cattle, his wife and newborn son, dead. There is no family. In *Lona Hanson*, Lona's enslavement and the Depression's desperation leave her alone—legacy of her name—in the grip of badass Joe Martin. *A Bargain*, his bestseller, ends thumbs up, with a big donation to the poor parish church; in *Trust in Chariots*, though, Sheldon Owen ends dead from the car crash. In *Power* cruel Phil—with more than a few traces of Savage and of Peter Gordon in him—dies cruelly: Savage's starkest rendition of gay violence in the West. *The Liar*, however, echoes *Bargain*'s sentimentality, with a nicely staged father-son reunion in Boston that doesn't strip the father, the liar, of his self-deception.

Daddy's Girl ends with protagonist Marty, a terminal alcoholic, improbably rescued by her otherwise absent father—a sudden retreat from life and friends; in *A Strange God* a random telephone ring postpones Jack Reid's suicide. In the next two novels, however, the telephone leads to family reunions and acceptance of responsibility. But in *Her Side of It* Liz Phillips, a terminal alcoholic like Marty in *Daddy's Girl*, dies. In *For Mary, With Love* impoverished Mary, with sudden news of a large bequest like an annunciation, plans to abandon her second husband, Peter Edwards. And in *The Corner of Rife and Pacific* Anne Metlen turns her back on Grayling/Dillon with $25,000 cash and sails for Paris with her young son, effectively thrusting her raised third finger at Savage's hometown.

If Savage was "America's best kept literary secret" in the mid-1970s, according to critic Roger Sale, one explanation for his sidelines position in sales and popular reputation derives from these quick synopses. He repeatedly told a harder story than many readers would find palatable, one that runs against the grain of the national imaginary as manifested in the western. Those readers want Louis L'Amour. And in Savage's story, gay or lesbian characters sometimes inhabit the edges of the bunkhouses or Boston streets, and their presence discomforts some among the heterosexual majority. But the discomfort never lasts as the queer characters are typically discarded or punished, in conformity with heteronormative expectations.

In his wide-ranging review of *Her Side of It*, Edgar Allen Beem glanced across Savage's career and used a remarkable marine metaphor to account for Savage's obscurity. The review, "The fortunes of an author—beware the 'guiling goddess'" (*Maine Sunday Telegram*, March 8, 1981), proposes a subversive explanation for the great-reviews-but-poor-recognition plot I have been tracing. For Beem, Savage writes neither "those big wooden arks (bestsellers) which ply the surface of popular American consciousness," nor fiction like Saul Bellow's "which allows for the exploration of great depths":

Instead, he sets adrift fictions that are like semi-submerged objects, buoyant and treacherous like depth charges or logs, which float just below the surface threatening either to explode or impale upon impact. So far, it seems that the public has not collided with his prose.

So a reviewer gets carried away. Savage would have been alternately disconcerted and sardonically amused by this conception of his fiction. If he read it, there is no record of his response. This unflattering if not unfortunate image whimsically suggests that reading Savage will metaphorically damage you, shake you up good—a dangerous jolt. Apart from the hyperbole, this novelist likely wanted his fiction to collide with mainstream sensibilities, particularly governing clichés about the Old or Not So Old West. And his best fiction—*Power,* say—packs an explosive punch.

I have argued that the energy of collision and, perhaps, explosion—following Beem's subversive image—derives directly from the details of Savage's unorthodox life. In denying bisexuality and swearing implicit allegiance to his queer identity, he refused to accept the notion that sexual minorities could head families. Gay *and* determined to have a family, he was a forerunner of the now accepted norm of outed gay men and lesbian women raising children. He bravely chose *not* to live a lie as did many gay men who married and sired families for generations. Yet in his fiction he usually followed the heteronormative lead in condemning sexual minorities, thus muting and masking, and pretending to punish, his own gay self. In one respect he sustained the lie, since he never outed himself to most friends, for instance. And at what cost? His surviving son, Russell, concluded: "He was a very great man in many, many, ways, courteous and kind—benevolent—but he was torn apart by his quintessential homosexuality and in the end it destroyed him." (email, September 18, 2014) Rather than destroying him, his core contradiction—gay man married and embracing the role of father, grandfather, even great-grandfather—provided the energizing tension of his career. His split root drove his fiction but created a complex family life that took a toll on Betty, his sons, and his daughter. Betty, above all, knew she made Tom happy—yet never wholly happy.

James Baldwin's remarkable *Giovanni's Room* (1956), published in the US the decade before Savage's destroyed gay novel and *Power*, shines a sympathetic light on the plight of the protagonist, a bisexual. David also feels torn at his roots: "Yet it was true...I wanted children. I wanted to be inside again, with the light and safety, with my manhood unquestioned, watching my woman put my children to bed...I wanted a woman to be for me a steady ground, like the earth itself, where I could always be renewed." (pp. 304-5, *Library of America* #97 ed.) Yet David's seasons in France, and specifically his love affair with the Italian waiter, Giovanni, symbolized by the safe space of the title, pulls him fiercely: "yet even this was not as real as my despairing sense that nothing was real for me, nothing would ever be real for me again— unless, indeed, this sensation of falling was reality." David exists in a confused free fall, a primary metaphor in the novel: "No matter how it seems now, I must confess: I loved [Giovanni]. I do not think that I will ever love anyone like that again." (p. 311)

On the one hand, "The beast which Giovanni had awakened in me would never go to sleep again; but one day I would not be with Giovanni anymore." (p. 288) On the other, when David tries to achieve romantic and sexual reunion with his fiancée, Hella, in Provence, he is repulsed: "I felt her watching and it made me wary and it made me hate her. My guilt, when I looked into her closing face, was more than I could bear." David lives at odds with contrary bodily desire, ripped between "the beast" and "my guilt." He exists across an unbridgeable gap: "I felt her body straining, straining to meet mine and I felt my own contracting and drawing away and I knew that I had begun the long fall down. I stepped away from her," and he takes a detached, clinical view: "From a great height, where the air all around me was colder than ice, I watched my body in a stranger's arms." (p. 353)

Baldwin's David, like Savage split at the root as though bisexuality is inconceivable and invalid, thrashes on the wrack of his own making. Marjorie Garber, incidentally, concludes that *Giovanni's Room* is not about bisexuality, believing bisexuality "a metaphor for exile, for marginality, for not belonging": "It is a novel in which bisexuality is what might be called an artifact—a device, a result of investigations aimed at other questions." (*Vice Versa*, p. 128) In staying loyal (post-dePaola) to wife and family, Savage fiercely tamped down his own desire. After

Betty Savage's death he could, in his mid-seventies, live the life he'd wanted with Tomie dePaola in the early 1960s.

Savage's loyalty to writing exceeded, if anything, his loyalty to family. As we have seen, only his work gave him self-worth. And in that career, he stayed faithful to his own tough rural West. Savage took to heart the lesson learned from his maternal grandmother, the Sheep Queen of Idaho. As a young woman Emma Russell had quit her native Illinois and traveled west by train (and stagecoach) in the mid-1880s to Idaho's Lemhi River Valley, a tiny part of the nineteenth century's great westering migration. In *The Sheep Queen* Savage recounts her archetypal experience of western space and remoteness during the unexpected train stop the second night out. It's a familiar American West trope, an epiphany that fundamentally expands the self:

> "So I stepped down off the train and smelled the sagebrush. You know how it smells after a little rain. I looked up at the millions of stars. You can't look at the western stars and be much concerned with your own death. We're all a part of things, dead or alive. And then for the first time in my life, I heard a nighthawk dive. It was as if Someone had cast a cord across the heavens and tightened it like a fiddle string, and plucked it."
>
> Her grandson, Thomas Burton, never forgot that. (p. 70)

Thomas Savage, oldest grandson, never forgot anything, apparently, especially his remote geographical inheritance in all its harsh facets. And Savage insisted upon a qualitative difference between his inheritance straddling the northern Continental Divide, symbolized by the nighthawk's dive, and those new "thoughts of big skies, tall timber and rolling prairies" that seize the eastern-educated "college men" like Wister, just arrived in the West.

In that qualitative difference, the always known should claim our interest far more than the newly romantically conceived, whatever the lure of the latter. It didn't work out that way for Savage, but this study seeks to return him to his rightful place in American letters, particularly to a prominent position in the literature of the Intermountain West. A primary feature of Savage's West concerns the size and influence of landscape, and in a generation and more during which not only gay and lesbian literature but ecofiction has flourished, claiming critical recognition and a larger audience, Savage's time has come.

In her afterword to *Power,* Annie Proulx defines "American landscape fiction," an older mode of ecofiction, as "a technique well suited to describing the then strikingly different regions of America, the pioneer ethos, the drive of capitalist democracy on the hunt for resources." (p. 285) Particularly in his species of near-historical novel we read about the small-town-and-ranch West unlike that in any other novelist. In his world that peculiar combination of high remote ranches (Horse Prairie, Montana, and Lemni, Idaho) and a pair of distant county seats (Dillon, Montana, and Salmon, Idaho) stamps character in decidedly anti- or unheroic ways. Savage's writing against the grain makes his counter-narrative—for example, over against the notion that Montana is the paradisal Last Best Place (the state literature anthology title, 1989)—all the more valuable. This native son always knew it ain't necessarily so. Far from it.

More than a generation has passed since the paradigm shift of New Western History, whose advent is often marked by the publication of Patricia Nelson Limerick's *The Legacy of Conquest* (1987). What has come to be called settler colonialism descends, in many regards, from Limerick's game-changing book. Savage's fiction tells a dark tale in the spirit of Limerick's paradigm shift. In his fiction, ranches wreck people and small towns often do as well. Happy endings are bad fiction. His incessant demand for a critical regional self-assessment merits a much bigger audience.

Novelist Tom McGuane knows more than a little about the literature of the northern Rockies, and his ranking of Savage just below Cather among the best writers about the American West represents a wake-up call for readers, teachers, and students. If this study closes, however slightly, the gap between his great reviews and his bad sales, it has met with success. Maybe posthumously, Savage can enjoy the status denied him during his long, productive career. Maybe more of those "highly educated" readers with "extreme sensitivity," in both his home region and elsewhere, will enjoy and publicize him. Certainly he demands a rewrite of Montana literary history.

Acknowledgments

AS AN ACADEMIC AND A WRITER, I've always valued immersing myself in the local literary landscape, wherever I've lived, so I think it was only a matter of time before I studied the best writer from southwest Montana.

This biography has grown slowly over more than a decade—much more slowly than one of Savage's novels. By the early 2000s I was reading back and forth in his career and teaching the recently (2001) re-released editions of *The Power of the Dog* and *Sheep Queen* [the new title], his two best novels. I began writing about Savage—no one else was, really—and from 2008 through 2017, published four articles. I also led the charge in getting Savage's first two novels back in print. Riverbend Publishing, in cooperation with the Drumlummon Institute (both Helena, Montana) republished *The Pass* (2009) and *Lona Hanson* (2011). I helped prepare the manuscripts and wrote the introductions. Additionally, I started leading tours through Thomas Savage Country, bending south between Dillon, Montana, and Salmon, Idaho, and crossing the Continental Divide in his home landscape. I've led book club tours, one Montana Preservation Alliance "On the Road" tour, and several UMW classes; one year I helped lead a Lemhi County Historical Society tour. I love showing folks Savage's high lonesome rural ground and walking it.

As some have attested, it takes a village to write a biography. Unsurprisingly, I have many to thank for their interest and generosity. My dedication recognizes two key players. Sandy James and his wife, Jeannie James, friends of decades, have been supportive in all kinds of ways. Over many years, every time I'm with Sandy, I've learned something new about his Uncle Tom, with whom he felt close. He has shared many letters and memorabilia. The late Sue Hart, the best encyclopedia of Montana literature, told me over twenty years ago to read Tom Savage, and so I did. Then I couldn't stop. At the second Montana Festival of the

Book (September 2002), she created a Tom Savage panel on which I was honored to be a member.

This biography wouldn't have been possible without the unflagging support of Betsy Savage Main, Savage's daughter and literary executor, and Russell Savage, Savage's surviving son. For a period of years, I enjoyed long, frank phone conversations with Betsy about her father and their family's life. We wrote letters back and forth. I admire Betsy for her candor and charm and wit. She has been a steady cheerleader and has shared a great deal with me, including photos, stacks of letters and the surviving manuscript of "Buddies," Savage's final, incomplete (and unpublished) novella from the 1990s. Russell has been similarly candid via email about his own life and his parents' marriage. I admire Russ for his keen memory and abilities as a writer. Because of Russ I know much more about the family life, and Savage's work habits, during the early 1950s and then the thirty years on Georgetown Island, Maine. And he has shared a crucial short story about him and his father that I reference in the book. I thank them as well for the full rights to use family estate photos in my work on their father.

More recently, I've benefited enormously from the unpublished memoir of Ellie (Eleanor) Savage Quigley, Brassil Savage's ex-wife and the Savages' first daughter-in-law. Ellie has also limned the character of Tom Savage through her folks' social involvement with the Savages and through her turbulent marriage (which lasted less than a decade) with Brassil. I've sure enjoyed my phone conversations with her. I admire Ellie for her hard focus on the Savages as she knew them in the mid- and late 1960s and early 1970s. She observed closely and remembers in painful detail.

Many relatives and friends have kindly provided me with files of letters. For example, because Jane Smiley (Kalispell, Montana) kept all of Savage's letters to her mother, Elizabeth (Bess) Carlson, in the 1935-36 period, we know a great deal about Tom's quickly shifting feelings about college life in Missoula and ranch life in Horse Prairie and beyond. Two relatives died during the writing of this book, and I wish to acknowledge them. Ralph Nichol, Savage's oldest male cousin (younger than Tom by five years), a rancher and a geologist, shared the billing with me on that Lemhi County Historical Society tour many summers ago. Nichol shared unpublished pieces with me about the Yearian grandparents (i.e., the Sheep Queen and her husband, Tom), as well as insightful opinions about Tom. Ralph, for instance, defined Tom as an "entertaining cowboy," as he remained far more interested in people than cattle. He remembered details from their childhood and his teenage summers working at the Brenner Ranch.

I also happily acknowledge the friendship and support of the late Liz (Elizabeth) Brenner Tourtelot Younggren, Tom's first cousin once removed. Liz, the only grandchild of Savage's Uncle Hal Brenner and, like Ralph Nichol, a geologist by training, wrote the Brenner history for the *History of Beaverhead County* book. Liz shared a trove of letters from her "wild" and alluring grandmother, Mary Skoning Brenner Kirk, with me. She knew the Savages well: during Tom's final hometown appearance (April 1983), he stayed at Liz's house in east Dillon, Montana, for example, and when she attended Wellesley College in the early 1960s, she spent a lot of weekends with the Savages in Maine. She knew Brassil well.

I only regret that this book did not reach the hands of Ralph and Liz in time. I also lament the death of Tomie de Paola while this book was in production. A famous children's book author and illustrator, he generously told the story of his liaison, as a young man, with Tom Savage. He was courteous and detailed, both on the telephone and in email, only asking that I treat him honestly. I only hope I have done so.

Other relatives or friends, for instance Janet N. S. Moore and Lucie Hagens, contributed letters and opinions which again took me well inside Tom's head. Professor John Scheckter, who has spent most of his career at Long Island University, Post Campus, was Savage's host during his final visit to Dillon, Montana, April 14–16, 1983. Scheckter also wrote and published the only scholarly article about Savage (*Western American Literature*, 1985) until my own work. He's shared letters and, even more importantly, the audiotapes of all his interviews with Savage during that visit, which I've digitalized. Because of Scheckter, I came home to Tom through his voice.

I want to single out at least a couple of other individuals. Emily Salkin Takoudes, at the beginning of her career in publishing (as an assistant editor at Little, Brown), courageously oversaw the reprinting, in handsome Back Bay paperback editions, of Savage's two best novels in 2001, only five months apart: *The Power of the Dog* in June, and *The Sheep Queen* (re-titled), five months later. Emily and her (then) fiancé, Greg Takoudes, came out to Missoula for that Tom Savage panel, where I first met her. The old author very much took this couple under his wing, and Emily has also been extremely generous with her recollections of Savage during his final years as well as her assessments of his literary quality.

I also want to shout out Hope Benedict, longtime director of the Lemhi County [Idaho] Historical Society, who's an eager student of the Yearian tribe and who's been a great cheerleader of this book. I so enjoyed my days studying Emma R. Yearian's (i.e., the Sheep Queen's) day journals in Salmon, Idaho. Hope would drop whatever else that needed her attention and research and send me copies of marriage licenses and death certificates that clarified for me the Yearian or Brenner genealogy. I have given more than one presentation about Tom Savage in Salmon, Idaho, and I salute Hope and her volunteer staff for their infectious enthusiasm.

As many other biographers have confessed, our work wouldn't be possible without the invaluable help of sundry special collections librarians. I want to thank Jim Merrick of Colby College's Miller Library, Special Collections, Waterville, Maine, for his sharing of many documents from the Colby Archives concerning Tom and Betty Savage, and Brassil and Russell Savage as well. Additionally, I thank Beth Schiller in Colby's Registrar's Office for sharing academic transcripts of Tom and Betty after I'd secured legal permission from Russell Savage. In Montana I thank Bonnie Holzworth and Joseph Hickman in the University of Montana, Missoula, Registrar's Office for searching the archives and providing transcripts of Tom "Brenner's" semesters at the "State University of Montana." Here at home I thank Victoria Haagenson of UMW's Lucy Carson Library for Interlibrary Loan assistance. And in my town I also thank the staff of the Beaverhead County Museum, particularly former staffers Lynn Giles and Jeannie James, both of whom provided many first-hand details about Dillon a century and half a century ago.

And in Dillon I also express my gratitude for the steady support of Donna Andrus Jones, whose family built (opened 1918) and operated (until 1969) the Andrus Hotel, Dillon's lead hotel. Donna and her son, Kreg, an architect, have generously shared family and hotel history with me, which is crucial in a biography of Savage. The Andrus (a.k.a. "Herndon House" and "Hotel Andrews"), currently being restored, became a cynosure in Savage's repeated reinvention of his hometown.

I also thank Dean M. Rogers, a special collections assistant at the Vassar College's Library, Poughkeepsie, New York, for securing a few documents related to Savage's year as an adjunct faculty member (1958–59). In addition, I thank Tara Craig of Columbia University's Rare Book and Manuscript Library, New York City, for providing a sheaf of letters from the estate of Blanche Gregory, longtime literary agent for both Tom and Betty Savage. I thank Susan Taylor, of the Georgetown [Maine] Historical Society, who sent both an audiotape and a transcription of a lengthy interview (1981) with Tom and Betty Savage, which provides more biographical detail about their domestic and writing lives.

I additionally thank Charles Skoning of Oshkosh, Wisconsin, who contacted me more than a decade ago with family history about his remarkable great aunt, Mary Skoning (Brenner Kirk), Savage's aunt and model for his penultimate novel. And in Langley, Washington, a "village by the sea" on southern Whidbey Island (Puget Sound), I thank Bob Waterman, co-author of the *Images of America* book about Langley, who led us on an historical walking tour of Langley and introduced us to the Savage's home (1985–89). We savored a few sunny hours in Langley a couple of summers ago. Bob put me in touch with Peggy Kimball, who knew the Savages during that period and shed some light on these grandparents and their three grandkids (i.e., Russell Savage's kids, who were living with them).

I also thank a pair of genealogists, Adele M. Murphy (another relative), of Find A Grave, and Michele Stephen-Hassard, of the Beaver Head Hunters Genealogical Society. Thanks to their research, I better understand the biography of Ben Savage, Tom's birth father, as well as Pat Hemenway, Tom's unknown sister who contacted and united with him in 1969.

I also thank my dear friend, Ken Egan, former executive director of Humanities Montana, for his eager support of the Tom Savage cause over many years. And I express deep gratitude for the interest and support of various friends in the Western Literature Association, a few of whom, such as David Peterson, have joined me on Savage panels. Egan and Peterson are among that coterie of Savage true believers, happy to spread the good news.

I also wish to thank the two readers of the University of Nevada Press who not only enthusiastically endorsed the book but, through their questions and comments, helped me make it a much stronger biography. And I thank W. Clark Whitehorn, former director of the Press, for his abiding interest in Montana letters and history, and his commitment to this book from his first day in Reno. I express my deep appreciation to the University of Nevada Press staff whose professionalism saw the book through: JoAnne Banducci, Sara Vélez Mallea, Paul Szydelko, Sara Hendricksen, Iris Saltus, and Jinni Fontana. You guys know my debt to you.

In the process of researching and writing Savage, I've drawn ever closer to the biographical subject. I vainly report that years ago, Betsy Main affirmed that her father would have heartily liked me. I deeply regret never getting to meet or know Tom Savage, particularly as we're able conversationalists, cynics, and classical music fanatics. I also love gin though not Tom's "milk punch." We would have compared notes from our vinyl collections. I've few other friends with whom I share our passion for composer Anton Bruckner: counter-balance to the Haydn and Mozart string quartets Savage and I love just as much. I have absolutely no question about our common points of view or his quality as a novelist.

Finally, I thank my dear wife, Lynn M. Weltzien, who's stood by me through various books and who told me, three years ago, to "get on" with this book, which I'd spoken of for several seasons, before I retire. As with most facets of our common life, I've followed her advice. She has read every word. More than once.

Any errors in fact or interpretation remain my own.

The Novels of Thomas Savage

TITLE	YEAR OF PUBLICATION	PROTAGONISTS
The Pass	1944; rpt. 2009	Jess and Beth Bentley
Lona Hanson	1948; rpt. 2011	Lona Hanson, Tom Bart, Ruth Bart
A Bargain With God	1953	Father Ferris
Trust in Chariots	1961	Sheldon Owen, Pal
The Power of the Dog	1976; rpt. 2001	Phil and George Burbank, Rose and Peter Gordon
The Liar	1969	Gerry Sawyer, Hal Sawyer
Daddy's Girl	1970	Marty Linehan, Chris
A Strange God	1974	Jack Reed
Midnight Line	1976	Tom Westbrook
I Heard My Sister Speak		
My Name (The Sheep Queen)	1977; rpt. 2001	Tom Burton, Beth and Emma Sweringen, Amy McKinney
Her Side of It	1980	Bill Reese, Liz C. Phillips
For Mary, With Love	1983	Mary Skoning Bower, Hal Bower, unnamed narrator
Corner of Rife and Pacific	1988	Zach and Anne C. Metlen

Dillon, Montana, is "Sentinel" (*Lona Hanson*); "Herndon" (*The Power of the Dog, The Liar*); and "Grayling" (*Midnight Line; The Sheep Queen; For Mary, With Love; and Corner of Rife and Pacific*).

Family Resemblances, Partial Representations

CHARACTER NAMES FOLLOWED BY ACTUAL NAMES

The Pass
Beth Bentley: traces of Beth Y. Brenner

Lona Hanson
Lona Hanson: Margaret Jean B. K. Orr; traces of Emma R. Yearian
    (the "Sheep Queen") and Isabel B. James
Ruth Bart: traces of Beth Y. Brenner
Tom Bart: traces of Thomas Yearian
Bert Bart: traces of John C. Brenner
Clyde Barrows: traces of Tom Savage
Joe Martin: traces of William Brenner

The Power of the Dog
The Old Gent and the Old Lady: John C. and Isabel W. Brenner
Phil Burbank: William Brenner
George Burbank: Charlie Brenner
Ruth Gordon: Beth Y. Brenner
Peter Gordon: Tom Savage

The Liar
Hal Sawyer: Benjamin H. Savage
Adele Burk: Emma R. Yearian
Anne Burk: Beth Y. Brenner
Howard Burk: Russell Yearian
Gerry Sawyer: Tom Savage
Herb Bond: Charlie Brenner
Old People: John C. and Isabel W. Brenner
Helen Sawyer: Elizabeth (Betty) F. Savage
Bozo Sawyer: Bob (Brassil) Savage, oldest child

Daddy's Girl
Marty Linehan: Betty Beresford, a Colby College friend
Chris: traces of Tom Savage
Jane: Betty Savage
Adele Burk: Emma R. Yearian

A Strange God
Jack Reed: traces of Tom Savage
Norma Reed: traces of Betty Savage
Martha Reed: traces of Betsy Savage, their daughter
Tim Reed: traces of Bob (Brassil) Savage
Chris: from *Daddy's Girl*, traces of Tom Savage

Midnight Line
Tom Westbrook: Tom Savage
Brief reappearances of Father Ferris (*A Bargain With God*), Jack Reed
    (*A Strange God*), and the Barts (*Lona Hanson*)

The Sheep Queen
Tom Burton: Tom Savage
Burton's wife: Betty Savage
Amy McKinney Nofzinger: Amy Patricia McClure Hemenway, Savage's
    newly found sister
Tom Sweringen: Thomas Yearian
Emma Sweringen: Emma R. Yearian
Beth Sweringen: Beth Y. Brenner
Tom-Dick Sweringen: Tom-Dick Yearian, who died at age eleven (1911)
Charlie Brewer: Charlie Brenner
Ed Brewer: William Brenner
Ben H. Burton: Ben H. Savage
Roberta Sweringen: Edwina ("Weenie") Y. Nichol, Savage's aunt
Maude Sweringen: Margaret ("Madge") Yearian, Savage's aunt
Pauline/Polly Sweringen: Helen ("Hellie") Y. Hanmer, Savage's aunt
Nora Whitwell: Nora Whitwell, Savage's great-aunt

Her Side of It
Bill Reese: traces of Tom Savage
Liz Chandler Phillips: Mary Kirk (minor novelist), traces of Tom Savage

For Mary, With Love
Mary Skoning Bower: Mary Skoning Brenner Kirk
Unnamed narrator: Tom Savage
Narrator's wife: Betty Savage
Harlow C. Bower: Henry ("Hal") Brenner
Beth Bower: Beth Y. Brenner
John ("Jack") Bower: Jack Brenner
Ed Bower: Charlie Brenner
John C. Bower: John C. Brenner
Belle Bower: Isabel W. Brenner
Tom Cummings: traces of Thomas Yearian
Adele Cloutier Cummings: traces of Emma R. Yearian

The Corner of Rife and Pacific

Chief Tendoy: Chief Tendoy (1835–1907)

Eagle Foot ("Jack"), son of Chief Tendoy: John (1865–1929)

John Metlen: traces of Joseph C. Metlen, pioneering Dillon, Montana, hotelier, and of Thomas Yearian

Lizzie Metlen: traces of Beth Y. Brenner

Martin Connard: traces of Martin Barrett, Dillon, Montana, business pioneer

Zach Metlen: traces of Harry Colter, part of the Andrus family

Anne Chapman Metlen: Anne Chapman, a Dillon, Montana, beauty of the 1920s

Bibliography

"A Special Program at the Portland [ME] Campus: Thomas Savage, Novelist." A feature in the University of Maine Portland Concert-Lecture Series, March 12, 1970.

"Amy P. McClure in the 1930 United States Federal Census." www.ancestry.com.

"Amy Patricia McClure in the Washington, Marriage Records, 1854-2013." www .ancestry.com.

Alleman, Irene S. "Novelist Finds Hingham Shift Ties in with Writing Schedule." *Quincy Patriot (MA) Ledger,* April 1944.

"Ansel Arthur Hemenway." www.legacy.com.

"Author Talks to B'Nai B'rith on Monday." *Quincy Patriot (MA) Ledger,* December 18, 1953.

Baldwin, James. *Giovanni's Room.* 1956. Reprint, New York City: Random House LLC, 2013.

Bateman, Geoffrey W., ed. *Queer Wests.* A special issue of *Western American Literature* vol. 5, no. 2 (Summer 2016).

Beaverhead County History Book Association. *The History of Beaverhead County 1800-1920,* vol. 1, 1990.

———. *More History of Beaverhead County Montana, 1800-1997.* Vol. 2, 1996.

Beem, Edgar Allen. "The Savages of Georgetown: Where a literary retreat beats a literal retreat." *Maine Sunday Telegram,* June 22, 1980.

———. "The fortunes of an author—beware the 'guiling goddess.'" Review of *Her Side of It. Maine Sunday Times,* March 8, 1981.

The Bells of St. Mary's. Director Leo McCarey, performances by Bing Crosby, Ingrid Bergman, RKO Radio Pictures, 1945.

Benedict, Hope. *Images of America: Lemhi County (ID).* Mount Pleasant, SC: Arcadia Publishing, 2006.

"Benjamin H. Savage." www.ancestry.com and Michele Stephen-Hussard, "Beaver Head Hunters." www.beaverheadhunters.com.

Birney, Hoffman. Review of *The Pass. New York Times,* April 23, 1944, 6.

Blasdel, Alex. "Ranch born," Review of *The Power of the Dog. Times Literary Supplement,* February 5, 2016.

"Books Briefly Noted." Review of *Corner of Rife and Pacific. New Yorker* August 15, 1989, 82-83.

"Brenner Funeral Rites Held at Episcopal Church." *Salmon [ID] Recorder Herald,* April 11, 1957.

"Brockton Chapter, Brandeis University: Thomas L. Savage." *Enterprise* (Brockton, MA), October 31, 1953.

Brokeback Mountain. Director Ang Lee, performances by Heath Ledger, Jake Gyllenhaal, Anne Hathaway, and Michel Williams, Focus Features and River Road Entertainment, 2005.

Bullock, F. H. Review of *Trust in Chariots*. *New York Herald*, September 3, 1961, 4.

Burr, Ben, and Tom Brown. Interviewers, "Tom Savage (TS) and Betty Savage (BS)." Georgetown [ME] Historical Society, July 16, 1981.

"Colby Authors." Review of *A Bargain With God*. *The Colby Alumnus* vol. 43, no. 3 (April 1954): 5.

Coltrera, Francesca. "Thomas Savage: A balladeer of the American scene his latest novel reflects the West of his Montana boyhood." *Publishers Weekly Interviews*, ed. Sybil Steinberg. *Publishers Weekly*, July 15, 1988, 45–46.

dePaola, Tomie. Personal communication. July 29, 2012.

Dunlop, Katherine. "Pastor of Boston Mission Makes 'Bargain with God.'" *The Philadelphia Inquirer*, August 16, 1953, 11.

Fellows, Will, ed. *Farm Boys: Lives of Gay Men from the Rural Midwest*. Madison: University of Wisconsin Press, 1996.

"Festival will feature artists, writers: Tom Savage is coming to the event which will include an art show." *Dillon Tribune-Examiner*, March 22, 1983, B1.

Fiedler, Leslie. *An End to Innocence: Essays on Culture and Politics*. Boston: Beacon Press, 1955.

"First Novel Acclaimed." *The Colby Alumnus* vol. 33, no. 7 (May 1944): 12–13.

Fitzgerald, F. Scott. *The Great Gatsby*. 1925. Reprint, New York City: Charles Scribner's, 2003.

Fleming, Thomas. Review of *Daddy's Girl*. *New York Times*, October 25, 1970, 56.

Forster, E. M. *Maurice*. Written, 1913–14. Published 1971. Reprint, RosettaBooks, 2019.

"Franconia College Faculty Member Has Novel Published." Lisbon (NH) *Courier*, March 23, 1967.

Garber, Marjorie. *Vice Versa: Bisexuality and the Eroticism of Everyday Life*. New York: Simon & Schuster, 1995.

"Georgetown Man Writes Novel of Montana Country." Review of *The Power of the Dog*. Savage, Thomas; Savage, Elizabeth 1918-89; and Maine State Library, "Thomas Savage Correspondence" (2015). https://digitalmaine.com/maine_writers_correspondence/495/.

Grevers, Mary McClure. "They live and write in a house by the sea." *Portland Sunday Telegram*, February 12, 1961, 1C.

Grumbach, Doris. "A State of Grace." *Washington Post*, September 16, 1984.

Guthrie, A. B., Jr. *The Big Sky*. 1947. Reprint, New York: Mariner Books, 2002.

———. *The Way West*. 1949. Reprint, New York: Mariner Books, 2002.

Hagens, Lucie, letters from Tom Savage, July 2, 1974–August 15, 1980; correspondence, August 21, 2009, and February 14, 2010.

Hart, Sue. *Thomas and Elizabeth Savage*. Boise: Boise State University, *Western Writers Series*, no. 119, 1995.

———. "Letters from the Savages." October 2009. In author's possession.

Howard, Joseph Kinsey, *Montana Margins*. New Haven, CT: Yale University Press, 1946.

"'Industry Wants Human Beings[,]' Students Told at Career Session." *The Colby Alumnu*, vol. 38, no. 6 (April 1949): 11.

Inspirations of Pen & Palette featuring Tom Savage. "A Look at Southwestern Montana Through Literature and Art." Dillon, MT, AAUW, Southwest Montana Art Gallery, April 14, 1983–April 16, 1983.

James, Alexander (Sandy). Recollections and letters, 2000-present.

Jones, Donna. Archive on the history of the Andrus Hotel ("news stories, 1918, and reminiscences, 1979").

Kelly, James. "Good and Evil in a Boston Church." Review of *A Bargain With God*. Source unknown.

Kirk, Mary Skoning Brenner. Correspondence with her granddaughter, Elizabeth (Liz) Brenner Tourtelot Younggren, December 4, 1969-August 6, 1979.

Kneeland, Paul F. "How to Write Novel for Which Movies Will Pay $50,000." New York: Burrelle's Press Clipping Bureau, May 9, 1948.

Lamb, Susan. "An independent sharing." *The Times Record* (Brunswick, ME), December 1, 1978.

Lehman, Tim. *Up the Trail: How Texas Cowboys Herded Longhorns and Became an American Icon*. Baltimore: Johns Hopkins University Press, 2018.

Lemhi County History Committee. *Centennial History of Lemhi County* (ID) vol. 3, 1992.

Levin, Martin. Review of *A Strange God*. *New York Times*, August 25, 1974, 31.

Lewis, Sinclair. *Main Street*. 1920. Reprint, New York City: Penguin Random House, 1996.

———. *Babbitt*. 1922. Reprint, New York City: Bantam Classics, 1998.

Limerick, Patricia Nelson. *The Legacy of Conquest: The Unbroken Past of the American West*. New York City: W. W. Norton, 1987.

Lofreda, Beth. *Losing Matt Shepard: Life and Politics in the Aftermath of Anti-Gay Murder*. New York City: Columbia University Press, 2000.

Maclean, Norman. *A River Runs Through It and Other Stories*. 1976. Reprint, Chicago: University of Chicago Press, 2017.

Main, Elizabeth (Betsy) Savage. Correspondence and Recollections, 2005-present.

"Man killed in freak accident identified." *Associated Press*, Virginia Beach, VA, June 4, 2001, C4.

"Many were honored." *The Colby Alumnus* vol. 43, no. 4 (July 1954): 10.

"Mary Skoning." www.AncestryLibrary.com, 1900 United States Federal Census; "Mary Skoning Kirk," California Death Index, 1940-1997.

Mann, Thomas. *Buddenbrooks*. 1901. Reprint, New York City: Random House, trans. John E. Woods, 2011.

———. *Death in Venice*. 1912. Reprint, Dover Thrift Editions, Dover Publications, 1995.

Moore, Janet N. S. Correspondence, 2008-15.

Morehouse, Stephen C., and the Beaverhead County Museum. *Images of America: Beaverhead County*. Mount Pleasant, SC: Arcadia Publishing, 2008.

Muir, Ross. "'Jackpot' Author Came to Colby From Ranch Country." Source unknown, May 3, 1948.

Murphy, Adele M. Find A Grave. Correspondence.

"New Bedford and Butte, Montana, Have Many Similarities, Says Visiting Westerner Now a Professor at Brandeis." *Sunday Standard-Times* (New Bedford, MA), February 7, 1954.

"New Novel by Georgetown Resident Gets Good Reviews." Review of *The Power of the Dog*. *Waterville* (ME) *Morning Sentinel*, 7/8/1967.

Nicholas, Liza J. "Ranching in Beaverhead County: 1863-1960: Transition Through Three Generations." M.A. history thesis, University of Montana, 1990.

Nichol, Ralph. "[Reminiscences of] 'Big Mom,'" Unpublished.

———. "[Reminiscences of] 'Big Pop, Pop, or Thomas.'" Unpublished.

———. Correspondence and Recollections, 2008–18.

Nordell, Roderick. Review of *A Strange God. Christian Science Monitor*, July 31, 1974, 11.

O'Connell, Shaun. "Elizabeth Savage at top of her form in 9th of series of remarkable novels." Review of *Toward the End, Boston Globe*, July 13, 1980.

Oliver, Myrna. "Thomas Savage, 88; Writer Best-Known for Western Novels Set in Montana. *Los Angeles Times*, August 30, 2003.

Olson, Karl. "West of Desire: Queer Ambivalence in Montana Literature." Ed. Brady Harrison, *All Our Stories Are Here*. Lincoln: University of Nebraska Press, 2009.

———. Rpt. "Writer Thomas Savage dies at 88." *Missoulian*, August 30, 2003, B3.

"Patricia M. 'Pat' Hemenway." www.findagrave.com.

Patton, Katherine. "Accomplished author greets hometown." *Montana Standard* "Time Out," April 30, 1983, 3.

Penson, Betty. "The Story of Idaho's Amazing Sheep Queen." *Idaho Statesman*, January 29, 1978, 10C.

"Pick of the Paperbacks." Review of *The Liar. Saturday Review*, September 26, 1970, 32.

Pritchard, William H. "Fiction Chronicle." *Hudson Review* vol. 21 (Summer 1968): 364–76.

"Prof. Savage to Address Brandeis Women Nov. 26." *Sunday Telegram* (Lowell, MA), November 18, 1951.

"Prof. Savage to Be Speaker." *Monitor & New Hampshire Patriot*, February 9, 1952.

Proulx, Annie, "Brokeback Mountain." *New Yorker*, October 13, 1997.

———. *Close Range: Wyoming Stories*. Reprint, New York City: Scribner Paperback Edition, Simon & Schuster, 1999.

———. Afterword to *The Power of the Dog*. Rpt. Boston: Little, Brown (Back Bay trade pb), 2001, 277–93.

Pruitt, Sarah. "How Gay Culture Blossomed During the Roaring Twenties." http://www.history.com, June 10, 2019.

Quigley, Eleanor (Ellie) Savage. Unpublished memoir manuscript.

———. Correspondence, 2018–present.

Review of *Lona Hanson. New York Herald Tribune*, October 17, 1948, 24.

Review of *Midnight Line. New York Times*, March 14, 1976.

Review of *I Heard My Sister Speak My Name*. ("MM"). *Boston Globe, Book Festival Supplement*, October 13, 1977.

Rolfe, John. "12th novel is powerful portrait of a woman," Review of *For Mary, With Love. Maine Sunday Telegram*, January 8, 1984.

Ross, Jean. *Contemporary Authors* interview, January 11, 1989. vol. 132, 364–67.

Saal, Hubert. Review of *The Liar. Saturday Review*, September 26, 1970.

Sale, Roger. "Unknown Novels." *The American Scholar*, vol. 43, no. 1 (Winter 1973–74): 86–104.

———. Review of *I Heard My Sister Speak My Name. New York Review of Books*, February 23, 1978, 42.

———. "Neglected Recent American Novels." *The American Scholar* vol., 48 no. 1 (Winter 1979); www.neglectedbooks.com.

Savage, Robert Brassil. "Twenty." Unpublished novel "Submitted in partial fulfillment of the requirements for the Senior Scholars Program at Colby College," 1966.

Savage, Elizabeth. *Toward the End*. Boston: Little, Brown, 1980.

Savage, Russell. Correspondence and recollections, 2014–present.

——. Unpublished story about his father, in author's possession.

Savage, Thomas. "The Geography of the World, and Other Jokes." ["by Tom Brenner": unpublished], New York City: McIntosh and Otis, Inc., 1936.

——. "Find the Orchestra." Ed. H. G. Merriam, *Frontier and Midland* vol. 17, no. 4 (Summer 1937): 276–77.

——. "The Bronc Stomper." ["by Tom Brenner"] *Coronet*, August 1937, 154–56.

——. *The Pass*. Garden City, NJ: Doubleday, 1944; rpt. Helena, MT: Riverbend Publishing, 2009.

——. *Lona Hanson*. New York: Simon & Schuster, 1948. Reprint, Helena, MT: Riverbend Publishing, 2011.

——. *A Bargain With God*. New York: Simon & Schuster, 1953.

——. "Review: '215.'" *Vassar Miscellany News* vol. 43, No. 5 (October 15, 1958).

——. *Trust in Chariots*. New York: Random House, 1961.

——. "Colby History & Dean Marriner." *The Colby Alumnus* vol. 52, no. 2 (Winter 1962): 22–25.

——. *The Power of the Dog*. Boston: Little, Brown, 1967. Reprint, Little, Brown (Back Bay trade pb), 2001.

——. *The Liar*. Boston: Little, Brown, 1969.

——. *Daddy's Girl*. Boston: Little, Brown, 1970.

——. *A Strange God*. Boston: Little, Brown, 1974.

——. "We Walked and Walked. *The Colby Alumnus* vol. 64, no. 3 (Spring 1975): 12–13

——. *Midnight Line*. Boston: Little, Brown, 1976.

——. *I Heard My Sister Speak My Name*. Boston: Little, Brown, 1977. Reprint, Little, Brown (Back Bay trade pb.), *The Sheep Queen*, 2001.

——. "Why a Pilgrim Traveled to Boston and His Implausible Arrival There." *A Book for Boston*. Boston: Godine, 1980, 13–19.

——. *Her Side of It*. Boston: Little, Brown, 1981.

——. *For Mary, With Love*. Boston: Little, Brown, 1983.

——. *Corner of Rife and Pacific*. New York: William Morrow, 1988.

——. "Buddies." Extant manuscript, in author's possession.

Saxon, Wolfgang. "Thomas Savage, 88, Novelist Drawn to the American West, dies." *New York Times*, August 25, 2003.

Sayers, Valerie. "Good Men, Beautiful Women and Cruel Bankers," Review of *Corner of Rife and Pacific*. *New York Times Book Review*, August 21, 1988, 12.

Scheckter, John. "Thomas Savage and the West: Roots of Compulsion." *Western American Literature* vol. 20, no. 1 (Spring 1985): 35–49.

——. Interviews with Tom Savage, Dillon, MT, April 14, 1983–April 16,1983.

——. Personal correspondence, 2012–2019.

Simon, Julie. "There's more to Tom Savage than his Beaverhead connection." *Dillon Tribune-Examiner*, April 12, 1983.

——. "We're lucky to have 'Pen and Palette.'" *Dillon Tribune-Examiner*, April 12, 1983.

——. "Savage comes home again." *Dillon Tribune-Examiner*, April 20, 1983, A1, A5.

——. "Arts festival was a big success." *Dillon Tribune-Examiner,* April 20, 1983.

Skoning, Charles. Personal communication, February 6, 2009.

Smiley, Jane. Correspondence between Clara Elizabeth ("Bess") Carlson and Tom Brenner [Savage], March 12, 1935–November 30, 1936.

Smiley, Jane. *A Thousand Acres.* 1991. Reprint, New York City: Anchor Books, 2003.

Sprague, Marshall. "The Burbank Spread." Review of *The Power of the Dog. New York Times,* April 9, 1967, 38.

Stephen-Hussard, Michele. Beaver Head Hunters Genealogical Society, correspondence, 2017- present.

Strachey, Lytton. *Queen Victoria.* 1921. Reprint, Kindle version, Amazon.com Services LLC, 2012.

Symondson, Kate. "E. M. Forster's gay fiction." www.bl.uk.20th-century-literature/articles/e-m-forsters-gay-fiction.

Takoudes, Emily Salkin. Correspondence, 2001–present.

"Teacher Sells His Novel to the Movies for $50,000." *New York Herald Tribune,* April 29, 1948.

The Last Best Place. Montana's state literature anthology. Helena: Montana Historical Society Press, 1989.

"Thomas Savage To Be Speaker at New Salem." *Sunday Republican* (Springfield, MA), June 13, 1954.

"Thomas L. [sic] Savage, western novelist." *Boston Herald,* August 27, 2003.

"Thomas H. Yearian, 99, Pioneer of Lemhi, Dies." *Salmon Recorder Herald,* December 19, 1963.

Waite, Thornton. *"Get Off and Push": The Story of the Gilmore and Pittsburgh Railroad.* Self-published, 2002.

Walker, Mildred. *The Curlew's Cry.* 1955. Reprint, Lincoln: Bison Books, 1994.

"Waltham Author's Book in Play Form on TV Tonight." *Waltham (MA) News-Tribune,* November 16, 1953.

Warren, Patricia Nell. *The Front Runner.* New York City: Wm. Morrow & Co., 1974. Reprint, Quality Paper Book Club, 2001.

——. *The Fancy Dancer.* New York City: Wm. Morrow and Co., 1976. Reprint, Wildcat Press, 1996.

Weltzien, O. Alan, and Scott L. Baugh, Donovan Gwinner, and Sara L. Spurgeon. "Conversing *Brokeback Mountain's* Varied Spaces and Contested Desires." *Intertext* vol. 10, no. 2 (Fall 2006), *Landscapes of Desire: Conversations on Brokeback Mountain,* 155–79.

——. "Thomas Savage, Forgotten Novelist." *Montana: The Magazine of Western History* vol. 58, no. 4 (Winter 2008): 22–41.

——. "Introduction to *The Pass.* Reprint, Helena: Riverbend Publishing, 2009, 5–14.

——. "Introduction" to *Lona Hanson.* Reprint, Helena: Riverbend Publishing, 2011, v–xvi.

——. "'Just Regular Guys': Homophobia, the Code of the West, and Constructions of Male Identity in Thomas Savage and Annie Proulx." In *All Our Stories Are Here: Critical Perspectives on Montana Literature,* edited by Brady Harrison. Lincoln: University of Nebraska Press, 2009, 117–38.

——. "Thomas Savage's Queer Country." *Western Writers Online,* February 2015. www.scholarworks.boisestate.edu.

———. "Literary Sociology in a Montana Town: Novelist Thomas Savage Rewrites Old Dillon." *Great Plains Quarterly* vol. 37, no. 2 (Spring 2017): 111-30.

Weston, Kate. "Get Thee to a Big City: Sexual Imaginary and the Great Gay Migration." *GLQ* vol. 2 (1995): 253-77.

Wister, Owen. *The Virginian.* New York City: Gramercy Books, 1902. Reprint, London: Oxford University Press, 1998.

Yardley, Jonathan. "The Loneliness of the Nightly Radio Confessor, Review of *Midnight Line. The Washington Post,* February 7,1976.

———. "The State of American Fiction: All in the Family," *Commonweal,* May 11, 1979, 265-66.

Yearian, Emma Russell. *Day Journals,* 1913-24, 1929-36, 1938-40, 1942, 1950-51. Salmon, ID: Lehmi County Historical Society.

Index

About the Author

O. ALAN WELTZIEN is a retired professor of English, specializing in American and Western American literature, at the University of Montana Western. He has published nine books, including studies of the work of John McPhee, Rick Bass, and Norman Maclean, as well as dozens of articles, two chapbooks, a memoir, and three poetry collections. He lives in Montana.